Research in Management
Volume 1 • 2001

RESEARCH IN MANAGEMENT

Volume 1 • 2001

Edited by

Chester A. Schriesheim
and
Linda L. Neider

Series sponsored by the Southern Management Association

INFORMATION AGE
PUBLISHING

80 Mason Street
Greenwich, Connecticut 06830

Library of Congress Cataloging-in-Publication Data

Measurement equivalence / edited by Chester A. Schriesheim and Linda L. Neide.
        p. cm. — (Research in management ; v. 1)
   Includes index.
   ISBN 1-930608-89-6 (hardcover) — ISBN 1-930608-88-8 (pbk.)
     1. Management—Research—Methodology. 2. Industrial sociology—
Methodology. I. Schriesheim, Chester. II. Neider, Linda L., 1953- III. Series.

HD30.4.M435 2001
658.4'038—dc21   2001003583

Printed in the United States of America

PAST PRESIDENTS

Tammy G. Hunt, University of North Carolina at Wilmington, 2001-2002
Pamela L. Perrewé, Florida State University, 2000-2001
Vida Scarpello, Georgia State University, 1999-2000
Chester A. Schriesheim, University of Miami, 1998-1999
Mark J. Martinko, Florida State University, 1997-1998
Rose Knotts, University of North Texas, 1996-1997
David D. Van Fleet, Arizona State University West, 1995-1996
Robert C. Ford, University of Central Florida, 1994-1995
J. Bernard Keys, Georgia Southern University, 1993-1994
Charles R. (Bob) Greer, Texas Christian University, 1992-1993
Daniel S. Cochran, Mississippi State University, 1991-1992
John A. Pearce, II, George Mason University, 1990-1991
J. G. Hunt, Texas Tech University, 1989-1990
W. Alan Randolph, University of Baltimore, 1988-1989
B. Wayne Kemp, University of Tennessee, Martin, 1987-1988
Achilles A, Armenakis, Auburn University, 1986-1987
W. Jack Duncan, University of Alabama at Birmingham, 1985-1986
William H. Holley, Jr., Auburn University, 1984-1985
Arthur G. Bedcian, Louisiana State University, 1983-1984
Dorothy N. Harlow, University of South Florida, 1982-1983
Dennis F. Ray, Mississippi Sate University, 1981-1982
Vince P. Luchsinger, Texas Tech University, 1980-1979
John E. Logan, University of South Carolina, 1979-1980
Ogden H. Hall, University of New Orleans, 1978-1979
Jay T. Knippen, University of South Florida, 1977-1978
James M. Todd, Memphis State University, 1976-1977
John T. DeVogt, Washington & Lee University, 1975-1976
Daniel T. Wren, University of Oklahoma, 1974-1975
Leon C. Megginson, Louisiana State University, 1973-1974
Richard J. Levin, University of North Carolina, Chapel Hill, 1972-1973
Max B. Jones, Old Dominion University, 1971-1972
Robert M. Fulmer, Georgia State University, 1970-1971
Bernard J. Bienvenu, University of Southwestern Louisiana, 1969-1970
Burnard H. Sord, University of Texas, Austin, 1968-1969
Claude S. George, Jr., University of North Carolina, Chapel Hill, 1967-1968
Herbert G. Hicks, Louisiana State University, 1966-1967
Charles R. Scott, University of Alabama, 1965-1966
William M. Fox, University of Florida, 1964-1965
Joseph L. Massie, University of Kentucky, 1963-1964

CONTENTS

CHAPTER 1

FOREWORD AND COMMENTARY

Chester A. Schriesheim and Linda L. Neider

Measurement equivalence has been a concern in organizational studies for a long time, perhaps beginning close to a century ago with attempts at establishing "alternate" or "parallel" forms of measures, so that research could assess change over time without the distortions caused by memory and pretest sensitization effects.

These early attempts at ensuring measurement equivalence have slowly been replaced by a broader and richer understanding and set of methodologies to assess or ensure measurement equivalence. This volume presents a compilation of research in this vein. As readers will see, measurement equivalence has different meanings (it is context-specific) and there are substantially different approaches that can be employed in its investigation. We have attempted to sample some of these differences in the chapters that are included in this volume.

However, before discussing each of the chapters in this volume, we should perhaps first explain how this volume (the first in an annual series) and this collaboration (between the co-editors) came about. We will then go on to briefly describe each of the chapters in this volume so that, hopefully, interest will be provoked about each contribution and readers stimulated to devour the entire contents of this volume.

This series is sponsored by the Southern Management Association (SMA) as part of its research and publication mission for SMA members, Academy of Management members, and the profession at large. We sincerely appreciate the work of former SMA President Pamela L. Perrewé (Florida State University) and the SMA Board of Governors in commissioning this series and in approving of this affiliation. As envisioned, the role of

1

this series is to complement and not compete with the SMA's scholarly journal, the *Journal of Management*. As part of the series' charter with the SMA, this series will publish the paper that wins the overall best paper award at the Annual SMA Meeting (subject to the author[s] consent). This best paper will appear as the first chapter in each volume and determine the general topic of the volume; the remaining chapters will then be invited from prominent scholars in the area and will be designed to complement the initial chapter and build a thematically coherent volume.

The series editors were selected by joint deliberations involving themselves, the SMA President and Board, and the publisher (George Johnson, Information Age Publishing, Inc.). We envision remaining as editors at least long enough to get the series off to a good start, perhaps staying on longer. Succession will be determined by the same process as the initial editor selection: joint deliberation between the SMA and the publisher. Neider and Schriesheim have collaborated on about a dozen articles over the past fifteen years and have enjoyed an excellent relationship during this time. Perhaps as a result of these prior collaborations, our writing style is also very similar (so that it is tough to tell who has written what). Schriesheim is listed as the first editor in Volume 1 due to his more active role in the initial start-up negotiations. However, Neider will be first editor for Volume 2, and the order of editorship will alternate with future volumes.

The winner of the SMA 1999 Annual Meeting Overall Best Paper Award is the first chapter in this volume, "Male and Female Interpretations of Bidirectional Work-Family Conflict Scales: Testing for Measurement Equivalence," by Bruce W. Eagle (St. Cloud State University), Edward W. Miles (Georgia State University), and Marjorie L. Icenogle (University of South Alabama). We sincerely appreciate the authors' willingness to allow their work to be published in this first volume and hope that they (and our other authors) are satisfied with the result.

Within the past three decades, measurement equivalence has been explored principally in two domains: research examining organizational change processes and cross-cultural or transnational research. However, there are clearly other domains where measurement equivalence *should* be a concern. Thus, the initial chapter by Eagle, Miles, and Icenogle is particularly apropos. In it, they test for measurement equivalence from a gender perspective, employing bidirectional work-family conflict scales in two separate samples. For those of us who are, or have been married, it will not come as a surprise that males and females interpret work-family conflict issues in different ways. However, the unique contribution of this aptly done study is to point out the fact that specificity in item wording is essential to increase common frames of reference across groups. It is also critical to construct scales that clearly separate work-family issues from more general work-related topics.

LIST OF CONTRIBUTORS

Wolfgang Beck

Colegio Alemán
Mexico City
E-mail: Wbeck@compuserve.com

Gordon W. Cheung

Department of Management
The Chinese University of Hong Kong
E-mail: GORDONC@CUHK.edu.hk

Bruce W. Eagle

Department of Management
St. Cloud State University
E-mail: bwemgmt@stcloudstate.edu

Betti A. Hamilton

Department of Management
University of Miami
E-mail: bhamilto@sba.miami.edu

James C. Hayton

W.T. Beebe Institute of Personnel and
    Employment Relations
Georgia State University
E-mail: gijehx@langate.gsu.edu

Marjorie L. Icenogle

Department of Management
University of South Alabama
E-mail: micenogl@jagnar1.usouthal.edu

Edward W. Miles

Department of Management
Georgia State University
E-mail: mgtewm@langate.gsu.edu

Linda L. Neider

Department of Management
University of Miami
E-mail: lneider@sba.miami.edu

Roger B. Rensvold

Department of Management
City University of Hong Kong
E-mail: MGRR@CityU.edu.hk

Hettie A. Richardson

Department of Management
The University of Georgia
E-mail: hrichard@arches.uga.edu

Christine M. Riordan

Department of Management
The University of Georgia
E-mail: criordan@terry.oga.edu

Terri A. Scandura

Department of Management
University of Miami
E-mail: scandura@miami.edu.

Vida Scarpello

Department of Management
Georgia State University
E-mail: mgtvvs@langate.gsu.edu

Bryan S. Schaffer

Department of Management
The University of Georgia
E-mail: schaffer@arches.uga.edu

Chester A. Schriesheim

Department of Management
University of Miami
E-mail: chet@miami.edu

Robert J. Vandenberg

Department of Management
The University of Georgia
E-mail: rvandenb@terry.uga.edu

Ethlyn A. Williams

Department of Management
University of South Florida
E-mail: ethlyna@aol.com

Xiaohua (Tracy) Zhou

Department of Management
University of Miami
E-mail: xzhou@sba.miami.edu

The second paper in this volume is an extension of the noteworthy earlier research by Roger B. Rensvold (City University of Hong Kong) and Gordon W. Cheung (Chinese University of Hong Kong), dealing with improving modeling processes for testing measurement invariance across groups. Specifically for this volume, Rensvold and Cheung succinctly present new procedures that will allow researchers to more effectively employ structural equation modeling (SEM) in investigating equivalence/inequivalence issues. The authors do note, however, that while they have helped to solve the classic standardization problem of SEM, the most valuable research dealing with equivalence issues starts with expository skills. This paper and the prior work of the authors should be required reading for all doctoral students in management (and their advisors, if they are not already familiar with this line of research).

Christine M. Riordan, Hettie A. Richardson, Bryan S. Scaffer, and Robert J. Vandenberg from the University of Georgia were selected to contribute the third chapter for this volume. The Riordan et al. theoretical paper, based on the now classic typology of alpha, beta, and gamma change, is one which raises numerous questions about management research methodology in general. Measurement equivalence issues become particularly troublesome in longitudinal designs with multiple samples, particularly in detecting beta change, and in some instances falsely assuming gamma change. The unique contribution of this particular chapter is making the reader aware of the instances in which measurement equivalence/nonequivalence may affect our assumptions concerning change over time. It is precisely in these instances that such equivalence becomes especially problematic and the authors' review is therefore particularly salient and timely.

The Terri A. Scandura (University of Miami), Ethlyn A. Williams (University of South Florida), and Betti A. Hamilton (University of Miami) contribution to this volume takes an international twist on the measurement equivalence problem. Given that surveys embedded with western biases tend to be frequently utilized in cross-cultural studies, such surveys may present severe limitations with respect to equivalence of measurement. Using items assessing political behaviors, the Scandura et al. team administered their survey to both United States and Middle East respondents. The confirmatory factor-analytic (CFA) results supported only one invariant item across these diverse groups, and the item response theory (IRT) analyses indicated highly differential results based on cultural context. This seems to suggest that prior recommendations to test for equivalence via CFA may not be sufficient. Instead, it appears that multiple methods or techniques (including IRT models) may be needed to assess measurement equivalence across culturally diverse samples.

The fifth paper in this volume is by Vida Scarpello and James C. Hayton (both of Georgia State University), and it examines equivalence issues across several popular measures of job satisfaction. Given the extensive use of job satisfaction instruments in management research, it is imperative to understand whether or not these measures are assessing the same construct. In trying to offer insight concerning the source of nonequivalence among these measures, Scarpello and Hayton found strong support for the omitted variables explanation for satisfaction measure nonequivalence. Specifically, it appears that measures which incorporate the assessment of occupational and career concerns seem to be the more inclusive measures of job satisfaction (than are those which do not). In other words, employees may respond to measures of job satisfaction based on whether or not they feel that their jobs fulfill more general career aspirations. Thus, Scarpello and Hayton's work provide the reader with insight into conceptual issues and explanations that may underlie equivalence and nonequivalence in job satisfaction instruments.

The final chapter in this volume, by Xiaohua (Tracy) Zhou, Chester A. Schriesheim (both of the University of Miami), and Wolfgang Beck (University of Heidelberg), again looks at measurement equivalence from a transnational perspective. Similar to the Scandura et al. chapter, this comprehensive study utilizes item response theory to elucidate some of the measurement equivalence issues inherent with cross-cultural samples. Specifically, influence tactics survey data were collected from graduate business school respondents in Germany and the United States. Again, the usefulness of IRT as a way of ensuring measurement equivalence was demonstrated. Coupled with Scandura et al.'s findings, these investigations indicate that IRT analyses may be more informative for measurement equivalence research than the more widely-used CFA approaches. However, given the diversity of contexts involved, additional studies are clearly needed to better determine appropriate analytic strategies for researchers to employ.

In conclusion, this volume highlights research and conceptual insights into one of the most basic, and yet, perplexing research issues in management—handling and assessing the comparability of our measurement devices across groups and measures. One of the most consistently difficult concerns in management research over the past three decades has been trying to reconcile measurement equivalence issues utilizing diverse samples. Given the emphasis on diversity in the human resources area and the internationalization of business and management, measurement equivalence is more of a general concern now than ever before. If we are not able to successfully address concerns about measurement equivalence, research examining differences between groups could be highly misleading and/or erroneous. Consequently, we hope that the thoughtful contributions of the scholars in this volume will help future scholars to better address measurement equivalence concerns.

CHAPTER 2

MALE AND FEMALE INTERPRETATIONS OF BIDIRECTIONAL WORK-FAMILY CONFLICT SCALES
Testing for Measurement Equivalence

Bruce W. Eagle, Edward W. Miles, and Marjorie L. Icenogle

Abstract. This study examines the measurement equivalence of three common scales designed to measure bidirectional work-family conflict, using responses of men and women in two separate samples. Each of the three scales contains items measuring two constructs, work-to-family conflict and family-to-work conflict. Results of the multiple group analysis using LISREL 8 suggest that the underlying factor structures on two of the three scales are invariant in both samples. Responses to the third scale show that in Sample 2 the responses of men and women are invariant; however, responses from Sample 1 show that the women in this sample perceive three underlying factors among the items, rather than the two underlying factors perceived by men. Implications are discussed for the future use of these and other scales designed to measure work-family conflict. The primary recommendation to researchers is to select scales that are specifically focused in order to reduce the probability of respondents perceiving different underlying constructs.

INTRODUCTION

Definitions of work-family conflict generally depict a bidirectional conceptualization: work-to-family conflict and family-to-work conflict (Carlson,

Kacmar, & Williams, 1998; Frone, Russell, & Cooper, 1992a). A rational view of work and family conflict which characterizes this bidirectional conceptualization was introduced by Gutek, Searle, and Klepa (1991). According to this view, the more time one spends in the roles associated with the domains of work or family, respectively, the more role conflict one will perceive in the other domain. Consequently, a distinction is made between work interfering with the family domain (work-to-family conflict or W=>F conflict) and family interfering with the work domain (family-to-work conflict or F=>W conflict).

Although evidence generally supports the bidirectional conceptualization, some researchers have extended this rational view to suggest that employed women will report more F=>W conflict than men, and that men will experience more W=>F conflict than women (Karasek, 1979; Pleck, 1977). Numerous studies (e.g., Berk & Berk, 1979; Denmark, Shaw, & Ciali, 1985; Pleck, 1985) have shown that women spend many more hours per week than men on family and household chores. By the rational view, this difference should lead to more F=>W conflict for women than for men. Evidence also shows that employed men spend more hours per week at work than employed women (Pleck, 1985). Likewise, this would suggest that men should experience more W=>F conflict than do women.

However, evidence supporting this difference between men and women is weak. For example, studies (Eagle, Miles, & Icenogle, 1997; Frone et al., 1992a; Gutek et al., 1991) show that both men and women who are employed full time report spending more hours per week in paid work than in family responsibilities and that both groups also report more W=>F conflict than F=>W conflict. In one study, Gutek et al. (1991) found that women reported more F=>W conflict than men, but found no difference between men and women in W=>F conflict. Other studies (Eagle et al., 1997; Frone et al., 1992b; Williams & Alliger, 1994) have found no difference. Still, employers believe that differences exist. Eagle, Icenogle, Maes, and Miles (1998) report that some employers can be reluctant to hire women with children, assuming that women are more likely than men to let the responsibilities of a family interfere with work.

The issue of which gender experiences more W=>F conflict or F=>W conflict is unresolved in the work-family literature. Many researchers and employers still suspect differences exist, although the evidence supporting such differences is fairly weak. We suggest that this issue may be unresolved because of the way W=>F and F=>W conflict is being measured. A most critical question concerns the extent to which men and women interpret the items that are designed to measure the constructs of work and family conflict. If men and women are interpreting the items differently, the items are not related to the constructs in the same way; therefore, comparisons of mean responses across the two populations are inappropriate (Cole & Maxwell, 1985).

One way to measure the equivalence of constructs between different groups is an analysis of covariance structures across the groups. Unequal variance-covariance matrices indicate a lack of measurement equivalence, which means a difference exists in the way the groups interpret the underlying constructs of the measurement instrument. A lack of measurement equivalence indicates that simple comparisons of mean scores, as is the common practice, would be both inappropriate and misleading. If the variance-covariance matrices for men and women are unequal, such inequalities would introduce error into results of previous studies, thereby confounding those results. This confounding may explain why studies have been unable to detect the differences predicted by Pleck (1977) and Karasek (1979). This study investigates three common measures of both W->F conflict and F=>W conflict to determine if men and women perceive the underlying constructs in the same way. Perceptual differences may have led to measurement inequivalence which, in turn, has confounded comparisons between men and women on issues related to W=>F conflict and F=>W conflict.

MEASUREMENT EQUIVALENCE

Two assumptions must hold for an instrument to be equivalent across two different groups (Labouvie, 1980). First, the instrument must evoke a constant conceptual domain across the two samples. The issue here is whether a measure relates to the underlying construct in the same way across both samples (Cole & Maxwell, 1985). If, because of life experiences or other causes, men and women do not see an intended measure of W=>F conflict and F=>W conflict as tapping the same underlying constructs, a comparison of means across those two samples would be meaningless and inappropriate (Golembiewski, Billingsley, & Yeager, 1976; Schmitt, 1982; Vandenberg & Self, 1993). In test theory, this form of equivalence would be called conceptual or congeneric equivalence (Cole & Maxwell, 1985; Linn & Werts, 1979). Congeneric equivalence can be operationalized by testing whether the instrument has the same number of underlying factors across samples (King & Miles, 1995; Riordan & Vandenberg, 1994).

Second, the instrument must be consistently calibrated across the two samples (Labouvie, 1980), which means that men and women use the same response metric. For example, on a five-point scale, if a value of "3" meant "neutral" to men, but "mild disagreement" to women, the instrument would not be constantly calibrated across the two samples. In this example, a simple comparison of mean scores might show no differences when differences truly existed. This form of equivalence is known in measurement theory as tau equivalence (Hattrup, Schmitt, & Landis, 1992; Cole & Maxwell, 1985). Tau equivalence can be operationalized by testing for equal factor loadings across the samples of men and women (King & Miles, 1995; Riordan & Vandenberg, 1994).

Of the two assumptions (congeneric equivalence and tau equivalence), the lack of congeneric equivalence is the most serious violation because, if it is not present, the difference is "so dramatic that we do not have comparable constructs" (Schaubroeck & Green, 1989, p. 895). For example, if a given measure appears to have one factor in a sample of men and three factors in a sample of women, then there is no meaningful way to compare means across samples. Thus, comparative analyses should stop when congeneric equivalence is not present.

If tau equivalence is not present, mean scores can be substantively compared only if the problem is recognized and the mean scores are adjusted to account for the inequivalence. (Vandenberg and Self, 1993, provide a review of this procedure.) If tau equivalence is not present in measures of W=>F and F=>W conflict, inappropriate conclusions may be drawn if the differences are not identified and adjusted. For example, an analysis of variance could find statistically significant differences where no "real differences" exist across samples. Likewise, an analysis of variance might find no statistically significant differences where "real differences" truly do exist across samples.

Pleck (1977) and Karasek (1979) have both proposed that men will experience more W=>F conflict than women and that women will experience more F=>W conflict than men. We propose that a reasonable explanation for the inconclusive nature of the evidence is the lack of measurement equivalence in some of the scales that measure bidirectional conceptualizations of W=>F and F=>W conflict.

Method

Measures

This study analyzes data collected from two samples, using the same measures of bidirectional work-family conflict. Three separate scales were used to measure the degree to which a person's job interferes with his/her family life (W=>F conflict) and the degree to which a person's family life interferes with his/her job (F=>W conflict). The individual items forming these scales are displayed in the Appendix.

Frone et al.'s (1992a) work-family conflict instrument contains two questions for each form of conflict that are answered using a 5-point, frequency-based response rating set (1 = almost never/never, 5 = almost always/always). Gutek et al.'s (1991) work-family conflict instrument contains four items measuring each form of conflict. The four items assessing W=>F conflict were originally developed by Kopelman, Greenhaus, and

Connolly (1983) and the four items assessing F=>W conflict were originally developed by Burley (1989).

Wiley's (1984, 1987) work-family conflict instrument contains six statements for W=>F conflict and six statements for F=>W conflict, some of which were reworded items taken from a scale originally developed by Burke, Weir, and DuWors (1980). Both the Gutek et al. (1991) and Wiley (1987) scales used a 5-point, Likert-based response rating set (1 = strongly disagree, 5 = strongly agree).

Sample 1

Procedures and Respondents. Data for Sample 1 were collected using paper-and-pencil surveys administered to undergraduate and graduate students who were enrolled in evening classes at a large, urban university in the southeastern United States. Course instructors and one of the researchers directly administered the surveys during class time and collected the completed surveys. Each questionnaire had a cover sheet that encouraged the students' participation, assured them of the anonymity of their responses, and thanked them for their involvement. A variety of occupations were represented within Sample 1; for example, accountants, attorneys, engineers, computer system analysts, consultants, financial services personnel, sales and marketing managers, manufacturing personnel, telecommunication specialists, hospitality staff, and retail employees. In exchange for the respondents' participation, descriptive summary results of the survey were provided at the end of the school term.

The selection criteria for inclusion in the study were similar to those employed by Frone et al. (1992b); that is, respondents must be: (a) employed at least 20 hours per week, (b) married (or living as married within a prolonged domestic partner relationship), or had children living at home, or both, and (c) able to provide complete data on the measures used in the study. Sample 1 consisted of 318 respondents meeting these criteria.

Complete responses were received from 192 men and 126 women. The average ages of the men and women were 31.9 and 31.5, respectively. With regard to Sample 1 as a whole, 44% were 29 years old and under, 43% were 30-39, and 13% were 40 and over. Forty-three percent of the sample had children living at home.

The majority of the respondents were married or living as married (94%), 4% were divorced with children, and 1% were single parents. Those who were married had been married an average of 6.9 years. Men in the study worked an average of 49.1 hours per week. Women in the study worked an average of 46.0 hours each week.

Sample 2

Procedures and Respondents. The participants in Sample 2 were employees of a large urban university located in the southeastern United

States. Data were collected using paper-and-pencil questionnaires distributed via interoffice mail to 1,100 university employees who worked 20 hours or more per week. These materials were sent to nonfaculty and faculty employees of the university's various colleges, as well as to administrative, clerical, and service personnel of the university. A cover letter which stated the purpose of the research accompanied each questionnaire, encouraged voluntary participation by the employees, assured the employees of the anonymity of their responses, provided instructions, and thanked them for their cooperation. Return envelopes addressed to the University Ombudsperson's Office (a cosponsor of the study) were included. Follow-up reminders were sent at one-week and two-week intervals after the initial distribution.

The same respondent selection criteria used for Sample 1 were also used to obtain Sample 2. Five hundred and fifty-eight completed questionnaires were returned (51%), but 165 were eliminated from the analysis because the respondents did not fit the selection criteria, leaving a final sample of 393 respondents.

Complete responses were obtained from 224 men and 169 women. The mean ages of the male and female participants were 45.7 and 41.8, respectively, and the age composition of the whole sample was 6% were 29 years old and under, 27% were 30-39, 38% were 40-49, 23% were 50-59, and 6% were 60 and over. Ninety-two percent of the respondents were married or living as married, 7% were divorced with children, and 1% were single parents. Those who were married had been married an average of 15.3 years.

Seventy-eight percent of the respondents had children living at home. Male respondents reported working an average of 54.9 hours per week. Female respondents reported working an average of 49.3 hours per week.

A broad spectrum of occupational types and levels were represented. More than 43% of the subjects were of nonfaculty-rank, including: 5% clerical and/or secretarial; 12% professional (e.g., engineers); 16% administrative/managerial; and 10% security, technical, and/or service personnel. Approximately 57% were of faculty-rank, including 12% administrative/managerial and 45% teaching and research personnel.

Statistical Analysis

The analysis to evaluate measurement equivalence followed three steps prescribed by Cole and Maxwell (1985). In each step, data from each instrument in each sample were analyzed separately, using the multiple group analysis features of LISREL 8 (Joreskög & Sorböm, 1996). These features allow comparisons between responses of men and women from each sample for each of the scales. Step 1 compared the covariance matrices of the individual scale items between men and women to determine if the matrices were equivalent. The null hypothesis in Step 1 is that the covariance matrices are equal; therefore, a significant chi-square value demonstrates a difference in the covariance matrices. Equivalence indicates that the covariance matrices from each group may be pooled so the researcher may analyze responses as if they are from a single group (Byrne, 1989; Cheung & Rensvold, 1999).

For this omnibus type of test, the chi-square is the only appropriate goodness of fit index used. Other indices are inappropriate because a structured, restricted set of parameters is not imposed on the data. Although a significant chi-square value provides evidence that the matrices are not equivalent, this omnibus test does not provide insight regarding sources of the differences. Subsequent analyses are required to identify the sources of the differences.

Recognizing that the global test of the equality of the variance-covariance matrices may yield contradictory results, Byrne (1989) and others (e.g., Rock, Werts, & Flaugher, 1978) suggest that, even if the test for inequality cannot be rejected, the analysis should proceed to subsequent tests to investigate invariance in the factor structure and item loadings. Therefore, we completed Step 1, Step 2, and Step 3 for both samples on each of the three measures.

Step 2 compared the underlying factor structure between men and women on each of the three scales (congeneric equivalence). The null hypothesis in the second step is that the number of underlying factors perceived by men and women are the same. The pattern of fixed and free loadings was based on the identification of items that loaded on specific factors in previous studies (Eagle, 1995; Frone et al. 1992a; Gutek et al., 1991), with the first item of each scale fixed and subsequent items freed. We used multiple goodness of fit indices because of the documented problems (Bollen & Long, 1993) in using the chi-square goodness of fit as the single criterion. These indices included the overall chi-square, the Tucker-Lewis index (TLI) and the normed fit index (NFI). Although there is no clear rule, TLI and NFI values of .90 or greater are generally interpreted as indicating a good fit (Sharma, 1996).

If significant differences in the factor structure were found in Step 2, Step 3 analyses were not conducted because it is not meaningful to test for equivalence of factor loadings if the factor structures are not equal. If the factor structures in Step 2 were not equivalent, the items in the scales were analyzed separately for men and women using maximum likelihood factor analysis in SAS to identify the appropriate number of factors. The intent of this factor analysis is to determine how many factors underlie the data in each sub-sample.

If Step 2 demonstrated that both men and women perceive an equal number of factors, the analysis advanced to Step 3 to compare the factor loadings of men and women by constraining the factor loadings of women to be equivalent to the men's factor loadings (tau equivalence). All goodness of fit indices used in Step 2 are used in Step 3, supplemented by examining the relative goodness-of-fit index (RGFI), and the change in chi-square. The TLI and the NFI are relative fit indices which compare the hypothesized model to a baseline model. Goodness-of-fit indices, such as the GFI, are based solely on the fit of the data to the hypothesized model. The goodness-of-fit index (GFI) and the expected goodness-of-fit index (EGFI) are affected by sample size and the number of indicators. As the sample size or the number of indicators increases, the value of the EGFI is likely to decrease. The relative goodness-of-fit index (RGFI) adjusts for sample size, as well as for the number of indicators and is therefore a more rigorous test of goodness-of-fit (Maiti & Mukherjee, 1990, Sharma, 1996). In Step 3, we are testing the equality of factor loadings, and therefore, as the number of indicators in the model increase, the RGFI offers a more rigorous test of fit. Change in chi-square is a meaningful statistic because each subsequent step in the analysis places additional constraints on the model. When constraints are inappropriately applied, a significant change in chi-square will result (Riordan and Vandenberg, 1994).

RESULTS

The results of Step 1, which included the tests for the equality of covariance matrices between men and women, are shown in Table 1. The only goodness of fit criterion used in Step 1 was whether the chi-square value was significant. In Sample 1, the only significant chi-square was for the Wiley (1987) scale. For the Frone et al. (1992a) and the Gutek et al. (1991) scales, the insignificant chi-square values indicate that the covariance matrices are invariant. In Sample 2, significant differences in the covariance matrices were found on all three scales, although the significance level for the Gutek et al. (1991) scale was marginal.

The Table 1 results suggest that, in four of the six tests, there is evidence to question measurement equivalence. However, consistent with the recommendation of Byrne (1989), we conducted Step 2 analyses for all instruments in both samples.

Table 1.   Tests for Equality of Variance-Covariance Matrices Between Men and Women on Three Work-Family Conflict Scales

Scale	Sample 1			Sample 2		
	df	χ^2	p	df	χ^2	p
Frone, Russell, & Cooper	10	12.23	0.27	10	25.12	0.0051
Gutek, Searle, & Klepa	36	39.37	0.32	36	49.85	0.0620
Wiley	78	108.59	0.013	78	123.06	0.0008

Step 2 of the analysis examined the equivalence of the factor structures of each scale. The results are shown in Table 2. In Sample 1, the three indices (chi-square, TLI, and NFI) are consistent for the Frone et al. (1992a) instrument: men and women perceived the same two underlying factors. However, for the Gutek et al. (1991) scales and the Wiley (1987) scales in Sample 1, the indices offer inconsistent results. Having inconsistency among the indices is common, and having the chi-square as the outlier is particularly common (Bollen & Long, 1993). Therefore, given that the TLI and NFI values are clearly above the .90 threshold, we failed to reject the null hypothesis of an equal number of underlying factors for the Gutek et al. instrument and for the Wiley instrument in Sample 1. Thus, the only scale that did not demonstrate congeneric equivalence in Step 2 was the Wiley (1987) instrument. In Sample 1, the three indices consistently indicated unequal factor structures and, therefore, in Sample 1 this instrument did not advance to Step 3.

Step 3, which compared the factor loadings between men and women, was completed for the Frone et al. (1992a) and Gutek et al. (1991) scales using both samples, and for the Wiley (1987) scales for Sample 2 only. The results of Step 3 analyses are shown in Table 3 and show five indices of goodness of fit. For one case—the Frone et al. instrument in Sample 2—all five indices indicate a good fit. For the other four cases, four of the five indices indicate a good fit, with each outlier being a chi-square. Thus, given the overall weight of the evidence, we conclude that all five cases in Step 3 demonstrate equal factor loadings, which is an indication of tau equivalence.

In summary, the Frone et al. (1992a) and Gutek et al. (1991) scales demonstrated both congeneric and tau equivalence in both samples. The Wiley (1987) scales demonstrated congeneric and tau equivalence in Sample 2, but not in Sample 1.

Since Step 2 revealed differences in the factor structures of the Wiley (1987) scales for Sample 1, the responses of the male and female sub-samples in Sample 1 were subjected to maximum likelihood factor analyses.

Table 2. Fit Indices for Congeneric Equivalence Between Men and Women on Three Work-Family Conflict Scales

Scale	Sample 1					Sample 2				
	df	χ^2	p	TLI	NFI	df	χ^2	p	TLI	NFI
Frone, Russell, & Cooper	2	2.03	0.36	1.00	1.00	2	3.26	0.20	.99	1.00
Gutek, Searle, & Klepa	38	56.26	0.028	.97	.93	38	102.61	0.001	.93	.93
Wiley	106	211.17	0.001	.89	.85	106	208.85	0.001	.94	.90

Table 3. Fit Indices for Tau Equivalence Between Men and Women on Three Work-Family Conflict Scales

Scale	Sample 1					Sample 2				
	$\chi^2(df)$	TLI	NFI	RGFI	$\Delta\chi^2(df)$	$\chi^2(df)$	TLI	NFI	RGFI	$\Delta\chi^2(df)$
Frone, Russell, & Cooper	8.40(4)	.97	.98	.99	6.37(2)*	4.67(2)	1.00	0.99	.99	1.41(2)
Gutek, Searle, & Klepa	63.54(44)*	.95	.93	.94	7.28(6)	112.50(44)**	0.94	0.92	.96	9.89(6)
Wiley						219.98(116)**	0.94	0.90	.98	11.13(10)

Note. TLI = Tucker-Lewis Index; NFI = normed-fit index; RGFI = relative goodness-of-fit index.

* $p < .05$; ** $p < .01$

This form of factor analysis was particularly appropriate because it can test the hypothesis that a specific number of factors are sufficient to explain the data. The test criterion for this hypothesis is the TLI. For each sub-sample, the hypothesis that two factors are sufficient was tested first. For the male sub-sample, the TLI of .95 indicated that two factors were sufficient to explain the data. However, for the female sub-sample, the TLI of .85 indicated that two factors were insufficient to explain the data. For the female sub-sample, a test of the hypothesis that three factors were sufficient yielded a TLI of .91, indicating a good fit to the data. In summary, the maximum likelihood factor analysis results indicate that, for the Wiley scales in Sample 1, males seem to view the scales as having two underlying dimensions while females seem to view the scales as having three underlying dimensions.

For each sub-sample, the factors were rotated using a VARIMAX rotation. Although there are differing opinions regarding what constitutes a meaningful factor loading (Ford, MacCallum, & Tait, 1986), we used the rule of Nunnally (1978) that loadings below .40 are too small to interpret. The resulting factor loadings are reported in Table 4.

Wiley (1987) suggested that her instrument includes six items designed to measure W=>F conflict and six items to measure F=>W conflict. Research, however, has shown that one item intended to measure W=>F conflict (listed as item 12 in Table 4 and in the Appendix) actually measures F=>W conflict (Eagle, 1995). This results in an instrument with five W=>F conflict items and seven F=>W conflict items. Results of the factor analyses on the Wiley scales showed that Factor 1 contained items 6 through 12 and that Factor 2 contained items 1 through 5 for the men in Sample 1.

The women's response pattern was somewhat different, with women responding according to the three underlying factors shown in Table 4. Factor 1 included six of the seven items intended to measure F=>W conflict—items 6 through 11. Factor 2 included four of the five items intended to measure W=>F conflict—items 1, 2, 3, and 5. Factors 1 and 2 seem to address *strain-based* issues. For example, item 3 refers to emotions while items 6 and 11 refer to mental and physical energy expended in one arena instead of the other. However, Factor 3 was composed of three items that had double loadings and items 4 and 12, which had single loadings on Factor 3. This factor may be a more general *time* factor based on dividing a finite amount of time between multiple demands. Of the five items that load on this factor, the term "time" is explicitly referred to in three of them (items 1, 7, and 12) but does not appear in other items in the scale. Another of those items (item 4) seems to implicitly address time concerns.

In summary, in Sample 1, men and women did not respond to the items of the Wiley instrument using the same underlying constructs. The men responded in a pattern that was the anticipated two-factor structure. The

Table 4.   Maximum Likelihood Factor Loadings for the Wiley Instrument: Sample 1

Items	Men Factor 1	Men Factor 2	Women Factor 1	Women Factor 2	Women Factor 3
1. My family often expresses unhappiness about the time I spend at work.		.62		.42	.51
2. My present job makes it difficult for me to relax when I'm away from work.		.83		.93	
3. I am sometimes angry and irritable at home because of things that happen at work.		.60		.52	
4. I often have to miss important family or social activities because of my job.		.71			.40
5. I often find myself thinking about work when I'm busy doing other things.		.62		.73	
6. When I am at work, I often find myself thinking about things outside of work and not paying attention to my job.	.42		.52		
7. My outside responsibilities make it difficult for me to spend as much time on job-related activities as my boss expects.	.71		.51		.53
8. Because of my family or school, I can't involve myself in my job as much as I would like.	.62		.58		
9. My family or personal life interferes with my job.	.75		.55		.50
10. I sometimes have to miss work to see that other responsibilities are met.	.46		.55		
11. I don't have much energy to devote to work because of all the other demands in my life.	.76		.77		
12. The time I have to spend on household activities makes it difficult for me to spend necessary time on job-related activities.	.62				.74

women responded in a pattern that indicated that a third factor, perhaps representing time, was present.

DISCUSSION

The primary purpose of this study was to determine whether measurement inequivalence exists in bidirectional measures of work-family conflict due to differences in men and women's interpretations of these scales. The results of this study indicate that measurement inequivalence can be a problem with this type of scale. Although the results do not show that a problem exists with every instrument in every population, the results do indicate that researchers should not take for granted that men and women will respond to measures of work-family conflict in the same manner.

Because one instrument (Wiley, 1987) had measurement equivalence problems in this study while the other two (Frone et al., 1992a; Gutek et al., 1991) did not, it is possible to compare these scales to see what the differences among them may be. Also, because we had samples from two different populations, comparisons may be made across samples as well. Three plausible explanations exist for the difference in the findings.

First, the scales vary in the degree to which they refer specifically to work-family issues or the broader category of work and nonwork issues. The Wiley (1987) instrument was the least specific. Some items refer to nonwork obligations in a very general way. For example, Wiley's item 7 is phrased "My outside responsibilities make it difficult for me to spend as much time on job-related activities as my boss expects." The "outside responsibilities" can certainly be in many arenas other than family. Another type of item in the Wiley instrument involves multiple references. For example, item 9 is phrased "My family or personal life interferes with my job." By contrast, the items of the Frone et al. (1992a) instrument refer specifically to family issues, not the broader category of nonwork. Frone et al.'s item 1 even goes as far as to list specific examples of "responsibilities at home."

We believe that, when scale items refer to the more general category of nonwork activities rather than the more focused category of family activities, there is more opportunity for men and women to interpret the scales using different frames of reference. The more specific the focus, the less opportunity there is to interpret the scales differently. We suggest that this difference may be one reason why the Frone instrument did not have measurement equivalence problems but the Wiley instrument did.

Second, the items that have multiple references may trigger different interpretations between men and women or differences in the salience of the multiple references. For example, item 8 of the Wiley instrument is phrased "Because of my family or school, I can't involve myself in my job as much as I would like to." A person who is not in school is likely to interpret this item solely as a family-work item. A person who is in school will have unknown proportions of family-work conflict and school-work conflict represented in his or her response.

Only 8% of Sample 2 was enrolled in school while 100% of Sample 1 was enrolled in school. This difference may very well have contributed to the finding of measurement equivalence for the Wiley instrument in Sample 2, but not in Sample 1. In Sample 1, the multiple reference items had a broader span of potential meanings than they did in Sample 2. This gave men and women more opportunity to interpret them differently.

Third, it may be that, in their responses, women distinguish more than men do between time-based conflict and strain-based conflict. Greenhaus and Beutell (1985) view time-based work-family conflict as the simple quantitative reality that time used in one arena is not available for use in the other arena. Strain-based conflict is a more qualitative concern; for example, emotions, state of mind, and energy expended in one arena influence how a person acts as he or she shifts to the other arena. The results of the factor analysis in Table 4 may be interpreted as the unanticipated third factor for women representing *time-based* conflict. Factors 1 and 2 seem to address *strain-based* issues. It may be that women are more prone to see time-based conflict and strain-based conflict as separate dimensions while men are less prone to see a distinction.

In contrast to the Wiley instrument, the Frone et al. instrument is only a time-based conflict instrument. The phrasing of the items (all items begin with "How often does . . . ") and the response anchors are oriented toward time-based conflict.

In summary, we have three recommendations to researchers who may be concerned about measurement equivalence in bidirectional measures of work-family conflict. (a) If work-family conflict is the specific interest, use instruments that are specifically focused on work-family instead of work and more general nonwork issues. We believe that the more general items provide more opportunity for differences in perceptions of underlying constructs to occur. Researchers who are interested in the more general issue of work and nonwork should be aware that there may be more opportunity for men and women to interpret those constructs differently. (b) Try to avoid scales that use multiple references in the same item. Different respondents will find some references to be more salient or more relevant than others will (i.e., multiple references are a source of error variance). (c) When appropriate to the research question, use instruments that focus on a single form (e.g., time-based or strain-based) of work-family conflict. Again, this degree of specificity leaves less opportunity for men and women to interpret the constructs differently. Alternatively, use instruments that clearly differentiate between forms of work-family conflict. Avoid instruments that mix forms of work-family conflict in the same dimensions.

Based on these recommendations, one key direction for future research is the development of more specifically focused bidirectional measures of work-family conflict. The measures developed should take care to separate work-family issues from more general work and nonwork issues. As specificity in item wording increases, the potential for common frames of reference increases across groups, even as the variety of demographic attributes in respondents increases. Additionally, researchers have the opportunity to develop instruments to measure other multiple dimensions of work-family conflict, such as time-based and strain-based conflict (Greenhaus & Buetell, 1985). This, too, should contribute to the commonality of conceptual frames of reference among respondents.

The present study has three noteworthy limitations. One limitation is the sole reliance on pencil and paper questionnaires that required respondents to reveal personal and sensitive information (e.g., cohabitation living arrangements). Since the accuracy of these responses could not be confirmed, respondents may have answered with the most socially acceptable responses. However, the anonymous collection of the questionnaires may have helped to minimize this weakness.

A second limitation is related to the generalizability of the results of this study. That is, the nature of the two samples. Students employed and enrolled in evening classes (Sample 1) and employees of an educational institution (Sample 2) may not be highly representative of the population of persons experiencing work-family conflict. However, given that the purpose of this study was to determine if measurement inequivalence can occur in these instruments, it would seem that this question can be appropriately answered with these two samples. Measurement inequivalence *is* a concern with bidirectional measures of work-family conflict. Still, samples of other populations will be necessary to determine the degree to which this problem is commonplace.

A third limitation is that this study addressed only one demographic attribute (gender) on three bidirectional measures of work-family conflict. Future studies should attempt to identify other demographic attributes that may contribute to differences in measurement equivalence (such as age, number of children, and socioeconomic status).

This study was designed to determine whether measurement inequivalence can occur in bidirectional measures of work-family conflict. The results of the study show that measurement inequivalence problems can occur. In general, we recommend that researchers avoid this problem by using measures that distinguish work-family conflict from work and nonwork issues and that distinguish among types of work-family conflict.

REFERENCES

Berk, R. & Berk, S.F. (1979). *Labor and leisure at home.* Beverly Hills, CA: Sage.

Bollen, K.A. & Long, J.S. (1993). *Testing structural equation models.* Newbury Park, CA: Sage.

Burke, R.J., Weir, T., & DuWors, R.E., Jr. (1980). Work demands on administrators and spouse well-being. *Human Relations, 33*, 253-278.

Burley, K. (1989). *Work-family conflict and marital adjustment in dual career couples: A comparison of three time models.* Unpublished doctoral dissertation, Claremont Graduate School, Claremont, CA.

Byrne, B.M. (1989). *A primer of LISREL.* New York: Springer-Verlag.

Carlson, D.S., Kacmar, K.M., & Williams, L.J. (1998). The development and validation of a multi-dimensional measure of work-family conflict. *Proceedings of the Academy of Management, USA, 98,* Research Methods Track, A1-A7.

Cheung, G.W., & Rensvold, R.B. (1999). Testing factorial invariance across groups: A reconceptualization and proposed new method. *Journal of Management, 25*(1), 1-28.

Cole, D.A., & Maxwell, S.E. (1985). Multitrait-multimethod comparisons across populations: A confirmatory factor analytic approach. *Multivariate Behavioral Research, 20,* 389-417.

Denmark, F.L., Shaw, J.S., & Ciali, S.D. (1985). The relationship among sex roles, living arrangements and the division of household responsibilities. *Sex Roles, 12,* 617-625.

Eagle, B.W. (1995). *A construct validity study of bidirectional measures of work-family conflict.* Unpublished doctoral dissertation, Georgia State University, Atlanta, Georgia.

Eagle, B.W., Icenogle, M.L., Maes, J.D., & Miles, E.W. (1998). The importance of employee demographic profiles for understanding experiences of work-family interrole conflicts. *The Journal of Social Psychology, 138,* 690-709.

Eagle, B.W., Miles, E.W., & Icenogle, M.L. (1997). Interrole conflicts and the permeability of work and family domains: Are there gender differences? *Journal of Vocational Behavior, 50,* 168-184.

Ford, J.K., MacCallum, R.C., & Tait, M. (1986). The application of exploratory factor analysis in applied psychology: A critical review and analysis. *Personnel Psychology, 39*(2), 291-314.

Frone, M.R., Russell, M., & Cooper, M.L. (1992a). Antecedents and outcomes of work-family conflict: Testing a model of the work-family interface. *Journal of Applied Psychology, 77,* 65-78.

Frone, M.R., Russell, M., & Cooper, M.L. (1992b). Prevalence of work-family conflict: Are work and family boundaries asymmetrically permeable? *Journal of Organizational Behavior, 13,* 723-729.

Golembiewski, R. T., Billingsley, K., & Yeager, S. (1976). Measuring change persistency in human affairs: Types of change generated by OD designs. *Journal of Applied Behavioral Science, 12,* 133-157.

Greenhaus, & Buetell (1985). Sources of conflict between work and family roles. *Academy of Management Review, 10,* 76-88.

Gutek, B.A., Searle, S., & Klepa, L. (1991). Rational versus gender role expectations for work-family conflict. *Journal of Applied Psychology, 76,* 560-568.

Hattrup, K., Schmitt, N., & Landis, R. S. (1992). Equivalence of constructs measured by job-specific and commercially available aptitude tests. *Journal of Applied Psychology, 77,* 298-308.

Joreskög, K., & Sorböm, D. (1996). *LISREL 8: User's Reference Guide.* Chicago: Scientific Software International, Inc.

Karasek, R. (1979). Job demands, job decision latitude and mental strain: Implications for job redesign. *Administrative Science Quarterly, 24*, 285-307.

King, W.C., Jr. & Miles, E.W. (1995). A Quasi-experimental assessment of the effect of computerizing noncognitive paper-and-pencil measurements: A test of measurement equivalence. *Journal of Applied Psychology, 80*(6), 643-651.

Kopelman, R.E., Greenhaus, J.H., & Connolly, T.F. (1983). A model of work, family, and interrole conflict: A construct validation study. *Organization Behavior and Human Performance, 32*, 198-215.

Labouvie, E.W. (1980). Identity versus equivalence of psychological measures and constructs. In L.W. Poon (Ed.), *Aging in the 1980s* (pp. 493-202). Washington, DC: American Psychological Association.

Linn, P.C., & Werts, C.E. (1979). Covariance structures and their analysis. In R. Traub (Ed.), *New directions for testing and measurement: Methodological developments* (pp. 53-73). San Francisco: Jossey-Bass.

Maiti, S.S., & Mukherjee, B.N. (1990). A note on distributional properties of the Joreskog and Sorbom fit indices. *Psychometrika, 55*, 721-726.

Nunnally, J.C. (1978). *Psychometric theory.* New York: McGraw-Hill.

Pleck, J.H. (1977). The work-family role system. *Social Problems, 24*, 417-427.

Pleck, J.H. (1985). *Working wives/working husbands.* Beverly Hills, CA: Sage.

Riordan, C.M., & Vandenberg, R.J. (1994). A central question in cross-cultural research: Do employees of different cultures interpret work-related measures in an equivalent manner? *Journal of Management, 20*, 643-671.

Rock, D.A., Werts, C.E., & Flaugher, R.L. (1978). The use of analysis of covariance structures for comparing the psychometric properties of multiple variables across populations. *Multivariate Behavioral Research, 13*, 403-418.

Schaubroeck, J., & Green, S.G. (1989). Confirmatory factor analytic procedures for assessing change during organizational entry. *Journal of Applied Psychology, 74*, 892-900.

Schmitt, N. (1982). The use of analysis of covariance structures to assess beta and gamma change. *Multivariate Behavioral Research, 17*, 343-358.

Sharma, S. (1996). *Applied multivariate techniques.* New York: John Wiley & Sons, Inc.

Vandenberg, R.J., & Self, R.M. (1993). Assessing newcomers' changing commitments to the organization during the first 6 months of work. *Journal of Applied Psychology, 78*, 557-568.

Wiley, D.L. (1984). *A systematic investigation of role conflict between work and nonwork roles.* Unpublished doctoral dissertation, The University of Tennessee, Knoxville, TN.

Wiley, D.L. (1987). The relationship between work/nonwork role conflict and job-related outcomes: Some unanticipated findings. *Journal of Management, 13*, 467-472.

Williams, K.J., & Alliger, G.M. (1994). Role stressors, mood spillover, and perceptions of work-family conflict in employed parents. *Academy of Management Journal, 37*, 467-472.

APPENDIX

Scale Items by Source

From Frone, Russell, & Cooper (1992a)
Work-to-Family Conflict

1. How often does your job or career interfere with your responsibilities at home, such as yard work, cooking, cleaning, repairs, shopping, paying the bills, or childcare?
2. How often does your job or career keep you from spending the amount of time you would like to spend with your family?
   Subscale Reliability Estimates (coefficient alpha); Sample 1: .88; Sample 2: .86.

Family-to-Work Conflict

3. How often does your home-life interfere with your responsibilities at work, such as getting to work on time, accomplishing daily tasks, or working overtime?
4. How often does your home-life keep you from spending the amount of time you would like to spend on job or career-related activities?
   Subscale Reliability Estimates (coefficient alpha); Sample 1: .77; Sample 2: .78.

   Response Anchors: 1 = almost never/never, 2 = occasionally, 3 = about half the time, 4 = frequently, 5 = almost always/always

From Gutek, B.A., Searle, S., & Klepa, L. (1991)
Work-to-Family Conflict

1. After work, I come home too tired to do some of the things I'd like to do.
2. On the job I have so much work to do that it takes away from my personal interests.
3. My family/friends dislike how often I am preoccupied with my work while I am at home.
4. My work takes up time that I'd like to spend with family/friends.
   Subscale Reliability Estimates (coefficient alpha); Sample 1: .82; Sample 2: .84.

Family-to-Work Conflict

5. I'm often too tired at work because of the things I have to do at home.

6. My personal demands are so great that it takes away from my work.
7. My superiors and peers dislike how often I am preoccupied with my personal life while at work.
8. My personal life takes up time that I'd like to spend at work.
    Subscale Reliability Estimates (coefficient alpha); Sample 1: .77; Sample 2: .81.

Response Anchors: 1 = strongly agree, 2 = agree, 3 = neither agree nor disagree, 4 = disagree, 5 = strongly disagree

From Wiley (1987)
Work-to-Family Conflict
1. My family often expresses unhappiness about the time I spend at work.
2. My present job makes it difficult for me to relax when I'm away from work.
3. I am sometimes angry and irritable at home because of things that happen at work.
4. I often have to miss important family or social activities because of my job.
5. I often find myself thinking about work when I'm busy doing other things.
    Subscale Reliability Estimates (coefficient alpha); Sample 1: .80; Sample 2: .81.

Family-to-Work Conflict
6. When I am at work, I often find myself thinking about things outside of work and not paying attention to my job.
7. My outside responsibilities make it difficult for me to spend as much time on job-related activities as my boss expects.
8. Because of my family or school, I can't involve myself in my job as much as I would like.
9. My family or personal life interferes with my job.
10. I sometimes have to miss work to see that other responsibilities are met.
11. I don't have much energy to devote to work because of all the other demands in my life.
12. The time I have to spend on household activities makes it difficult for me to spend necessary time on job-related activities.
    Subscale Reliability Estimates (coefficient alpha); Sample 1: .83; Sample 2: .85.

Response Anchors: 1 = strongly disagree, 2 = disagree, 3 = neutral, 4 = agree, 5 = strongly agree

CHAPTER 3

TESTING FOR METRIC INVARIANCE USING STRUCTURAL EQUATION MODELS
Solving the Standardization Problem

Roger B. Rensvold and Gordon W. Cheung

Abstract: This chapter discusses the standardization problem that arises in structural equations modeling when variables are tested for between-group metric invariance. Thus, this chapter is essentially a recapitulation of one of our earlier works, with some revisions and additions. Basically, we changed much of our nomenclature to conform to better usage. Additionally, we describe two new procedures for identifying sets of non-invariant items. These supplant our earlier "triangle heuristic," which relied upon the researcher's powers of observation and his/her ability to manually rearrange the rows and columns of a matrix. The new procedures are straightforward and unambiguous, and yield all sets of reference indicators (e.g., survey items) that are invariant with respect to the groups being studied.

INTRODUCTION

This chapter discusses the so-called standardization problem, which arises when variables are tested for between-group metric invariance (Horn &

McArdle, 1992). The test is performed by researchers wishing to ensure that the variables used in a between-group comparison "mean the same thing" to members of both groups (see Vandenberg & Lance, 2000, for a thorough review). The problem arises because of circularity. Invariance testing using structural equation modeling (SEM) requires a measurement model. Estimating the model requires the specification of a referent (or "reference indicator;" Vandenberg & Lance, 2000), which must be invariant. Researchers are thus forced to assume, a priori, a portion of what they wish to test. If the assumption is false, then the results of the test are likely to be incorrect.

Metric invariance is particularly important when the indicators are items on a survey or questionnaire, and the groups being compared have different cultures and languages. Not even the most careful translation strategy (e.g., Brislin, Lonner, & Thorndike, 1973) can ensure that items have the same meanings for members of both groups, or that they have equivalent weights as indicators of the constructs being measured. However, the problem is not limited to international or cross-cultural studies. Whenever two groups are not randomly drawn from the same population, metric invariance failure is possible. In the context of survey research, metric invariance testing is aimed at identifying the non-invariant (problematical) items, and constructing sets of invariant (useable) items.

We first described this problem and proposed a solution two years ago (Cheung & Rensvold, 1999; Rensvold & Cheung, 1998). It has attracted little attention to date, despite its obvious implications for a large number of published studies. Re-analyzing the studies could (and in our view, should) become a major research program, both for the original authors and for others. In addition to either substantiating or refuting the original conclusions, the procedures we describe could provide new, potentially important sources of information about between-group differences.

Thus, this chapter is essentially a recapitulation of Cheung and Rensvold (1999), with some changes and additions. We have changed much of our nomenclature to conform to Vandenberg and Lance (2000). Measurement equivalence/invariance (ME/I) is a new field, bedeviled with idiosyncratic terminology; Vandenberg and Lance's important review offers an opportunity to achieve some standardization. (We have, however, retained a few of our own quirks; e.g., "referent" instead of "reference indicator.") In addition, we describe two new procedures for identifying sets of non-invariant items. These supplant the so-called "triangle heuristic" (Cheung & Rensvold, 1999; Rensvold & Cheung, 1998), which relied upon the researcher's powers of observation, and his/her ability to manually rearrange the rows and columns of a matrix. The new procedures are straightforward and unambiguous, and yield all sets of reference indicators (e.g., survey items) that are invariant with respect to the groups being studied.

Deciding what to explain and what to assume was difficult. One group of readers, with limited prior exposure to structural equation modeling

(SEM), may find parts of the chapter overly technical. We apologize, offering as a defense our need to use the same vocabulary as others working in this area. Another group of readers may find other parts of the chapter a simplistic rehash of what everybody already knows. Again we apologize, offering as a defense the needs of the first group. Both groups are urged to make full use of the references, which include detailed, elementary treatments, as well as some that are more concise and advanced.

MEASUREMENT EQUIVALENCE/INVARIANCE (ME/I)

Measurement equivalence is a prerequisite for comparison. When a variable is measured, it must mean the same thing with respect to all the entities being compared. In many cases, a measurement is so manifestly equivalent that it is never questioned, much less tested. We expect a thermometer to always work the same way, regardless of the medium in which it is immersed, and we readily accept that 80° C water is just as hot as 80° C maple syrup.

Between-group comparisons are central to science. Comparing two single entities (stars, plants, cells, rocks, managers, etc.) may be informative and even entertaining, but *between-entity* differences are not generalizeable. We only feel we have discovered something important when we observe systematic, *between-group* differences that cannot reasonably be attributed to chance (i.e., sampling error). The invention of techniques for assessing the likelihood of observed between-group differences (e.g., Student's *t* statistic, 1908) marked the birth of statistics as a science.

Between-group measurement equivalence is usually trivial with respect to inanimate objects. Sometimes, it is also trivial with respect to people. Income, years of education, and five-year survival rate following cancer therapy are all examples of well-operationalized variables that obviously have the same meaning for everyone. However, the issue of ME/I tumbles from triviality into deep complexity when the measurement involves a psychological or an attitudinal object, such as organizational commitment. Unlike five-year survival, organizational commitment cannot be measured by checking records. Group members have to be asked how satisfied they are with their jobs. Usually, the "asking" takes the form of giving them multi-item instruments to complete. If ME/I exists, then members of both groups interpret the items in the same way. Various aspects of ME/I testing form the subject matter of this chapter.

ME/I has been studied in many different contexts, such as cross-cultural organizational psychology (e.g., Triandis, 1994), cross-cultural management (Janssens, Brett, & Smith, 1995; Reise, Widaman, & Pugh, 1993; Riordan & Vandenberg, 1994; Windle, Iwawaki, & Lerner, 1988), across groups with different levels of academic achievement (Byrne, Shavelson, &

Muthén, 1989), different industries (Drasgow & Kanfer, 1985), genders (Byrne, 1994), experimental versus control groups (Pentz & Chou, 1994), and self-ratings of performance versus ratings by others (Cheung, 1999). Vandenberg and Lance (2000) provide an extensive list of similar studies.

LEVELS OF ME/I

ME/I exists at several different levels, only some of which may be relevant to a particular study. In order to place the following discussion in context, and to provide a starting point for readers who may be unfamiliar with the field, we provide a brief overview of the ME/I levels most frequently discussed in the literature (Vandenberg & Lance, 2000).

Researchers have taken various approaches to the ME/I, including item response theory (e.g., Maurer, Raju, & Collins, 1998; Millsap & Everson, 1993; Reise et al., 1993) and generalizability theory (e.g., Brennan, 1983; Cronbach, Gleser, Nanda, & Rajaratman, 1972; Marcoulides, 1996, 1998). Current practice, however, favors confirmatory factor analysis (CFA) of the measurement model, using SEM. Although the measurement model is discussed at length elsewhere (e.g., Bollen, 1989; Bollen & Long, 1993; Jöreskog & Sörbom, 1993), we briefly review its terminology and basic concepts.

Figure 1 shows a six-indicator, two-group measurement model with two correlated latent variables, or factors. The indicators (e.g., survey item responses) are the entities labeled X_i^g (i = 1 to 6, g = 1 to 2). The subscript identifies the indicator, and the superscript identifies the group from which the data were collected. In Figure 1 we use the numbers 1 and 2 to identify the groups, written in parentheses to avoid confusion with exponentiation. The indicators are the only "real" part of the model. All the other parameters are estimated using the model specification, and the data.

The value of each X_i^g indicator is conceptualized as being due to the value of an unobserved, estimated ξ_j^g factor (e.g., job satisfaction), plus the indicator's unique variance (δ_i^g). The strength of the relationship between ξ_j^g and X_i^g is given by the value of the factor loading parameter, λ_{ij}^g. The factors ξ_j^g also possess variance ϕ_{ij}^g and covariance. The two factors ξ_1^g and ξ_2^g in Figure 1 have covariance ϕ_{12}^g.

Figure 2 shows the relationship between the X_i^g indicators and the ξ_j^g factors in more detail. The λ_{ij}^g factor loading parameters can be conceptualized as the slopes of the lines obtained by regressing the factors on each of the indicators. In addition, each regression line has an intercept τ_i^g, which is the value of X_i^g when ξ_j^g is zero. Each ξ_j^g also possesses a latent mean κ_j^g, which we shall not discuss further, except to note that the null hypothesis $\kappa_j^{(1)} = \kappa_j^{(2)}$ cannot be tested using all the X_i^g indicators unless

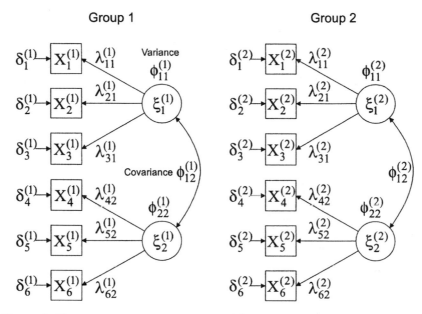

Figure 1. Two-group measurement model.

$\lambda_{ij}^{(1)} = \lambda_{ij}^{(2)}$ and $\tau_i^{(1)} = \tau_i^{(2)}$ for each indicator. The equation for each indicator X_i^g can be written as

$$X_i^g = \tau_i^g + \lambda_{ij}^g \xi_i^g + \delta_i^g \tag{1}$$

Vandenberg and Lance (2000) list eight specific types of ME/I. Byrne et al. (1989) refer to the first five levels as measurement invariance, and the last three as structural invariance. Using the nomenclature introduced above, these levels are as follows:

1. Omnibus equality of the covariance matrices across group, i.e., $\Sigma^{(1)} = \Sigma^{(2)}$. This is the highest level of ME/I. Normally, it would be expected only if groups 1 and 2 consisted of two samples randomly drawn from the same population. If omnibus equality exists, no further ME/I tests are necessary.
2. Configural invariance (Vandenberg & Lance, 2000), also known as "weak factorial invariance" (Horn & McArdle, 1992). Each group displays the same pattern of factor loadings. In other words, the same indicators are associated with the same factors for both groups. Configural invariance is a prerequisite for further ME/I tests.

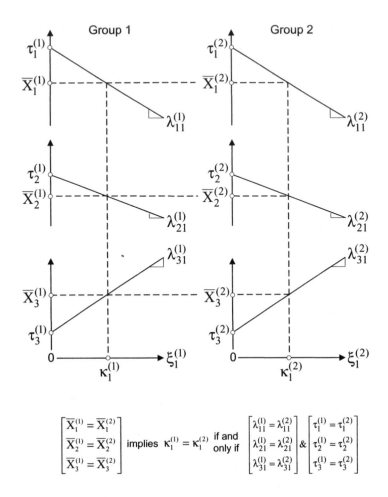

Figure 2. Two-group measurement model: Intercepts and latent means.

3. Metric invariance (Horn & McArdle, 1992). Equality of factor load-
    ings ($\lambda_{ij}^{(1)} = \lambda_{ij}^{(2)}$ for all i, j). In the first instance, the entire model is
    tested for metric invariance. If the model fails, then each factor is
    tested. Each factor that fails is then tested at the level of the separate
    indicators, to find the specific sources of non-invariance. We discuss
    the procedure in more detail below. The model must display metric
    invariance with respect to at least some indicators, or subsequent
    tests for ME/I are not meaningful.
4. Scalar invariance (Meredith, 1993; Steenkamp & Baumgartner,
    1998). Equality of indicator intercepts ($\tau_i^{(1)} = \tau_i^{(2)}$ for all i).
5. Homogeneity of unique variances. Between-group equality of the
    unique variance associated with each indicator ($\delta_i^{(1)} = \delta_i^{(2)}$ for all i).

6. Equality of construct variances ($\phi_{jj}^{(1)} = \phi_{jj}^{(2)}$ for all j).

7. Invariance of construct covariances ($\phi_{jk}^{(1)} = \phi_{jk}^{(2)}$, $j \neq k$; in Figure 1, $\phi_{12}^{(1)} = \phi_{12}^{(2)}$).

8. Invariance of factor means ($\kappa_i^{(1)} = \kappa_i^{(2)}$, for all i).

Vandenberg and Lance (2000) list 67 studies that either address ME/I issues, or invoke some level of ME/I as a test of a substantive hypothesis. As an example of the applicability of ME/I concepts to a management issue, we briefly recount Cheung's (1999) work on the sources of disagreement concerning self-ratings and ratings by others.

Discovering that you and your boss have different perceptions of your work performance is a common source of workplace stress. Both self-raters and external raters (e.g., bosses) possess implicit models of performance, in which various behaviors, such as attendance and punctuality, serve as indicators of performance dimensions (factors), such as reliability. Cheung associates various types of rating disagreement with specific ME/I failures between the two models.

Self-raters and external raters may have different implicit theories of the job, manifested in different performance dimensions and different indicators. This would be manifested as configural non-invariance (level 2, above). Self-raters and external raters who agree on desired behaviors and critical performance dimensions may still attach different weights to the behaviors as indicators of the dimensions. This state of affairs would result in metric non-invariance (level 3). If the self-raters and external raters do not have access to the same information concerning the self-raters' performance, then differences in rating consistency may be observed, which could be manifested as heterogeneity of unique indicator variances (level 5). Leniency on the part of self-raters may result in range restriction for self-ratings, leading to a between-rater difference in performance dimension variability (level 6). If external raters are unduly influenced by an overall impression, their ratings may display considerable halo or horn effects when compared with self-ratings. The halo or horn effect would be detectable as a between-group difference in the correlations between performance dimensions (level 7). This one paragraph scarcely scratches the surface of Cheung's analysis, but it makes a point. The various levels and aspects of ME/I are not statistical curiosities. They are indicative of real-world measurement problems having a wide range of practical implications.

TESTING FOR METRIC INVARIANCE

Structural equation models are evaluated on the basis of *fit* (e.g., Bollen, 1989; Bollen & Long, 1993; Jöreskog & Sörbom, 1993). The model to be tested implies a particular pattern of covariances among the observed variables, represented by the fitted covariance matrix. This is compared to the covariance matrix of sample data. The discrepancy between the two is operationalized as a fit index (FI), of which over 30 have been proposed. The fit is acceptable if the FI is above (or below, depending on the FI) some criterion value. Good fit indicates that the model is a satisfactory representation of the relationships among the variables, at least on the basis of the sample data. (For a discussion of the "fit" concept see Tanaka, 1993.)

The original FI is the χ^2 statistic, defined as

$$\chi^2 = (N-1)\hat{F}_{min} \tag{2}$$

N is sample size, and $\hat{F}_{min}$ is the minimum of the fit function, estimated via an iterative procedure. A *non-significant* value of χ^2 indicates *good* fit, that is, failure to reject the null hypothesis that the fitted covariance matrix is identical to the population covariance matrix. This is counterintuitive, but not really a problem. A problem does arise, however, because of the dependence of χ^2 upon N. One can choose an N that produces a significant value of χ^2 for any value of the fit function. It follows that for large sample sizes, χ^2 provides a highly sensitive *statistical* test of fit, but not a *practical* test. Owing to this and other considerations, many alternatives to have been proposed; some in common use are the comparative fit index (CFI; Bentler, 1990), Tucker-Lewis Index (TLI; Tucker & Lewis, 1973), normed fit index (NFI; Bentler & Bonett, 1980), and root mean square error of approximation (RMSEA; Steiger, 1989). Algebraic definitions and properties for these and other FIs, including rules of thumb for evaluating model fit, can be found in Arbuckle and Wothke (1999) and Hu and Bentler (1998). Tanaka (1993) provides an excellent conceptual discussion of fit and fit indices.

FIs indicate overall fit; differences in FIs are used to indicate ME/I. In current best practice, tests of between-group ME/I involve comparing constrained and unconstrained models (Vandenberg & Lance, 2000). The researcher selects the parameters(s) to be tested. In the unconstrained model,[1] the parameter is permitted (via the model specification) to assume different values for the two groups. In the constrained model, the parameter is required to be the same for both groups. If the FI of the constrained model is "worse" than the FI of the unconstrained model, then the constraint is "wrong." In other words, the parameter being tested should not be constrained to have the same value when the model is estimated using data from the two different groups. The parameter therefore fails the ME/I test.

We put quotation marks around "worse" in the preceding paragraph because the construct is problematical. To simplify the discussion, we define the between-group difference in a fit statistic, DFI, as

$$\Delta FI = FI_{con} - FI_{uncon} \tag{3}$$

where FI_{con} and FI_{uncon} are the fit indices of the constrained and unconstrained models respectively. The value of ΔFI can be either positive or negative, depending upon the FI being used to compare the models; for example, better fit is indicated by smaller values of RMSEA and χ^2, but larger values of CFI and TLI. More importantly, there is still controversy about what value of a particular ΔFI indicates ME/I failure.

The most commonly used ΔFI is the chi-squared difference (Bollen, 1989), defined as

$$\Delta\chi^2 = \chi^2_{con} - \chi^2_{uncon} \tag{4}$$

evaluated with Δdf degrees of freedom, where

$$\Delta df = df_{con} - df_{uncon} \tag{5}$$

Like the χ^2 index of overall fit, $\Delta\chi^2$ is a significance test of the null hypothesis of no difference. Like χ^2, it is also sensitive to sample size. If the combined sample size for the groups being compared is large, then even a small difference between the fit functions of the constrained and unconstrained models may result in a significant value of $\Delta\chi^2$. This would indicate that the null hypothesis ought to be rejected, even when the difference may be trivial.

Despite this difficulty, the $\Delta\chi^2$ statistic is widely used because of one virtue; it has a known distribution. Assume that the constrained model, compared with the unconstrained model, has one additional parameter that is required to be equal across groups (the parameter being tested for ME/I). Then $\Delta df = 1$, and any value of $\Delta\chi^2$ greater than 10.83 is significant at the .001 level. Such an unambiguous rule is not available for the differences in other fit indices. For example, one can define $\Delta CFI = (CFI_{con} - CFI_{uncon})$, but there is at present no generally accepted rule for determining what value of ΔCFI indicates ME/I failure. The $\Delta\chi^2$ statistic is used in the remainder of this chapter.

METRIC INVARIANCE AND THE STANDARDIZATION PROBLEM

Metric invariance has special standing among the several varieties of ME/I described above. Metric invariance, along with configural invariance, must exist before other tests for ME/I are meaningful (Vandenberg & Lance, 2000). Further, metric invariance has particular significance as a prerequisite for between-group comparisons of summated (or mean) scale scores (Bollen, 1989). The remainder of this chapter focuses on metric invariance, with particular attention to the identification problem mentioned in the first paragraph.

At last we approach the main argument. Testing for ME/I involves comparing two CFA models, a constrained model and an unconstrained model. However, in the process of estimating a CFA model, the researcher must assign units of measurement to the factors (latent variables) by using some sort of standardization procedure (Jöreskog & Sörbom, 1989). All such procedures embody a tacit assumption of invariance. Since the reason for estimating the models in the first place is to test for invariance, this creates a problem.

We return to the model in Figure 1, and consider the first factor ξ_1^g. (Identical arguments apply to the second factor, or to any of the other factors in a more complex measurement model.) Two standardization methods (plus minor variants) are in general use. Type 1 standardizes factor variance across groups; i.e., $\phi_{11}^{(1)} = \phi_{11}^{(2)} = 1$. Type 2 standardization involves selecting an indicator, other than the one being tested for invariance, and setting its factor loading equal to unity. If, for example, indicator X_2^g is being tested for metric invariance ($\lambda_{21}^{(1)} = \lambda_{21}^{(2)}$), then X_1^g could be selected as the standardization indicator ($\lambda_{11}^{(1)} = \lambda_{11}^{(2)} = 1$). Factor ξ_1^g would then be estimated using indicator X_1^g's unit of measurement. It is convenient shorthand to refer to the standardization indicator (X_1^g) as the *referent*, and the indicator being tested for ME/I (X_2^g) as the *argument* (Rensvold & Cheung, 1998).

Type 1 standardization (e.g., Bandalos, 1993) is the less common of the two procedures. Standardizing the factor defines the metric that is applied to the estimated factor loadings of that group (MacCallum & Tucker, 1991). If the factor variance is not actually the same for both groups, then tests for metric invariance may be biased because the factor loadings for each group are expressed in terms of different scales. For example, setting $\phi_{11}^{(1)} = \phi_{11}^{(2)} = 1$ when the data indicates otherwise may result in erroneously rejecting the ME/I hypothesis $\lambda_{11}^{(1)} = \lambda_{11}^{(2)}$ when it is actually true. In addition, Type 1 standardization produces a test for *strict* metric invariance (Meredith, 1993), in which both the factor loadings and the factor variances are invariant (e.g., Aiken, Stein, & Bentler, 1994; Byrne, 1994). This is unnecessarily stringent for many investigations. In an earlier paper (Cheung & Rensvold, 1999, Appendix A) we show algebraically that Type 1 standardization may result in an ambiguous test of metric invariance.

Type 2 standardization is the more common procedure (Vandenberg & Lance, 2000; Riordan & Vandenberg, 1994; Smith, Tisak, Bauman, & Green, 1991; Van de Vijver & Harsveld, 1994). By setting a referent factor loading parameter equal to unity across groups, Type 2 standardization tacitly assumes that the factor loading *is* equal across groups. If incorrect, this assumption can lead to inaccurate estimates of other model parameters (Bollen, 1989), and bias ME/I tests of other indicators. Our earlier paper

(Cheung & Rensvold, 1999; Appendix B) presents a detailed mathematical demonstration of this point.

A variation of Type 2 standardization, referred to here as Type 2a, (Drasgow & Kanfer, 1985) begins by setting the variance of one factor equal to unity. Then the whole sample, without regard to group membership, is used to estimate factor loadings. The indicator having the largest factor loading is then used as the referent. Although the loading of the referent is not constrained to be identically equal to unity, it is still required to be the same for both groups. Therefore, Type 2 and Type 2a standardization suffer from the same problem.

A second variation of Type 2 standardization, which we call Type 2b, was suggested by Reise (1993). This technique standardizes the variance of one factor, and then selects a referent. The metric for the first group is set by standardizing the factor, and the same metric is extended to the second group by way of the referent. Like Type 2 standardization, the Type 2b procedure assumes that the referent is invariant across groups.

In summary: Type 1 standardization is overly restrictive for most applications, and assumes that the variances of the factors are equal across groups. There are three varieties of Type 2 standardization, each of which makes an *a priori* assumption about the metric invariance of the referent. Unfortunately this is an untestable assumption since only the invariance of the *ratios* of factor loadings can be tested for invariance across groups (Bielby, 1986; Williams & Thomson, 1986). We propose a solution based upon Type 2 standardization, which we refer to as the factor-ratio test. Instead of using only one item as a referent, the procedure uses *all* of them, following an iterative scheme.

SOLVING THE SPECIFICATION PROBLEM: THE FACTOR-RATIO TEST

The factor-ratio test is a test of the between-group equality of the factor loading parameters for separate indicators in the model. The researcher approaches it through a series of preliminary tests. First, the researcher may conduct an omnibus test for the equality of the group covariance matrices (level 1, above). If the null hypothesis of equality is not rejected, then no further ME/I tests are required. Next comes the test for configural invariance (level 2). An unconstrained model, also known as the baseline model, is estimated using the data for both groups, with parameters being allowed to vary across groups. (Referents must be fixed across groups, but the requirement poses no problems at this point.) If the fit is satisfactory, then configural invariance is established.

Next comes the test for overall metric invariance (level 3). An overall constrained model is estimated, in which all factor loading parameters are constrained across groups. If the ΔFI of the unconstrained and globally constrained models is larger than some critical value (e.g., a significant value of $\Delta\chi^2$), then metric non-invariance exists somewhere in the model, and testing continues.

Metric invariance is then tested at the level of each factor. In Figure 1, for example, a model would be estimated with between-group constraints imposed on all the factor loadings associated with ξ_1^g. If the ΔFI of this model and the unconstrained model is larger than the critical value of ΔFI, then one or more of the indicators associated with ξ_1^g are non-invariant. That is, one or more of the following equalities is not valid: $\lambda_{11}^{(1)} = \lambda_{11}^{(2)}$, $\lambda_{21}^{(1)} = \lambda_{21}^{(2)}$, $\lambda_{31}^{(1)} = \lambda_{31}^{(2)}$.

Metric invariance testing continues at the level of each indicator. A constrained model is estimated for each of the equalities listed above. At this point, however, the situation is complicated by the need to choose a referent. That is, one of the three equalities must be *assumed* to be true (e.g., $\lambda_{11}^{(1)} = \lambda_{11}^{(2)} = 1$) before one of the other two indicators can be constrained for the purpose of the test (e.g., $\lambda_{21}^{(1)} = \lambda_{21}^{(2)}$).

In general, it follows that there is not just one, but rather two constraints associated with every indicator-level constrained model of this type; that is,

$$\lambda_{ij}^{(1)} = \lambda_{ij}^{(2)} \quad \text{(the test constraint)} \tag{6}$$

and

$$\lambda_{i*j}^{(1)} = \lambda_{i*j}^{(2)} = 1 \quad \text{(the standardization constraint),} \tag{7}$$

where $i \neq i*$.

In order to test all X_i for invariance, it is necessary to construct and test a model for *each combination* of X_i and X_{i*}, subject to the constraints above. This is an extension of Byrne et al.'s (1989) procedure, but it is a far-reaching extension. Technical details supporting the recommendation are given in Cheung and Rensvold 1999 (Appendix B), where it is shown that each model produces a test for the null hypothesis

$$\frac{\lambda_{ij}^{(1)}}{\lambda_{i*j}^{(1)}} = \frac{\lambda_{ij}^{(2)}}{\lambda_{i*j}^{(2)}} \tag{8}$$

The systematic examination of all combinations of referents and arguments, across all groups, is called the factor-ratio test.

For a non-invariant factor with N indicators, a total of $N(N-1)/2$ constrained models are required. Each indicator is taken as the referent, and the remaining indicators (arguments) are constrained one at a time. For a factor with three indicators (Figure 1), the three constrained models are as follows:

Model	Referent	Argument
1	1	2
2	1	3
3	2	3

The fit of each constrained model is compared with the fit of the globally unconstrained model. If ΔFI exceeds the critical value, then the listed argument is non-invariant when the constrained model is estimated using the listed referent. *The test is symmetrical with respect to argument and referent.* That is, if A is non-invariant when B is used as the referent, then B is non-invariant when A is used as the referent. Under these conditions, A and B constitute a *non-invariant indicator pair.*

As another example, consider a non-invariant construct with five indicators. Ten indicator-level constrained models are required to locate the non-invariant indicator(s). Each constrained model is compared with the unconstrained model using the χ^2 statistic. Hypothetical results are as follows:

Model	Referent	Argument	$\Delta\chi^2$
1	1	2	.21
2	1	3	4.81*
3	1	4	.02
4	1	5	5.20*
5	2	3	1.32
6	2	4	.20
7	2	5	.01
8	3	4	.34
9	3	5	.00
10	4	5	.08

The asterisks indicate significant values of $\Delta\chi^2$ with Δdf = 1 (p < .05). The following referent/argument pairs are therefore non-invariant: 1 and 3, 1 and 5. To introduce the nomenclature used below, we write these non-invariant pairs as (1,3)* and (1,5)*.

IDENTIFYING SETS OF NON-INVARIANT ITEMS

The purpose of metric invariance testing is not to identify the indicators we *cannot* use (although that is necessary), but rather to identify the indicators we *can* use to test between-group differences. Once all non-invariant pairs have been identified, therefore, the next step is to identify subsets of invariant indicators. Each subset consists entirely of indicators that display metric invariance across both groups. That is, every indicator in the subset displays metric invariance when any other indicator in the subset is selected as the referent. Clearly, a subset of indicators satisfying this property cannot contain *both* members of a non-invariant indicator pair.

We have described a procedure that uses non-invariant pairs to identify invariant sets (Cheung & Rensvold, 1999; Rensvold & Cheung, 1998). This procedure, called the triangle heuristic, uses a matrix having one column for each referent, one row for each argument, and cells containing the p-statistic (significance) of the ΔFI associated with each argument/referent pair. To use the procedure, a researcher manually swaps the rows and columns of the matrix to obtain triangular patterns of non-significant ΔFIs. These patterns identify the invariant subsets. Finding all of the subsets depends upon the user's skill and powers of observation.

We will describe two alternative procedures for generating the required subsets. Unlike the triangle heuristic, both are highly mechanical and, if used correctly, automatically produce all non-redundant subsets. Both can be automated, but the occasional user will probably be satisfied to use one or both of them manually.

The List-and-Delete Procedure

This procedure has three rules.

Rule 1: List all combinations of the N indicators. The combinations have cardinality N, N-1, N-2, down to 2.

Rule 2: For each non-invariant pair, delete all combinations of indicators (from rule 1) containing both elements of that pair.

Rule 3: Eliminate all combinations that are subsets of larger combinations.

Table 1 illustrates this procedure for the example introduced in the section above, a set of five indicators having two non-invariant pairs, (1,3)* and (1,5)*. Note that the indicators are numbered 1 through 5 for convenience. They could just as easily be labeled 31 through 35, A through E, VI

Table 1.   The List-and-Delete Procedure

Five indicators numbered 1 through 5.

Non-invariant indicator pairs (1,3)* and (1,5)*

Proceeding from left to right →

Original candidate combinations	Eliminate combs. Containing 1 and 3	Eliminate combs. Containing 1 and 5	Eliminate subsets
1 2 3 4 5	1 2 3 4 5	1 2 3 4 5	1 2 3 4 5
2 3 4 5	2 3 4 5	2 3 4 5	2 3 4 5
1 3 4 5	1 3 4 5	1 3 4 5	1 3 4 5
1 2 4 5	1 2 4 5	1 2 4 5	1 2 4 5
1 2 3 5	1 2 3 5	1 2 3 5	1 2 3 5
1 2 3 4	1 2 3 4	1 2 3 4	1 2 3 4
3 4 5	3 4 5	3 4 5	3 4 5
2 4 5	2 4 5	2 4 5	2 4 5
2 3 5	2 3 5	2 3 5	2 3 5
2 3 4	2 3 4	2 3 4	2 3 4
1 4 5	1 4 5	1 4 5	1 4 5
1 3 5	1 3 5	1 3 5	1 3 5
1 3 4	1 3 4	1 3 4	1 3 4
1 2 5	1 2 5	1 2 5	1 2 5
1 2 4	1 2 4	1 2 4	1 2 4
1 2 3	1 2 3	1 2 3	1 2 3
4 5	4 5	4 5	4 5
3 5	3 5	3 5	3 5
3 4	3 4	3 4	3 4
2 5	2 5	2 5	2 5
2 4	2 4	2 4	2 4
2 3	2 3	2 3	2 3
1 5	1 5	1 5	1 5
1 4	1 4	1 4	1 4
1 3	1 3	1 3	1 3
1 2	1 2	1 2	1 2

Notes: Sets of invariant items are (2,3,4,5) and (1,2,4)

through X, etc. The first column in Table 1 shows the result of applying rule 1; that is, listing all combinations of the indicators. The second column shows the result of applying rule 2 to the first non-invariant pair (1,3)*, which eliminates combinations (1,2,3,4,5), (1,3,4,5), (1,2,3,5), plus others. The third column shows the result of applying rule 2 again, using non-invariant pair (1,5)*. Additional deletions include combinations

(1,2,4,5), (1,4,5), plus others. The fourth column shows the result of apply-ing rule 3, which eliminates (3,4,5) as a subset of (2,3,4,5), (1,4) as a subset of (1,2,4), and several others. We are left with two remaining subsets of invariant items, (2,3,4,5), and (1,2,4).

The procedure is straightforward for six or fewer indicators. The six-or-fewer qualification is not very stringent. Hinkin (1995) examined 277 scales used in 75 organizational studies, and found that 200 (72%) of them had six or fewer indicators. Table 2 lists the starting combinations for these groups, which correspond to the first column of Table 1.

Unfortunately, the procedure rapidly becomes unsuitable for hand cal-culation as the number of indicators increases beyond six. For N indica-tors, the number of starting combinations C_{start} is

$$C_{start} = 1 + N + C(N, N - 1) + C(N, N - 2) + \dots + C(N, 2). \qquad (9)$$

As usual, $C(M,N)$ is the number of combinations of M distinguishable objects taken in sets of size N. If $N = 10$, then $C_{start} = 1013$; if $N = 12$, then $C_{start} = 4063$. Getting past rule 1 becomes a problem. Under these condi-tions, we recommend the following alternative procedure.

The Stepwise Partitioning Procedure

This procedure has four rules.

Rule 1: Write down all N indicators. This is the first input combination.
Rule 2: Produce output combinations from each input combination by using a non-invariant pair. If the input combination contains *both* elements of the pair, write two output combinations, as fol-lows. The first output combination is the input subset, minus the *first* element of the pair; the second output combination is the input subset, minus the *second* element of the pair. If the input combination does not contain both elements of the non-invariant pair, then it becomes the output combination *without change.*
Rule 3: Output combinations become input combinations. Apply rule 2, using the next non-invariant pair. When all non-invariant pairs have been used, go to
Rule 4: Eliminate all combinations that are subsets of larger combina-tions.

These rules are easier to demonstrate than to enunciate. Figure 3 illus-trates the process, using the same input as above. The first input combina-tion is (1,2,3,4,5). Applying rule 2 with the first non-invariant pair (1,3)*,

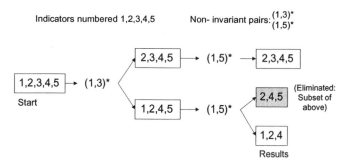

Figure 3.   Finding Sets of Invariant Items

produces two output combinations. The first is simply the starting combination, minus indicator 1: (2,3,4,5). The second is the starting combination minus 3: (1,2,4,5). These output combinations become the input combinations for the next round of partitioning. Rule 2 is applied to each of the input combinations, using the second non-invariant pair (1,5)*. The first input combination (2,3,4,5) contains 5, but not 1; therefore it is copied without change. The second input combination (1,2,4,5) contains both 1 and 5. Consequently, two output combinations are produced: (2,4,5) and (1,2,4). This exhausts the non-invariant pairs. Rule 4 eliminates (2,4,5) because it is a subset of a larger combination, (2,3,4,5). We are left, as before, with the two remaining subsets of invariant items (2,3,4,5), and (1,2,4).

The stepwise partitioning procedure is procedurally more complex than the list-and-delete procedure, but arguably less labor-intensive. The two authors are divided concerning the relative merits of the two procedures. We would welcome input from readers.

Programming the stepwise partitioning procedure is quite simple, and makes a nice project for a Sunday afternoon. Those who feel they have better things to do with their weekends are invited to download "STEPWISE.EXE" from the first author's website (http://personal.cityu.edu.hk/~mgrr), where it will be available until 30 June 2003.

Readers wishing to test their understanding can work through the following exercise, using both procedures. Find the invariant sets of six indicators having the three non-invariant pairs (1,3), (1,4), and (2,4). Answer: (3,4,5,6), (2,3,5,6), (1,2,5,6). (Hint: Work through the list-and-delete procedure using a photocopy of Table 2.)

A NUMERICAL EXAMPLE

The following example uses the "Work Orientations" data set published in 2000 by the International Social Survey Program (ISSP, 2000), an interna-

Table 2. Indicator Combinations, Three through Six Indicators

123	1345	14	1345	135
23	1245	13	1256	134
13	1235	12	1246	126
12	1234		1245	125
	345		1236	124
	245		1235	123
1234	235	**123456**	1234	56
234	234	23456	456	46
134	145	13456	356	45
124	135	12456	346	36
123	134	12356	345	35
34	125	12346	256	34
24	124	12345	246	26
23	123	3456	245	25
14	45	2456	236	24
13	35	2356	235	23
12	34	2346	234	16
	25	2345	156	15
	24	1456	146	14
12345	23	1356	145	13
2345	15	1346	136	12

tional project begun in 1984. This analysis compares two groups, Americans (N = 755) and Japanese (678). The model to be tested consists of a single construct measuring organizational commitment, measured using four indicators scored on a five-point Likert-type scale (1 = strongly disagree, 5 = strongly agree). The indicators are as follows:

1. I am willing to work harder than I have to in order to help the firm or organization I work for succeed.
2. I am proud to be working for my firm or organization.
3. I would turn down another job that offered quite a bit more pay in order to stay with this organization.
4. I am proud of the type of work I do.

Indicator variances and covariances for the two nationalities are shown in Table 3.

The sequence of tests for ME/I is shown in Table 4. The omnibus test was not performed, since there was no expectation that the covariance matrices $\Sigma^{(USA)}$ and $\Sigma^{(JAP)}$ would be equal. Configural invariance was

Table 3.   Variance/Covariance Data

Items	USA (N = 755)				Japan (N = 678)			
	1	2	3	4	1	2	3	4
1	.65				1.39			
2	.35	.65			.59	1.32		
3	.31	.38	1.24		.33	.53	2.23	
4	.25	.40	.27	.77	.49	.99	.54	1.36

tested by estimating an unconstrained model. The same pattern of factor loadings was specified for each group, but the factor loadings themselves were not constrained to be equal. Configural invariance was established by satisfactory model fit, with RMSEA = .051, TLI = .98, and CFI = .99. Chi-squared was significant ($\chi^2 = 11.38$, df = 4, p < .01), which would ordinarily be interpreted as indicating poor fit. In this case, however, the significance of χ^2 is attributable to the large sample size, a result that illustrates the problematical nature of this statistic.

ME/I was tested by estimating a fully constrained model. In addition to the configural constraints, factor loadings were constrained to be equal across the two nationalities. The fully constrained model displayed weaker fit than the unconstrained model, with RMSEA = 0.77, TLI = .97, and CFI = .98. The fully constrained model could not be considered poor on the basis of these statistics, but comparison with the unconstrained model clearly indicated a failure of ME/I ($\Delta\chi^2 = 24.23$, df = 3, p < .001).

A series of tests were performed to isolate the sources of ME/I. In each test, a model was estimated that had a particular combination of referent and argument constrained, while the other parameters were not constrained. The constrained model was then compared with the unconstrained model. In the first test, for example, indicator 1 was the referent ($\lambda_{11}^{(USA)} = \lambda_{11}^{(JAP)} = 1$) and indicator 2 was the argument ($\lambda_{21}^{(USA)} = \lambda_{21}^{(JAP)}$). Model chi-squared was 15.90 with five degrees of freedom. The difference in fit between this model and the unconstrained model was tested using a Bonferroni-adjusted critical value of .008, and was found not to be significant ($\Delta\chi^2 = 4.52$, df = 1, p = 0.34). As noted above, the same result would have been obtained if indicator 2 had been the referent, and indicator 1 had been the argument; therefore, indicators 1 and 2 were invariant with respect to the two nationalities. Similar tests produced opposite results, owing to significant values of $\Delta\chi^2$; in particular, indicators 1 and 4 were found to be non-invariant, as well as indicators 3 and 4. To use our earlier terminology, the four indicators of organizational commitment had two non-invariant pairs, (1,4)* and (3,4)*. Applying the list-and-delete procedure and double-checking by using the stepwise partitioning procedure, we identified two sets of invariant indicators; (1,2,3) and (2,4).

Table 4.   Constrained and Unconstrained SEM Models, Organizational Commitment

	χ^2	df	$\Delta\chi^2$	Δdf	p	RMSEA	TLI	CFI
Unconstrained Model	11.38	4	-	-	.010	.051	.98	.99
Fully constrained Model	35.51	7	24.13	3	.001*	.077	.97	.98
Models with single item constraints[1]								
Referent Argument								
1 2	15.90	5	4.52	1	.034	.055	.98	.99
1 3	12.18	5	.80	1	.371	.045	.99	1.00
1 **4**	25.29	5	13.91	1	.008**	.076	.97	.99
2 3	18.19	5	6.81	1	.009	.060	.98	.99
2 4	15.11	5	3.73	1	.053	.053	.98	.99
3 **4**	27.13	5	15.75	1	.008**	.078	.96	.98
PFI Model	20.28	6	8.90	2	.012	.058	.98	.99

Notes: [1]Referent/argument pairs in bold are non-invariant.

* Significant at p < .001

** Significant at Bonferroni –adjusted $p = .05/6 = .008$

What do these results mean? Providing a definitive answer would require more data than we have available, but a close examination of the invariant sets provides some clues. Indicators (1,2,3) all specifically mention the subject's firm or organization, and some action with respect to the organization ("(W)ork harder...be working...stay with"). Indicators (2,4) both invoke a subjective response toward the organization by using the word "proud." The one indicator common to both sets, number 2, refers to the subject's "firm or organization," and also uses the word "proud."

The original four-indicator measure of organizational commitment, which (presumably) possessed simple factor structure when originally developed, bifurcates across cultures. The two sets of invariant indicators are subtly different. The first set speaks more about the subject's expected actions with respect to the organization, the second more about his or her pride in the organization and work. This distinction may be more salient in Japanese culture, for reasons that we do not have the expertise to discuss. Whatever the reason, the results point to a researchable question concerning Japanese-American cultural differences. They also indicate that not all four items should be *uncritically* used in any study comparing Japanese and American organizational commitment. Either indicators (1,2,3) or indicators (2,4) should be used, depending upon which meaning is more relevant to the study. If all four indicators are used, the researcher should justify his or her decision to do so in light of the ME/I test results.

In this instance, the results obtained using partial factorial invariance (PFI) support the use of all four items. Under PFI, all factor-loading parameters are fixed across groups, except for those that have been previously identified as being non-invariant (Bryne et al., 1989; Steenkamp & Baumgartner, 1998). The latter are allowed to assume group-specific values. Fit statistics for the PFI model are shown at the bottom of Table 4. The FIs are better than those for the fully constrained model (e.g., RMSEA .058 versus .077). The TLI and CFI statistics are the same for both the PFI model and the unconstrained model (.98 and .99 respectively). Retaining all of the original indicators in a measurement model is often desirable for theoretical reasons, and the doctrine of PFI permits doing so, as long as it has no practical effect on the model. This is certainly true for the current example. Before PFI can be invoked, however, the non-invariant indicators must be unambiguously identified, and their effects assessed.

DISCUSSION

Although ME/I has been discussed for over 30 years (cf. Meredith, 1964a, b), invariance testing using CFA has only recently become widespread. The development of LISREL, Amos, and similar tools produced an awareness on the part of researchers of the importance of ME/I in the study of between-group differences. Earlier, a typical procedure comparing the organizational commitment between American and Japanese workers would have gone as follows: Check scale reliabilities (ignoring any difference, as long as Cronbach's alpha is greater than 0.70 for each group), calculate scale scores, find the scale score difference, and check for significance. The outcome of this procedure is ambiguous. If a significant difference is observed, one cannot tell if it is due to something substantive, such as a culturally related attitudinal difference towards employers, or to something exogenous, such as subjects' interpretations of scale items. On the other hand, failure to observe a significant difference is equally ambiguous. One group might respond strongly to one subset of indicators that reflects a particular aspect of the construct, whereas the other group may respond equally strongly to a separate subset. Although there may be no significant difference in overall response, there may be significant differences at the indicator level. These differences are detectable using CFA.

ME/I testing, specifically metric invariance testing, poses several problems for the researcher. Several different tests have appeared in the literature, although tests based on CFA appear to be current best practice (Vandenberg & Lance, 2000). One problem concerns the selection of model standardization constraints, or referents. Using the factor-ratio test, as described above, solves this problem. Another problem is the inherent complexity of the procedure. It involves multiple steps with decisions at each step. Although there is no single fix for this problem, Rensvold and Cheung (1998) proposed to cut through some of the complexity by using simplified nomenclature, which they described and illustrated with an extended sample. (The new nomenclature was pointedly omitted from this chapter, which has quite enough in it already.) A final difficulty is computational (although clerical might be a better description). Generating the requisite LISREL code for testing the constrained models is a non-trivial exercise, especially for factors having large numbers of indicators. Rensvold and Cheung (1998) discuss this problem, and offer DOS-based software to help cope with it.

Although ME/I testing poses problems, it also offers opportunities. The decomposition of indicators into invariant subsets is a new tool for learning about between-group differences. In some instances, direct between-group comparisons using a single summated scale may not be feasible because the scale "shatters" when subjected to the test for metric invariance. Just the same, the content of the various "pieces" (invariant subgroups) may be profoundly informative, since they indicate which constructs are comparable. In an earlier article (Cheung & Rensvold, 1999) we argued that non-invariant indicators should not be summarily eliminated or ignored, since they may constitute the only source of information concerning between-group differences. The present chapter extends that notion by including, as sources of information, the subsets on invariant indicators that remain when the non-invariant indicators are systematically removed. We hope that this perspective will eventually supplant the current one, which views ME/I failure solely as a problem to be solved, and not as an opportunity to be exploited.

We close on a cautionary note. Tests for metric invariance can detect non-invariance, but they cannot prove invariance. A successful test for metric invariance only demonstrates that the same indicators covary in roughly the same way for members of each group. Japanese responses to four survey items may be highly correlated; American responses to the same items may also be correlated. This suggests, but does not prove, that the same construct is producing the pattern of correlations in both cultures. A particular value of ΔFI, by itself, cannot make that argument. It is left to the investigator to make it, based upon his or her detailed understanding of the research context.

In addition, demonstrating metric invariance does not prove that a construct has the same domain for the members of both groups. One can imagine a construct tentatively labeled "Importance of interpersonal relations." A scale intended to operationalize this construct may consist of items addressing relationships between the subject and his/her friends, parents, and others. Such a scale might adequately represent the construct in a Western culture, but be deficient in an Eastern culture. In China, for example, the Five Cardinal Relations of Confucianism are between sovereign and subject, father and son, elder brother and younger brother, husband and wife, friend and friend (Bond & Hwang, 1995). Clearly, the "interpersonal relationships" construct is more highly elaborated in the East than in the West. A scale that taps only a few of the many facets of interpersonal relationships may display a high degree of metric invariance with respect to those few facets, yet be totally uninformative regarding larger, more interesting questions. Further, low regard for "interpersonal relationships" would arguably have a wider range of behavioral implications for a Chinese subject than for a Western subject, owing to the larger number of indicators that covary with levels of that construct.

To summarize: ME/I has received inadequate attention from researchers performing between-group research. SEM provides a powerful tool for studying ME/I, but SEM's largely unappreciated standardization problem casts doubt upon the results of many studies. The procedures described here solve the standardization problem, and help make ME/I a powerful analytical tool in its own right. Still, SEM and ME/I in no way diminish the need for critical and expository skills on the part of researchers. As the first author's father, a research chemist, was fond of repeating, "The numbers *never* speak for themselves."

NOTE

1. Sometimes referred to as the "baseline" model; Bagozzi and Edwards (1998); Marsh (1994); Riese et al. (1993).

REFERENCES

Aiken, L.S., Stein, J.A., & Bentler, P.M. (1994). Structural equation analyses of clinical subpopulation differences and comparative treatment outcomes: Characterizing the daily lives of drug addicts. *Journal of Consulting and Clinical Psychology, 62,* 488-499.

Arbuckle, J.L., & Wothke, W. (1999). *Amos 4.0 user's guide.* Chicago: Smallwaters.

Bagozzi, R.P., & Edwards, J.R. (1998). A general approach to representing constructs in organizational research. *Organizational Research Methods, 1,* 45-87.

Bandalos, D.L. (1993). Factors influencing cross-validation of confirmatory factor analysis models. *Multivariate Behavioral Research, 28,* 351-374.

Bentler, P.M., & Bonett, D.G. (1980). Significance tests and goodness of fit in the analysis of covariance structures. *Psychological Bulletin, 88,* 588-606.

Bielby, W.T. (1986). Arbitrary metrics in multiple-indicator models of latent variables. *Sociological Methods and Research, 15,* 3-23.

Bollen, K.A. (1989). *Structural equations with latent variables.* New York: John Wiley & Sons.

Bollen, K.A., & Long, J.S. (1993). *Testing structural equation models.* Newbury Park, CA: Sage.

Bond, M.H., & Hwang, K.K. (1995). The social psychology of the Chinese people. In M.H. Bond (Ed.), *The psychology of the Chinese people* (pp. 213-266). New York: Oxford University Press.

Brennan, R.L. (1983). *Elements of generalizeability theory.* Iowa City, IA: American College Testing.

Brislin, R.W., Lonner, W., & Thorndyke, R.M. (1973). *Cross-cultural research methods.* New York: Wiley.

Byrne, B.M. (1994). Testing for the factorial validity, replication, and invariance of a measurement instrument: A paradigmatic application based on the Maslach Burnout Inventory. *Multivariate Behavioral Research, 29,* 289-311.

Byrne, B.M., Shavelson, R.J., & Muthén, B. (1989). Testing for the equivalence of factor covariance and mean structures: The issue of partial measurement invariance. *Psychological Bulletin, 105,* 456-466.

Cheung, G.W. (1999). Multifaceted conceptions of self-other ratings disagreement. *Personnel Psychology, 52,* 1-36.

Cheung, G.W., & Rensvold, R.B. (1999). Testing factorial invariance across groups: A reconceptualization and proposed new method. *Journal of Management, 25,* 1-27.

Cheung, G.W., & Rensvold, R.B. (1998). Cross-cultural comparisons using non-invariant measurement items. *Applied Behavioral Science Review, 6,* 93-110.

Cronbach, L.J., Gleser, G.C., Nanda, H., & Rajaratnam, N. (1972). *The dependability of behavioral measurements: Theory of generalizeability scores and profiles.* New York: John Wiley.

Drasgow, F., & Kanfer, R. (1985). Equivalence of psychological measurement in heterogeneous populations. *Journal of Applied Psychology, 70,* 662-680.

Hinkin, T.R. (1995). A review of scale development practices in the study of organizations. *Journal of Management, 21,* 967-988.

Horn, J.L., & McArdle, J.J. (1992). A practical and theoretical guide to measurement invariance in aging research. *Experimental Aging Research, 18,* 117-144.

Hu, L., & Bentler, P.M. (1998). Fit indices in covariance structure modeling: Sensitivity to underparameterization model misspecification. *Psychological Methods, 3,* 424-453.

ISSP (2000). *International Social Science Program: Work Orientations, 2000* [Computer file]. Ann Arbor, MI: Inter-university Consortium for Political and Social Research [distributors], 1992.

Janssens, M., Brett, J.M., & Smith, F.J. (1995). Confirmatory cross-cultural research: Testing the viability of a corporation-wide safety policy. *Academy of Management Journal, 38,* 364-382.

Jöreskog, K.G., & Sörbom, D. (1993). *LISREL 8: Structural equation modeling with the SIMPLIS command language.* Chicago: Scientific Software International, Inc.

MacCallum, R.C., & Tucker, L.R. (1991). Representing sources of error in the common-factor model: Implications for theory and practice. *Psychological Bulletin, 109,* 502-511.

Marcoulides, G.A. (Ed.). (1998). *Applied generalizeability theory models.* Mahwah, NJ: Lawrence Erlbaum.

Marcoulides, G.A. (1996). Estimating variance components in generalizability theory: The covariance structure analysis approach. *Structural Equation Modeling, 3,* 290-299.

Marsh, H.W. (1994). Confirmatory factor analysis models of factorial invariance: A multifaceted approach. *Structural Equation Modeling, 1,* 5-34.

Maurer, T.J., Raju, N.S., & Collins, W.C. (1998). Peer and subordinate performance appraisal measurement equivalence. *Journal of Applied Psychology, 83,* 693-702.

Meredith, W. (1964a). Notes on factorial invariance. *Psychometrika, 29,* 177-185.

Meredith, W. (1964b). Rotation to achieve factorial invariance. *Psychometrika, 29,* 187-206.

Meredith, W. (1993). Measurement invariance, factor analysis and factorial invariance. *Psychometrika, 58,* 525-543.

Millsap, R.E., & Everson, H. (1991). Confirmatory measurement model comparisons using latent means. *Multivariate Behavioral Research, 26,* 479-497.

Pentz, M.A., & Chou, C. (1994). Measurement invariance in longitudinal clinical research assuming change from development and intervention. *Journal of Consulting and Clinical Psychology, 62,* 450-462.

Reise, S.P., Widaman, K.F., & Pugh, R.H. (1993). Confirmatory factor analysis and item response theory: Two approaches for exploring measurement invariance. *Psychological Bulletin, 114,* 552-566.

Rensvold, R.B., & Cheung, G.W. (1998). Testing measurement models for factorial invariance: A systematic approach. *Educational and Psychological Measurement, 58,* 1017-1034.

Riordan, C.M., & Vandenberg, R.J. (1994). A central question in cross-cultural research: Do employees of different cultures interpret work-related measures in an equivalent manner? *Journal of Management, 20,* 643-671.

Smith, C.S., Tisak, J., Bauman, T., & Green, E. (1991) Psychometric equivalence of a translated circadian rhythm questionnaire: Implications for between- and within-population assessments. *Journal of Applied Psychology, 76,* 628-636.

Steenkamp, J.E.M., & Baumgartner, H. (1998). Assessing measurement invariance in cross-national consumer research. *Journal of Consumer Research, 25,* 78-90.

Tanaka, J.S. (1993). Multifaceted conceptions of fit in structural equation models. In K.A. Bollen & J.S. Long (Eds.), *Testing structural equation models* (pp. 10-39). London: Sage Publications Ltd.

Triandis, H.C. (1994). Cross-cultural industrial and organizational psychology. In H.C. Triandis, M.D. Dunnette, & L.M. Hough (Eds.), *Handbook of industrial and organisational psychology* (Vol. 4, 2nd ed.). Palo Alto, CA: Consulting Psychologists Press, Inc.

Tucker, L.R., & Lewis, C. (1973). The reliability coefficient for maximum likelihood factor analysis. *Psychometrika, 38,* 1-10.

Van de Vijver, F.J.R., & Harsveld, M. (1994). The incomplete equivalence of the paper-and-pencil and computerized versions of the General Aptitude Test Battery. *Journal of Applied Psychology, 79,* 852-859.

Williams, R., & Thomson, E. (1986). Normalization issues in latent variable modeling. *Sociological Methods and Research, 15,* 24-43.

Windle, M., Iwawaki, S., & Lerner, R. M. (1988). Cross-cultural comparability of temperament among Japanese and American preschool children. *International Journal of Psychology, 23,* 547-567.

CHAPTER 4

ALPHA, BETA, AND GAMMA CHANGE
A Review of Past Research with Recommendations for New Directions

Christine M. Riordan, Hettie A. Richardson, Bryan S. Schaffer, and Robert J. Vandenberg

Abstract: Golembiewski, Billingsley, and Yeager introduced the typology of alpha, beta, and gamma change in 1976. Twenty-five years after its inception, however, we have made little progress toward full integration of this typology into change research. Therefore, the purposes of this paper are first to describe the theoretical premise of the ABG typology. We then review research that has been conducted on ABG and compare methodologies associated with assessing ABG change. Finally, we discuss directions for future research.

INTRODUCTION

To operationalize individual change in employees, researchers have generally relied upon comparisons of self-report measures of attitudes captured at one time period, with the same attitudes measured again at some later point(s) in time. Within these comparisons, differences in mean values of the measured variables across time have typically been accepted as an indication of individual change. Yet it is apparent that an accurate assessment of change is crucial when longitudinal designs are used. To address this need for accuracy, Golembiewski, Billingsley, and Yeager (1976) introduced the alpha, beta, and gamma (ABG) typology for operationalizing individual attitude change across time. However, since its introduction twenty-five years ago and even though researchers continue to employ longitudinal designs, very few have truly incorporated the typology as a means of assessing individual change.

Given that a quarter century has passed, it is appropriate to revisit Golembiewski et al.'s (1976) conceptualization of change, and ask ourselves what we have learned, and from this, to define directions for new research. To this end, we begin with the definitions underlying the ABG components, followed by an overview of the substantive research on this typology. Subsequently we review the research on the methodologies typically used to assess ABG change. Finally, we propose a number of theoretical and methodological directions needed to advance this conceptualization of the change process.

DEFINITION AND THEORETICAL PREMISES OF ABG CHANGE

A close examination of theories characterizing the conceptual domains of applied psychology and organizational behavior reveals that most have "change" as an underlying premise (Lance, Vandenberg, & Self, 2000; Vandenberg & Lance, 2000). As used here, the term "change" refers to employees reinterpreting and revising both the meaning of work as it pertains to a particular organization and the view of themselves as functioning members of their organizations (Hulin, 1991; Lance et al., 2000). Change can occur as the result of purposeful organizational efforts (i.e., interventions) or simply by the phenomenological processes of experiencing work (i.e., the day-to-day exposure to new and different ways of undertaking work).

Positive change occurs to the extent that the revisions and reinterpretations result in actions that are mutually beneficial to both the person and organization. Negative change is reflected in a weakened linkage or bond between the person and organization (Mowday, Porter, & Steers, 1982; Vandenberg & Seo, 1992). This view of individual change or adjustment is prominent in many conceptual frameworks within applied psychology and organizational behavior, such as those concerning work socialization (Feldman, 1976; Louis, 1980; Schein, 1968), the Theory of Work Adjustment (Dawis & Lofquist, 1993), realistic job previews (Wanous, 1992), the study of the antecedent conditions driving organizational commitment (Mowday et al., 1982; Meyer, Bobocel, & Allen, 1991), and the attraction-selection-attrition hypothesis (Schneider, Goldstein, & Smith, 1995). Although these frameworks focus on different substantive areas, they share a common concern of longitudinal change. That is, employees are expected to change in the way that they relate to their work context over time, and inferences about their positive or negative adjustment to the work place are based on these changes.

The operationalization of change has been a long-standing and controversial topic (Burr & Nesselroade, 1990; Collins, 1996; Cronbach & Furby, 1970; Hertzog, 1996). The practice of operationalizing change (i.e., the methodological/statistical procedures) cannot be truly understood, however, without first addressing the theoretical or conceptual issues. Golembiewski et al. (1976) were one of the first to note that change has several conceptual facets, which they labeled alpha, beta, and gamma change.

Alpha change refers to a change in the level of a variable from one measurement period to the next period. That is, alpha change corresponds to an absolute quantitative change in a given variable. For example, assume that we take an assessment of individual organizational commitment at Time 1. We then implement an intervention focused on strengthening organizational commitment. After its implementation, we take another index of employees' commitment at Time 2. We then conduct a t-test for related measures to determine whether there is a statistically significant difference between the two means (T_1 and T_2), and we hypothesize that the postintervention value will be the higher of the two. Traditionally, the difference in mean values would be interpreted as a change in the level of commitment to the organization as a function of the intervention. Using Golembiewski et al.'s (1976) terminology, this is an example of *alpha change*.

Golembiewski et al. (1976), however, noted that there are other forms of change that may occur in addition to the traditional alpha change. Specifically, encounters with a new organizational environment (any type of change) may influence workers such that they reconstitute their interpretations of that organization (Schaubroeck & Green, 1989). The reconstitution of work-environment perceptions may take two forms (Golembiewski et al., 1976). One form, *beta change*, occurs when the respondents recalibrate the intervals anchoring the measurement continuum. In other words, experiences and encounters (including, but not limited to, the intervention) between T_1 and T_2 alter how the rating scale for a measured variable such as organizational commitment (e.g., the values of a 5-point Likert scale) is interpreted. Thus, respondents perceive a difference between the intervals underlying the scale across the time periods (Vandenberg & Self, 1993). For example, a "4" at T_2 may be defined by respondents in the same manner as was a "3" at T_1, and although a statistically significant difference exists between the two values, this difference possesses no meaning because in reality, the two values are perceptually identical. Beta change is not a low probability event. Using the example above where low commitment existed prior to the intervention, the "5" may not have even been an option perceptually for the respondents, and thus a "3" (which from our viewpoint as researchers is neutral) was the highest level of commitment any employee would have possessed. Assuming the intervention is successful, it is the "1" or perhaps "2" now which may not be an option perceptually. Thus, the 4 is now the lowest value given by the majority of employees. Simply stated, the point is that the instrument did not remain calibrated from pre- to postintervention, in the sense that the values of the underlying scale are anchored differently at both time periods.

The final form of reconstitution is gamma *change*, in which the respondent reconceptualizes the conceptual domain of the measured variable (Golembiewski et al., 1976). Specifically, the conceptual domain underlying the instrument is assumed to be constant across measurement periods that have alpha and beta changes. However, experiences under the new conditions may change employees to such a degree that they actually use a different construct at each time period to respond to the measurement instruments. Responses to items at both time periods, therefore, are made relative to different conceptual frames of reference (Vandenberg & Self, 1993). As such, comparisons between time periods are meaningless under gamma change since the instrument now operationalizes a different construct at each of the two time periods.

Using the example above, employees prior to the intervention may not have even had a concept of organizational commitment. Hence when faced with the preintervention measure, they completed it relative to a conceptual frame of reference that had little to do with the researcher's view of commitment (and upon which the measure is based). The "successful" intervention, though, now provides employees with the conceptual frame of reference traditionally attributed to the items in the instrument. Thus, any direct comparison of mean values for organizational commitment from T_1 and T_2 cannot be undertaken, as they do not represent equivalent constructs.

Both beta and gamma change are threats to the validity of alpha change. That is, if either beta and/or gamma change(s) is/are present, then any obtained differences in mean values on the instrument of interest may not necessarily be due to alpha change (Millsap & Hartog, 1988; Vandenberg & Lance, 2000; Vandenberg & Self, 1993). Interpretation of mean-level differences is meaningless if the instrument is not calibrated constantly or the construct is not conceptualized consistently across the time periods.

Based on the ABG typology, a common operative question in the study of individual change becomes, "to what extent are beta and gamma changes present, and if present, how do they influence an ability to accurately interpret alpha change or mean differences in levels of variables across time?" It is important to assess the presence of beta and gamma change prior to interpreting our traditionally desired forms of alpha change. However, this question assumes that alpha change is always the most desired type of change, and this is not always the case. In some circumstances, beta and/or gamma change may be desired.

In the following section, we review previous research on ABG change as it pertains to each of these issues. Specifically, we examine research that plans for intentional alpha change. Additionally, we review research that plans for intentional beta and gamma change. And finally, we examine the extent to which studies have assessed beta and gamma change as threats to their alpha change results (checking for unintentional beta and gamma change).

A REVIEW OF THE RESEARCH ON ABG

In 1976, Kilmann and Herden presented a model for evaluating the effectiveness of OD interventions. Around the same time period, other authors similarly devoted attention to understanding the impacts of change-interventions in organizations (e.g., Porras & Berg, 1978). While these works focused primarily on macrolevel issues, a noticeable shift in researchers' agendas occurred around the same time that Golembiewski et al. (1976) presented alpha, beta, and gamma change (Armenakis, Bedeian, & Pond, 1983). Researchers started to adopt more of a micro-perspective when looking at change in organizations. This research stream largely focused on longitudinal examinations of changes in individual-level constructs, as the result of some type of planned intervention, or by some "unplanned" event that took place within the organization.

Longitudinal research involves the collection of data on variables across two or more distinct time periods. The main purpose of this type of research is to describe patterns of change. While the advantages of this type of design seem obvious, there has been the concern that because of the differences in time within a longitudinal study, it is often unclear whether the results of a study are due to true changes or to mere differences in orientations on the part of the respondents (Menard, 1991). This is the essence of the message that Golembiewski et al. (1976), and other researchers, were relaying in their discussions of alpha, beta and gamma change.

For examples of how the study of change has been dealt with in organizational research, we reviewed studies from five academic journals for the years 1976 through 2000. These journals were the *Academy of Management Journal, Administrative Science Quarterly, Journal of Applied Psychology, Journal of Management,* and *Personnel Psychology.* In total, 266 studies were selected (see appendix). Relevant articles were identified by searching through abstracts for terms such as "change," "longitudinal," "time," and "field-" or "quasi-experiment." Specifically, we looked for longitudinal studies with designs that included planned intentional changes in the constructs of interest. This would include planned alpha change, planned beta change, and/or planned gamma change. We also looked for studies that incorporated techniques for dealing with the complexities of unintentional beta or gamma changes. We discuss our findings below, and provide examples for clarification.

Planned Intentional Alpha Change

In most of the studies (94%), the researchers' purpose was to examine the variation in a construct over two or more time periods, while incorporating an underlying assumption that the measurement intervals of scales, and the respondents' conceptual frames of reference regarding the constructs, remained constant. While these assumptions were often not addressed in the study explicitly, we considered the omission of any discussion of such issues to mean that the researchers did in fact hold such assumptions, or in some cases, that the researchers were naïve as to the implications of other types of change besides alpha change.

Symbolically, studies examining planned intentional alpha change commonly use one of the following designs;

$$\overline{O_1 \, X \, O_2} \qquad \overline{O_1 \, O_2 \, X \, O_3 \, O_4} \qquad \left| \quad \begin{array}{c} \overline{O_1 \, X \, O_2} \\ \overline{O_1 \quad\; O_2} \end{array} \right.$$

(One Group Pretest-Posttest)   (Untreated Control Group
                                                          Pretest-Posttest)

where O_i represents an observation of the construct of interest in the i_{th} time period, and X represents the planned intervention or event that was hypothesized to bring about a change in the construct (see Golembiewski et al., 1976; Cook & Campbell, 1976). The majority of the studies reviewed used a one-group pretest-posttest design, with measurements of the relevant construct taking place once before and once after the intervention or event.

For example, Hui, Lam, and Law (2000) examined changes in organizational citizenship behavior, as a function of the announcement of a promotion decision. A finding was that employees who perceived OCB to be instrumental to their promotion, and who did receive a promotion, were more likely to decline in their OCB after the promotion than were other employees (Hui et al., 2000). Self-evaluations and supervisor ratings of OCB were collected at two time periods—once before the promotion announcement and once after the promotion announcement. The variable of "time" (dummy coded as: 1 = before promotion decision; and 2 = after the promotion decision) was incorporated into the hierarchical regression analyses to determine differences in T_1-OCB and T_2-OCB.

In this study, the researchers did not account for or discuss possible changes other than alpha-type changes. For example, consider the possibility that a supervisor might respond differently to an OCB question about an employee after that employee receives a promotion. In responding to the T_1 survey-item, "does not take unnecessary time off [from] work," suppose the supervisor gives the employee a rating of "4" (out of "5"). However, after the promotion announcement, the supervisor might conceptually use a different scale on which to judge this employee; one based upon higher expectations she or he has for the employee due to the employee's promotion (beta change). The postpromotion rating for the same level of behavior may now be a "3" instead of a "4."

Alternatively, after the promotion the supervisor may reconceptualize what OCB means as it applies to the employee, as opposed to what OCB means before the promotion. For the supervisor, the T_2 concept of "unnecessary time off [from] work" might have included the behavior of going home to care for a sick child, while "abusing the absence policy" might have been part of the T_1 assessment. In this respect, comparisons of OCB perceptions across the two time periods would be difficult to make, since the T_1 and T_2 constructs would not be conceptually equivalent (gamma change).

In another longitudinal study, Frayne and Geringer (2000) examined the changes in salespersons' self-efficacy, outcome expectancies, and performance, as a result of a training intervention. Changes in these variables from pretraining to posttraining were examined, and among the findings was the conclusion that training had a positive effect on outcome expectancies (this was one of many findings in the study, and we isolate it here for illustrative purposes). Measurement periods in this study included one pretraining period (T_1), and four posttraining periods (T_2, T_3, T_4, and T_5), each separated by 3 months. Outcome expectancies, which increased significantly from the pretraining to the posttraining period, were measured with items such as "I will increase my sense of accomplishment." This was one of 15 items that made up the outcome expectancy scale. The salesperson was asked to rate these items on a 9-point Likert-type scale ranging from "1" (very unlikely) to "9" (very likely), designating how likely she or he thought it was that such outcomes would result from his or her own sales behaviors.

As with Hui et al. (2000), beta or gamma changes were not considered or discussed in this study. Consider the possibility that the term "sense of accomplishment" might have one meaning for a salesperson that had completed training, and a different meaning for a salesperson that had not gone through training. Prior to training, a sales representative might think that "accomplishment" is a very broad term encompassing general behaviors that are related to a variety of sales activities. On the other hand, a sales representative who has completed training might have a clearer and more concise definition of "accomplishment," which incorporates the specific content of the training program, and mirrors more accurately the expectations that the company has for him or her. In this respect, comparisons of pretraining and posttraining responses to this survey item may be misleading, given that other types of change (gamma in this case) have not been addressed.

The preceding examples seem to be representative of many longitudinal studies in organizational research (e.g., Garst, Frese, & Molenaar, 2000; Spector, Chen, & O'Connell, 2000; Weitlauf, Smith, & Cervone, 2000), where the focus has been solely on alpha change. To their credit, some researchers explicitly recognized that gamma and beta change were potential concerns for the validity of their alpha change results. For example, in a study examining work attitudes of employees in autonomous work groups, Cordery, Mueller, and Smith (1991) recognized that gamma change probably should have been accounted for in their study. They suggested that they could not discount such a type of change, since they did not methodologically test for it in their study design. Similarly, in a study measuring affective dispositions over the lifetimes of individuals, Staw, Bell, and Clausen (1986) recognized that it was unclear whether the construct of affect remained constant over time. They recognized this as a concern in their study, but they did not introduce procedures to empirically discount it.

Planned Intentional Beta/Gamma Change

Interestingly, out of the 266 studies in our sample, only 16 (6%) examined planned beta and/or gamma change. In reviewing the literature for examples of how researchers tested for intentional beta or gamma changes, two categories of studies emerged. The first included those in which the researchers' hypotheses and study designs had the effects of testing for beta and/or gamma changes, even though such objectives were not explicitly stated. The second included those in which the researchers specifically stated that their objectives included an examination of these changes.

In the first category, the majority of the research consisted of longitudinal studies that examined issues related to rater training for performance appraisals. These studies inherently tested for intentional beta change. Specifically, researchers who have tested for rater errors and biases across time periods (e.g., leniency), found that such rating biases can be reduced with training (e.g., Friedman & Cornelius, 1976; Bernardin, 1978; Sauser & Pond, 1981; Vance, Winne, & Wright, 1983). These changes in rater biases represent beta changes, because they are directly related to how raters interpret scale intervals on the performance appraisal instrument. For example, if a rater assigned high ratings to all employees in T_1 (leniency bias), and the effects of training caused him or her to recalibrate the training instrument and assign less biased scores in T_2, then this reduction of leniency bias would represent beta change.

Ivancevich (1979) expected that rater training would serve to reduce these types of psychometric errors, and his pretraining/posttraining measurement design serves as a good example of testing for intentional beta change. He examined the effects of rater training on a sample of supervisory engineers, to see if the training would increase effectiveness in the use of the organization's performance appraisal scales. A longitudinal design was used to study rater errors six months before training (T1), six months after training (T2), and 12 months after training (T3). Using analyses of variance and covariance, Ivancevich (1979) found that individuals who received the training performed significantly better than individuals who did not receive training, in terms of reducing leniency and halo error.

Similar research designs and objectives were observed in Sauser and Pond (1981), Hedge and Kavanagh (1988), and Stamoulis and Hauenstein (1993). It should be noted that in these studies, the researchers did not discuss their designs in terms of Golembiewski et al.'s (1976) conceptualization of alpha, beta, and gamma change. However, their objectives of reducing rater errors provide nice illustrations of intentional beta change in practice.

In another line of research, studies that examine organizational culture, and changes to organizational culture, seem inherently to address gamma change. Although no examples of such studies were found in our sample, we nonetheless discuss the issue here to heighten the reader's awareness. In these studies, the methodology is not typically presented in terms of ABG, but the changes do represent examples of gamma change. In a case study of a change initiative at Westco, Inc., Ogbonna and Harris (1998) documented change in employees' reinterpretations or reorientations with respect to the values and the culture of the company. One interviewed employee stated: "Westco Millenium has completely changed the way I think about my job. I can't believe that I used to think of myself as a Front-End Supervisor—my job is about keeping our customers happy—nothing else matters!" (Ogbonna & Harris, 1998, p. 284). While this study was qualitative and did not test for changes in constructs empirically across different time periods, it still represents an example of intentional gamma change.

Unlike the examples above, in some instances researchers have specifically stated that their objectives included generating some type of beta or gamma change. In these studies, the researchers' intentions to bring about these changes are based in theory, because such changes are part of the researchers' hypothesized relationships. For example, Bartunek and Franzak (1988) examined how organizational restructuring changed members' cooperation with each other (alpha change). They also examined how changes in understandings of concepts related to restructuring and collaboration (gamma changes) affected the success of restructuring efforts.

Similarly, Buono, Bowditch, and Lewis (1985) examined gamma change when they showed how a merger of two banks and the corresponding restructuring effort shifted the way that bank employees viewed their coworkers, creating a we-they attitude that was not present before. Second, Rice and Contractor (1990) tested for intentional beta and gamma changes when they examined the effects of a new office information system on the way that organizational members conceptualize office work. Their results provided evidence for both types of change: "The implementation of the integrated office information system had modest but statistically significant effects, but not in the traditional way as measured by alpha change. Rather, the significant effects occurred in the way organization members conceptualize generic office activities; over time, those activities were seen as integrated or unidimensional" (Rice & Contractor, 1990, p. 314).

Checking for Unintentional Change

In some studies that tested for the presence of beta and gamma changes, researchers viewed these changes as confounding effects that could complicate the analysis of the true relationships that they were trying to test. In our sample, 15 studies (6% of the total sample) that focused on alpha change as their primary objective also checked for unintentional beta/gamma change. Importantly, checking for intentional beta/gamma change is theoretically different than checking for unintentional beta/gamma change. The key distinction is that in the first case, beta or gamma changes are expected and serve as part of the theoretical basis of the study. For the second case, however, the relationship hypotheses primarily specify alpha type changes, and the researchers seek to ensure that their observed relationships are not invalidated through the presence of other types of change.

As mentioned earlier, most studies that have used longitudinal designs have focused primarily on alpha changes, and have largely neglected examinations of beta and gamma changes. Specifically, of the studies that focused solely on alpha change, 94% did not check for the effects of unintentional beta or gamma change. To counter this trend, three examples are provided in this section to serve as models that researchers might emulate in examining change over time in a more comprehensive manner.

Randolph (1982) examined the effects of an OD intervention at a college student counseling organization, to see whether there would be changes in such variables as communication, supervisory relations, and the use of management by objectives. Randolph explicitly described the procedures he used to test for the presence of gamma and beta changes. While the specific methodology he used is not discussed in this section, it is important to note that he examined alpha changes only after gamma and beta changes were discounted. His results showed that for the variables of communication and supervisory relationships, there were no gamma or beta changes across the preintervention and postintervention time periods, a fact, which strengthened the support for the alpha change that he observed in these two variables.

Vandenberg and Self (1993) recognized the importance of different types of change in their examination of newcomers' entry and adjustment into the organization. They noted that it may be misleading to operationalize newcomer change by simply comparing mean values of commitment (organizational commitment, organizational identification, affective commitment, and continuance commitment) at entry and at some later points in employment (see also Schaubroeck & Green, 1989). In other words, their interest was in examining how the interpretations of alpha change might be constrained by the presence of gamma and beta changes (Vandenberg & Self, 1993). The results of the study revealed the presence of both beta and gamma changes in two of the variables, thus making it difficult to compare means across time periods. In discussing their results, Vandenberg and Self (1993) offered the following advice:

> Indeed, the findings suggest that tests for the presence of beta and gamma changes may need to become a standard practice and treated as a preliminary analytical step in studies in which change is a focal issue. (p. 566)

In another study that examined the process of newcomers adapting to the organization, Chan and Schmitt (2000) used a latent growth modeling (LGM) approach to check for unintentional changes. In looking at changes in constructs such as technical information seeking, referent information seeking, and relationship building, they recognized that as a prerequisite for such a study, researchers must establish measurement invariance across the time periods in each of the constructs. In other words, they wanted to ensure that each construct was being measured with the same precision across time, and that each construct held the same factor structure and factor loadings across time (Chan & Schmitt, 2000). Their approach accounted for non-alpha type changes by modeling intraindividual changes in newcomers, across four equal time periods, following their entry into the organization.

Summary

Table 1 presents a descriptive categorization of the studies we reviewed. Despite recommendations that change should be viewed from the multiple

Table 1.   Substantive Studies Published Between 1976 and 2000 that Assess Alpha, Beta, and Gamma Changes (N = 266)

Category of Study	Number of Studies
I. Examined planned alpha change:	250 (94%)
Planned alpha change studies that did not check for the presence of beta and gamma change:	235 (88%)
Planned alpha change studies that did not check for the presence of beta and gamma change, but mentioned these changes as possibilities:	5 (2%)
Planned alpha change studies that checked for the presence of unintentional beta and gamma change:	15 (6%)
II. Examined planned beta and/or gamma change:	16 (6%)

perspectives underlying ABG, our review reveals that many studies failed to do this. While the studies focused predominantly on alpha change, very few checked for the unintentional effects of gamma or beta change. Also, only a few studies have focused exclusively on planned gamma or beta change.

STATISTICAL METHODS FOR DETECTING ABG CHANGE

To date, the majority of ABG research has focused on developing and testing statistical methods for identifying the three types of change. Since Golembiewski et al. (1976) first defined ABG change, five major methodological techniques have been proposed for identifying the existence of ABG change. These techniques are Ahmavaara's technique, actual-ideal difference measures, retrospective accounts, confirmatory factor analysis (CFA) with and without control groups, and latent growth modeling (LGM).

As Milsap and Hartog (1988) point out, there has been much disagreement regarding these methods, and regarding which is the best choice for detecting ABG change (see also Armenakis & Bedeian, 1982; Terborg, Maxwell, & Howard, 1982). Indeed, Tennis concluded in his review of the ABG literature that "no single method has emerged as decidedly superior" (1989, p. 145). The one point of agreement among researchers examining ABG change is that Time 1 and Time 2 difference scores are not sufficient to distinguish among the three types of change (Milsap & Hartog, 1988). In this section we describe the major methodological techniques, and the primary limitations and advantages of each.

Ahmavaara's Technique

The Ahmavaara technique was the initial method proposed by Golembiewski et al. (1976) for measuring beta and gamma change. This approach is based on the underlying operational definition of gamma change as a shift in the conceptualization of a given construct represented by a change in the Times 1 and 2 factorial structures for that construct (Milsap & Hartog, 1988). The premise is that both the number of factors and their patterns of loadings operationalize the frame of reference that respondents use in answering items. Quite simply, Ahmavaara's technique rotates Time 1 and Time 2 factor pattern matrices to maximum similarity. As a first step, Time 1 and Time 2 data are factor analyzed. Then either the Time 1 or Time 2 factor matrix is rotated into the other matrix in such a way as to maximize the degree of correspondence between the two (Ahmavaara, 1954). According to Golembiewski et al., the Ahmavaara rotation "efficiently reduces the effects of noise, or the exogenous influence inherent in prior rotations of either matrix" (1976, p. 31).

At this point the two matrices can be compared directly using indices of congruence (e.g., coefficient of similarity; Tucker, 1951). Absence of beta and gamma change is inferred from a high degree of congruence between the two factor structures, while a lack of congruence suggests that beta or gamma change may be present. One rule of thumb for interpreting the coefficient of similarity is that any coefficient over .80 is acceptable, while any coefficient below .50 is unacceptable (Harman, 1976). Coefficients falling between .50 and .80 are questionable. An example of a study using Ahmavaara's technique was reported by Griffin (1981), who measured respondents' perceptions of their job characteristics (i.e., feedback, autonomy, identity, and variety) at two time periods that were three months apart. Because none of the congruency coefficients were below .80, Griffin concluded that the Time 2 factors were not substantially different from the Time 1 factors. As an alternative to coefficients of congruence, interclass correlation coefficients and product-moment correlation coefficients can be computed between the Time 1 and Time 2 factor loadings (Golembiewski et al., 1976). Interclass class correlation coefficients that are closer to 1.0 indicate factors that are similar in pattern and magnitude across times. Product-moment correlation coefficients that are closer to 1.0 indicate only a similarity of patterns between two factors.

Ahmavaara's technique represents a major contribution to our understanding of how to recognize non-alpha change. However, as one of the first techniques proposed, it also suffers from some important limitations. Though low congruence suggests that non-alpha change may be present, Ahmavaara's technique does not allow researchers to identify specifically whether the change is beta or gamma in nature (Golembiewski et al., 1976; Golembiewski & Billingsley, 1980; Schmitt, 1982). Furthermore, Lindell and Drexler (1979, 1980) argue that low congruence could occur because of alpha change, not just beta or gamma change. Thus, while the Ahmavaara technique was a useful first-step, it is a very imprecise method for identifying change. The remaining techniques all attempt to clarify identified change as specifically alpha, beta, or gamma.

Actual/Ideal Measures

Zmud and Armenakis (1978) proposed the use of "ideal" measures in order to assess alpha and beta change. At Times 1 and 2 respondents report actual perceptions of themselves or conditions and also provide "ideal" ratings for every item used as Time 1 and Time 2 measures. For example, a respondent rating his/her job satisfaction would first rate his/her current real job satisfaction, then respond to the same questions in terms of how he or she would answer them if his/her satisfaction was at an ideal level. The reasoning behind this approach is that any change in respondents' ideal ratings between Time 1 and Time 2 represents some form of respondent recalibration of the measurement scale. Again using job satisfaction as an example, a respondent with an average ideal job satisfaction rating of 3.0 at Time 1 and 5.0 at Time 2 is most likely recalibrating the scale for the job satisfaction items. Because we would not expect a respondent's ideal level of job satisfaction to change over time, it is possible that, in this case, the respondent's tendency toward rating strictness changed over time. Zmud and Armenakis (1978) describe five hypothetical situations that suggest alpha change, beta change, both, or neither. Beta change is believed to have occurred when actual perceptions between Time 1 and Time 2 and ideal perceptions between Time 1 and Time 2 are both different. Beta change is also thought to have occurred when ideal perceptions between Times 1 and 2 and difference scores between Times 1 and 2 are both different. Alpha change has occurred when difference scores, actual scores, and ideal scores have changed between Times 1 and 2 and also when only difference and actual scores have changed between Times 1 and 2.

As another technique for identifying beta change using ideal scores, Bedeian, Armenakis, and Gibson (1980) suggest regressing Time 2 ideal scores onto Time 1 ideal scores. The beta weights and intercepts for the resulting regression equations can then be examined to determine whether they are significantly different from 1 and 0, respectively. If the beta coefficient is not significantly different from 1 and alpha is not significantly different from 0, this suggests beta change has occurred. The logic behind this conclusion can best be illustrated by examining the regression equation for Time 2 regressed onto Time 1, with an alpha 0 and a beta of 1:

$$\text{Time } 2 = 0 + 1(\text{Time } 1).$$

In this equation, Time 1 is clearly equal to Time 2, suggesting that recalibration of the scale has not occurred between Times 1 and 2. Also, gamma change in the actual/ideal measures approach is assessed much as it is in the Ahmavaara approach described above. That is, factor structures between times are compared using a coefficient of congruence.

The main advantage of the "ideal" approach over the pure Ahmavaara technique is that the addition of the ideal measures allows researchers to identify more precisely whether an observed change is alpha, beta, or gamma. Nonetheless, there are still some important weaknesses to the actual/ideal technique. Schmitt et al. (1984) report that this technique leads to conclusions different than those suggested by either retrospective accounts or CFA (both discussed below). These authors also suggest a ceiling effect for ideal ratings. In their study, respondents tended to rate the ideal state as the positive endpoint of the scale. According to Schmitt et al. (1984), rating the ideal as the endpoint means there is no room for change in the ideal measure, making any observed response shift potentially artifactual. Finally, because respondents must provide an "ideal" rating for every measure included on a data collection instrument, this approach significantly increases the time and effort required of respondents.

Retrospective Accounts

In 1980, Terborg, Howard, and Maxwell suggested collecting retrospective "then" measures at Time 2 of the same variables measured at Time 1 as one means of assessing ABG change. That is, at Time 2 each subject first reports current perceptions of self or conditions; then immediately reports retrospective perceptions (i.e., "then" measures) of self or conditions for the time prior to the intervention, doing so for every item used as a Time 1 *and* Time 2 measure. The logic of this suggestion is that any shifts in measurement calibration or reconceptualization will be reflected in the difference between subjects' Time 1 and retrospective responses. Likewise, because Time 2 and "then" measures are made concurrently, they should be from the same perspective and relatively free from gamma and beta change, and the difference between the two should represent alpha change.

Unlike the techniques discussed in the previous sections of this review, this one can be used to test for the presence of gamma and beta change at both the individual and group levels. At the individual level, a significant difference between an individual's mean score across items on the Time 1 and "then" measures reflect beta change. Gamma change, on the other hand, is identified via pairwise comparison of the Time 1, Time 2, and "then" ratings per construct using profile shapes (correlations) and profile dispersions (standard deviations). Gamma change can be identified from these profile comparisons in two ways. First, gamma change is believed to be present if the correlations between Time 2 and "then" measures are greater than those between Time 1/Time 2 measures and between Time 1/"then" measures. Second, gamma change is likely to have occurred if the standard deviations of the Time 2 and "then" profiles are not substantially different from one another but are different from the Time 1 standard deviation profiles. The strongest support for gamma change is obtained when both the correlation and standard deviation profile comparisons suggest its existence.

At the group level, alpha change can be diagnosed by assessing the difference between Time 2 and "then" scores for each participant, employing t-tests for these scores at the individual level. The resulting t-values can be used as dependent variables in a comparison of the difference between treatment and control groups. Terborg et al. (1980) suggest using either the Mann-Whitney U Test (for two groups) or the Kruskal-Wallis H Test (for more than two groups) for this comparison. A significant difference between treatment and control groups, with the treatment group having higher t-values, suggests an alpha change. Group-level beta change is assessed similarly. In this case, the Mann-Whitney U or Kruskal-Wallis H Tests are used on the ranked t-values that were determined by comparing Time 1 and "then" profile means. To assess gamma change, scores are constructed from differences either in pairs of profile correlations or in pairs of profile standard deviations.

There are several important advantages to this approach. Among them, it is the only approach that allows for assessment at both the individual and group levels. As Terborg et al. (1980) argue, lack of attention to individual change may confuse the interpretation of group effects. For example, if there are relatively large changes for only a few individuals, this might result in statistical evidence of group-level change, but does not really suggest group-wide change. The examination of individual effects has a practical advantage from an OD perspective as well: feedback to an organization need not be a broad-brush approach and can be tailored to the individual. Another advantage is that this approach allows researchers to investigate the three types of change more independently than is possible under the two previously proposed methods. According to Terborg et al., "Any possible permutation of none, some, or all three types of change can be found and described for each individual subject in the study" (1980, p. 118). Finally, this analysis can be used even with very small samples.

However, this approach also has several limitations. A major limitation is that it uses significance tests in unconventional ways (Schmitt et al., 1984). Thus statistical significance tests at the individual level are not meaningful, thereby requiring the researcher to make subjective judgments about what represents a "practically" significant difference (Terborg et al., 1980). For example, how similar or different must the correlations be among the Time 1, Time 2, and "then" measures in order to infer that gamma change at the individual level has occurred? Another methodological limitation is that this approach assumes no change in the control group, thus it only tests for change in the treatment group (Schmitt, 1982). Because problems with external validity can cause changes in the control group, it is important to ascertain whether such changes have occurred. Finally, there are also interrelated practical research limitations to this approach. First, it is only appropriate for use with measures that are comprised of many items. As such it requires the use of fairly lengthy data collection instruments. Second, the addition of "then" measures requires even further lengthening of instruments and may increase the frustration of already fatigued respondents. Additionally, the use of retrospective accounts is often called into question because of the reliance on the memories of respondents.

Confirmatory Factor Analysis

Much recent interest has turned to CFA methods to assess ABG change. There are two CFA approaches for this task. One is the original method proposed by Schmitt (1982), which employs only one subject group for analysis, and the other involves CFA for research with both treatment and control groups (Milsap & Hartog, 1988). We will first describe the basic CFA method and then explain how this method can be adapted for use with multiple groups (for a comprehensive review see Vandenberg & Lance, 2000).

As described by Schmitt (1982) and Schmitt et al. (1984), the CFA method of detecting ABG change proceeds in at least four steps, each of which represents the test of a particular hypothesis. The first hypothesis is that the variance-covariance matrices between Times 1 and 2 are equal: these serve as an initial indication of the possibility of beta and/or gamma change. A significant difference in variance-covariance matrices implies one or more of the following: (a) some unspecified gamma change, (b) some form of beta change, or (c) different uniquenesses. More detailed information about the nature of the change is provided in the remaining steps (cf. Vandenberg & Lance, 2000).

The second hypothesis concerns the equality of factor patterns and involves a test of invariance between factor patterns for Time 1 and Time 2 latent variables. As with Ahmavaara's technique, the underlying assumption of CFA analysis is that gamma change can be operationalized as a shift in factor structures between Times 1 and 2 for a given construct: as such, the purpose of this step is to test those structures for gamma change. If Time 1 and Time 2 measures are operationalizing the same underlying construct, the Time 1 and Time 2 factor structures will be the same, suggesting no occurrence of gamma change. Likewise, if the hypothesized factor structure adequately describes both the Time 1 and Time 2 data, then the chi-square value for the difference between the observed and reproduced matrices should be insignificant, and other measures of fit (e.g., non-normed fit index) should be strong (Jöreskog, 1969; Schmitt, 1982; Schmitt et al., 1984).

The third hypothesis is also a test of gamma change, and proposes that the covariance matrices of common factors are equal between Times 1 and 2. The logic underlying this step is that the covariances among factors should remain at the same level across time if a reconceptualization has not occurred at T_2. That is, the relationship pattern among the factors should not shift across time unless a reconceptualization in one set of constructs has occurred which then alters how the constructs covary with each other. If this model does not differ significantly in fit from the previous one, then gamma change is presumed not to have occurred.

The fourth step or hypothesis is that the factor loadings are identical for like items across time. This is primarily a test of beta change. Following the logic of other methods that test for beta change, CFA proposes that beta change can be operationalized as a change of scale between Times 1 and 2 among the latent variables that underlie observed test variables. Consequently, this step focuses on equalizing scaling units in the factors, which is accomplished by setting the Time 1 and Time 2 loadings to be equal. To the degree that a nonsignificant worsening of fit is observed in this model relative to the previous one, beta change is said not to have occurred, hence the respondents calibrated items to the underlying latent variable to the same degree at both time periods. As a fifth step, one further test of beta change is to constrain the factor variances of like factors to be equal across time. The logic underlying this restriction is that factor variance represents the degree to which respondents use the full range of the underlying construct when responding to items. Therefore a recalibration would be detected if the factor variance of a construct were much smaller or much greater at T_2 than at T_1. This would be supported if this model resulted in a significantly worse fitting model relative to the other two.

Schmitt et al. summarize the entire CFA process as follows: "gamma change is assessed by comparing the difference between the chi-squares produced in testing Hypotheses 2 and 3, and beta change is determined by comparing the difference between the chi-squares for tests of Hypotheses 3 and 4" (1984, p. 250). This summary suggests some of the proposed advantages of the CFA approach over other methods for detecting beta and gamma change. Unlike Ahmavaara's technique and actual/ideal measures, the statistical comparison of hypotheses and changes in fit provide *statistical* evidence of beta and gamma change (i.e., as evidenced by fit statistics), rather than relying upon *subjective* determination of acceptable coefficients of congruence or upon a review of factor structures and loadings.

The Milsap and Hartog (1988) technique is very similar to Schmitt's original methods but introduces the use of a control group for additional comparisons, and also introduces the use of structural models. Time 1 and Time 2 data is gathered from both the treatment and control groups, and a structural model is specified in which Time 2 measures are regressed onto Time 1 measures for both groups. Again, hypotheses about beta and gamma change are tested via a series of nested models. As with the original Schmitt method, adequate fit of the baseline model suggests no gamma or beta change, while poor fit suggests the need for further investigation. If the Time 1 measures for the two groups are similar, but the Time 2 measures are different, this indicates gamma change has occurred for at least one group and that the two groups have changed in different ways. If Time 1 measures for the groups are different yet Time 2 measures are similar, this suggests that gamma change has occurred in both groups and the change is similar for both groups. Beta change is determined by specifying a structural model in which Time 2 measures are regressed onto Time 1 measures for both groups. If beta change is present it will alter the regression in one of two ways: (a) producing a nonlinear function, or (b) altering the size of the regression coefficients.

One major advantage of both CFA techniques is that they, like the Terborg et al. (1980) test, allow for relatively independent examination of all three types of change, thereby providing more precise information as to what types of change have occurred. As Milsap and Hartog (1988) explain, "An advantage of the confirmatory approach, in comparison with other rotational procedures, is the availability of statistical tests of fit and detailed information on departures from the hypothesized structure" (1988, p. 582). In addition, while it does not guarantee that the researcher will be able to link change specifically to an intervention, the use of control groups in CFA analyses helps researchers to do so more directly. In other words, the other techniques only indicate whether change occurred and what type of change exists. They provide no information as to what the source of the change is (i.e., whether it is a function of a particular intervention or of some extraneous influence). The Milsap and Hartog (1988) technique takes advantage of experimental design when attempting to isolate the source of the change—be it alpha, beta, or gamma change.

There are, of course, limitations to both CFA approaches as well. As a general rule, CFA analysis requires sample sizes of at least 150-200. However, the primary fit statistic (i.e., chi-square) on which the comparison of models (e.g., the model associated with step 2 vs. the one associated with step 3) is based can be misleading when large sample sizes are used. In particular, with large samples the chi-square test can indicate statistically poor fit of the data to the hypothesized model when, in fact, the variation between the two is practically quite small (Bentler & Bonnett, 1980). Likewise, both the Schmitt (1982) and Milsap and Hartog (1988) techniques can indicate beta change when none actually exists, and also, the Milsap and Hartog (1988) procedure cannot detect beta change that is linear in nature. Though very little research has been conducted to compare these techniques to other methods for detecting ABG change, Schmitt et al. (1984) do report that their technique results in conclusions that are quite similar to those from the Terborg technique.

Latent Growth Modeling

The most recent methodological development for assessing change over time is latent growth modeling (LGM). One important difference between LGM and the methods described above is that LGM focuses primarily upon accuracy for assessing alpha change. The other methods described herein have primarily emphasized detection of beta and gamma change, while assuming that, in the absence of beta and gamma change, alpha change can be detected accurately through conventional methods. Conventional means of assessing alpha or "true" change include: computing a difference score between data collected at two times; using residual change scores; and doing regression estimates of true change.

As Chan (1998) and others (see, for example, Edwards, 1994; Tisak & Smith, 1994a, b) point out, difference scores—perhaps the most common method for assessing alpha change—have been criticized as being unreliable and invalid and frequently negatively correlated with Time 1 measures. Regardless of the limitations of difference scores, any method of assessing alpha change that relies upon only two time periods can provide only limited information about change over time (Chan, 1998). By relying on data from only two time periods, researchers are provided with only two snapshots during continuous change processes, and important questions remain unanswered, such as, "Does true change proceed gradually or does it occur through large shifts at each time interval?" and "Is the nature of the change nonlinear?" (Chan, 1998; Lance et al., 2000). Unlike conventional methods of assessing alpha change, LGM can provide answers to these questions by actually modeling true change, its predictors, and its outcomes. More specifically, LGM allows researchers to specify and test hypotheses about individual predictors and (1) individual differences in initial states and (2) individual differences in the rate of change (Chan & Schmitt, 2000). LGM also allows researchers to test hypotheses regarding the impact of true change on individual outcomes (Lance et al., 2000).

Lance et al. (2000) describe LGM as a two-stage process that imposes a CFA structure on longitudinal variables. In the first stage, within-individual change is modeled by fitting individual-level growth (or change) trajectories for constructs that are measured at multiple points in time (Chan, 1998, 2000; Lance et al., 2000). This stage is accomplished by specifying the model in Figure 1. To illustrate, suppose this model represents a

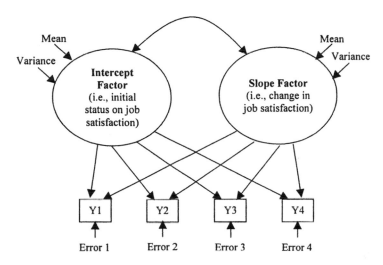

Figure 1. An example of stage one of the LGM approach with job satisfaction as the focal construct.

change in job satisfaction over time. The latent construct "Intercept" represents individuals' initial status, or their level of job satisfaction at Time 1, and it is constant for any given individual across time. The latent construct "Slope" represents the rate of change (i.e., in terms of increase and decrease), if any, over time. The measurement of job satisfaction at four different time periods is indicated by the variables "Y1" through "Y2."[1] According to Chan and Schmitt (2000), true change in this model is indicated by a latent mean for the slope factor that is significantly different from 0. The sign of the latent mean indicates the direction of the change. Likewise, a small slope factor latent mean indicates a gradual change over time, while a large slope factor mean indicates large magnitude change (Chan, 1998).

An extension of this basic, stage-one LGM model can be achieved by treating the intercept and slope factors as second-order constructs which, in turn, represent multiple first-order constructs of the focal construct of interest (e.g., job satisfaction) as measured by multiple manifest indicators within each time period (Lance et al., 2000). There are two advantages to this second-order change over the basic model (Lance et al., 2000). First, it corrects the intercept and slope factors for attenuation that arises from unreliability in the longitudinal measurement of the focal construct. Second, the second-order model allows the researcher to incorporate tests for beta and gamma change (as described in the CFA section above) and, provided evidence of such change is found, to correct for partial measurement nonequivalence when measures are not strictly invariant over time. For example, the second-order model permits corrections for a gamma change that is not found between Times 1 and 2 but is found between Times 2 and 3. This second advantage is critical because, like all methods of detecting alpha change, the accuracy of LGM rests entirely on the correctness of the assumption that beta and gamma change are not present (Chan, 1998; Lance et al., 2000).

The second stage of the LGM process introduces predictors of the individual differences in longitudinal growth trajectories established in stage one. Whereas stage one focused on within-individual change, Lance et al. (2000) refer to this second stage as the "between-individuals" stage. Figure 2 illustrates stage two. Still using job satisfaction as our example, the model in Figure 2 proposes that two variables measured at Time 1 are predictors of individual differences in initial job satisfaction and change in job satis-

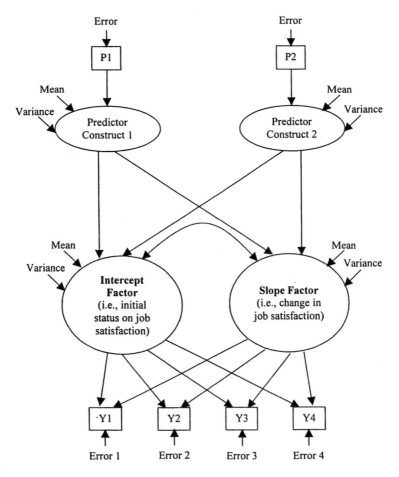

Figure 2. An example of stage two of the LGM approach with job satisfaction as the focal construct.

faction over time. According to Lance et al. (2000), hypothesized effects of the predictor variables on the intercept factor represent hypothesized static (i.e., no-change) relationships. Because the slope factor represents true longitudinal alpha change in the focal construct, hypothesized relationships between the predictor variables and the slope factor represent moderator effects. In other words, a significant structural relationship between the predictor variables and the slope construct suggest that change in the focal construct is contingent upon the predictor variables. Using much the same structural logic as is used for the predictor variables, Lance et al. (2000) also describe how outcomes of initial status (i.e., the intercept factor) and change (i.e., the slope factor) in the focal construct can be specified.

As a final note about LGM, it is important to point out that LGM models can also be specified for multiple groups within the same data set (Chan, 1998). As such, the advantages of the Milsap and Hartog control group CFA technique can be incorporated into the LGM approach. Given this possibility and the potential for incorporating tests for gamma and beta change into LGM models, it is appropriate to consider LGM as a means for extending the CFA technique to assess change.

Summary

The techniques described in this section represent multiple approaches to test for ABG change, all of which vary in complexity and sophistication. Each approach has its advantages and disadvantages. The major features of each approach are summarized in Table 2. Little research has been conducted comparing the approaches and their utility to one another. Thus at this time it is not entirely clear which method is the most appropriate for assessing ABG change. However, as of this writing both the CFA and the latent growth modeling approaches seem to garner the most support among researchers.

One factor to consider is that the methodological technique should match the research question and design. Given the variety among the aforementioned methodologies, there is likely to be a feasible and appropriate technique for every longitudinal data collection situation and research need. For example, if a researcher is primarily interested in increasing the confidence with which he or she can draw conclusions regarding alpha change, and merely wants to rule out beta and gamma change, then the Terborg or Schmitt tests might be optimal choices. Likewise, if a researcher has specific hypotheses about the nature of alpha change (e.g., that it occurs gradually over time), the LGM approach makes the most sense—again, provided that beta and gamma change can be ruled out. Which approach the researcher ultimately chooses would

Table 2.   Summary of Major Features for Each Statistical Technique

Technique	Requires Large Sample	Adds Length to Survey Instrument	Requires Multiple Samples	Can Link Change to Intervention	Analyses Can be Conducted at Individual Level	Allows Relatively Independent Testing for Each Change Type
Ahmavaara	No	No	No	No	No	No
Actual/Ideal Measures	No	Yes	No	No	No	Somewhat
Retrospective Accounts	No	Yes	Yes	No	Yes	Yes
CFA	Yes	No	No	No	No	Yes
CFA, with control group	Yes	No	Yes	Yes	No	Yes
LGM	Yes	No	No	No	Yes	Yes
LGM, with control group	Yes	No	Yes	Yes	Yes	Yes

depend upon his/her sample size, as well as the number of variables under investigation and the specific research questions under investigation. On the other hand, if a researcher is interested in planned beta and gamma change and wants to determine whether such change is due to a particular intervention, then the Milsap and Hartog technique would probably be preferable. Therefore we urge researchers to consider the methodological implications of their theoretical interests regarding change, and to design their research so that they will be able to use the right technique for their needs, and to use it appropriately.

RECOMMENDATIONS FOR FUTURE RESEARCH

Since the hallmark presentation of ABG by Golembiewski et al. in 1976, great strides have been achieved with respect to both the conceptual underpinnings of the change concepts and the analytical tools used to detect their presence. ABG has evolved from a rather abstract notion that, while acknowledged by researchers as a concern, remained analytically unreachable. Today, it is a more concrete application that can be incorporated in most designs. Despite this progress, there remain a number of issues that need to be researched to advance our understanding of the change concepts.

Substantiation of the Analytical Tools

While our recommendation is to use the CFA approach, we are unaware of any studies to date that have convincingly substantiated the validity of this approach for detecting the changes, particularly gamma and beta change. Namely, the sensitivity of the CFA approach needs to be carefully examined. Doing so will require a series of methodologically oriented studies in which the CFA approach itself is the focal issue. For example, a number of experiments should be undertaken in which a conceptual frame of reference toward some entity is formed and subsequently altered in participant-subjects, and the tools used for detecting gamma change are then examined as to their ability to detect this change. As it stands right now, we are accepting on faith that the tools for uncovering gamma change are indeed doing so.

Similarly, experiments that alter the calibration of scale items (as indicators of the underlying construct) are required to evaluate the tools for detecting beta change. These studies need to be supplemented by a series of Monte Carlo simulations so that the distributional properties of the tools are also scrutinized. Again, the need for this work is driven by the fact that we currently do not know how sensitive the tools are to these forms of change. For example, how much beta change is required in order to be detected by the tools (is it a small amount or a large amount)? What happens to analytic sensitivity as sample size increases or decreases? Similar questions need to be addressed in terms of gamma change.

There are other methodological issues as well. For example, Cheung and Rensvold have noted that the selection of the reference indicator (a requirement for identification in CFA approaches) for each of the scales has major implications for detecting beta change in particular. There is the potential to grossly over- or underestimate the severity of beta change if the wrong reference indicator is selected. Dr. Larry Williams (personal communication; Center for the Advancement of Research Methods and Analysis, Virginia Commonwealth University) also notes that the techniques may be casting "too large a net." We may infer gamma change from research findings when, in fact, there may be some other undetected systematic source of influence (e.g., some form of individual difference or common-method construct) that is actually causing the findings. That is, we may be falsely assuming gamma change when, in fact, if another source of influence were removed, we would see that the conceptual frame of reference is indeed stable.

Finally, a set of studies that directly compares all of the ABG methodologies is needed for researchers and practitioners to determine the relative utility of each, especially for the measurement of beta and gamma change. Soon after the ABG typology was introduced, a number of researchers actively pursued methodologies to test for beta and gamma change (Armenakis, Buckley, & Bedeian, 1986; Milsap & Hartog, 1988; Schaubroeck & Green, 1989 Zmud & Armenakis, 1978). As indicated earlier, there are advantages and disadvantages for each of the methodologies. Yet, to date, only one study has compared and contrasted some of the methodological techniques (Schmitt, Pulakos, & Lieblien, 1984). Conducting a set of comparative studies would permit us to "lay to rest" once and for all the question as to which indeed is the best method for detecting ABG changes.

Need to Develop Theory and Conduct Research on Intentional Beta and Gamma Change

As depicted in Table 3, to date, there have been at least ten studies that specifically address how to avoid beta and gamma change effects (e.g., Armenakis & Smith, 1978; Porras & Singh, 1986; Zmud & Armenakis, 1978). While in many cases we do not want to find beta and gamma change because they represent a threat to the traditionally desired alpha change, there may also be times when we desire a complete reconstitution of the work environment or individual attitude. As noted in our review, there

Table 3.   A History of ABG Theory and Methods

	1975	1976	1978	1979	1980	1982	1983	1984
Introduction of ABG concept	Golembiewski et al.	Golembiewski et al.						
Theoretical articles				Lindell & Drexler	Golembiewski & Billingsly; Lindell & Drexler	Terborg et al.; Armenakis & Bedeian	Armenakis et al.	
Methodological articles			Zmud & Armenakis		Terborg et al.; Bedeian et al.	Schmitt		Schmitt et al.

	1985	1986	1988	1989	1993	1996	2000
Introduction of ABG concept	Van de Viert et al.	Golembiewski					
Theoretical articles				Tennis; Golembiewski; Bedeian & Armenakis		Thompson & Hunt	
Methodological articles			Millsap & Hartog	Randolph & Elloy; Schaubroeck & Green	Vandenberg & Self		Chan & Schmitt; Vandenberg & Lance

have been very few studies that have intentionally tried to create beta or gamma change. This is an area that is fruitful for future theorizing and research.

There are many situations in which a dramatic reconceptualization of a construct such as that associated with gamma change could be desired. For example, diversity training by its nature typically tries to produce a fundamental shift in individuals' attitudes. That is, diversity training may try to change fundamentally how individuals "view" or "conceptualize" different groups of people. This type of fundamental attitude shift is not likely to be captured solely with tests of alpha change. In these cases, gamma change may be desired as the result of the diversity training intervention.

More researchers need to recognize the usefulness of beta and gamma change for capturing and creating the types of change actually desired by an intervention. Most of our theories focus solely on alpha change. This implies that there is plenty of room for developing new theory associated with beta and gamma change.

CONCLUSION

Twenty-five years ago, Golembiewski et al. (1976) introduced the typology of alpha, beta, and gamma change. Yet, we have made little progress toward incorporating this typology into our assessments of change. It is not clear why there has been resistance to the incorporation of this model of change within our research. Speculation suggests that it could be the difficult nature of the typology in terms of its requirements for testing, that it is a threat to planned and desired alpha change interventions, or that it is not demanded by reviewers of change research. Nevertheless, we need to be more systematic and diligent in our efforts toward addressing alpha, beta, and gamma change within our research.

As indicated in our review, many of the studies that examined change over time did not include tests of beta and gamma change prior to testing for alpha change (the mean difference across a variable over time). While several researchers hinted at the possibility that beta or gamma change *could* have influenced their results, empirical tests were not conducted to confirm or disconfirm these types of change (e.g., Cordery, Mueller, & Smith, 1991; Gavin & McPhail, 1978; Gavin & Montgomery, 1983).

It has been acknowledged widely that if either beta or gamma change has occurred, then the difference scores calculated through the traditional tests of alpha change can be misleading (Milsap & Hartog, 1988; Vandenberg & Lance, 2000). Yet, as researchers and reviewers of manuscripts, we rarely require that tests of beta and gamma change be conducted to eliminate threats to the validity of alpha test results. These types of screening tests for beta and gamma should become standard practice, much like confirmatory factor analyses for assessing the validity of scales within our studies. Vandenberg and Self (1993) provide a good example of testing for beta and gamma changes prior to their tests of alpha change. They, in fact, found that due to the presence of beta and gamma change, they were unable to conduct some of the traditional tests that they had originally planned for assessing alpha change. Two-hundred and forty out of 255 (94%) studies did not check for the presence of beta or gamma change before proceeding with tests of alpha change. This lack of recognition for the potential effects of beta and gamma change on the validity of alpha results is significant and should be more readily recognized and addressed by future research in this domain.

NOTE

1. As represented in Figure 1, true change is modeled as a linear function. However, Figure 1 can be modified to model true change as nonlinear (e.g., curvilinear) as well (Chan, 2000). See Chan (2000) for examples of nonlinear modifications to the basic LGM change model.

REFERENCES

Ahmavaara, Y. (1954). Transformation analysis of factorial data. *Annals of the Academy of Science Fennicae* (Series B), *881*, 54-59.

Armenakis, A.A., & Bedeian, A.G. (1982). On the measurement and control of beta change: Reply to Terborg, Maxwell, and Howard. *Academy of Management Review, 7*, 296-299.

Armenakis, A.A., Bedeian, A.G., & Pond, S.B. (1983). Research issues in OD evaluation: Past, present, and future. *Academy of Management Review, 8*(2), 320-328.

Armenakis, A.A., Buckley, M.R., & Bedeian, A.G. (1986). Survey research measurement issues in evaluating change: A laboratory investigation. *Applied Psychological Measurement, 10*, 147-157.

Armenakis, A.A., & Smith, L. (1978). A practical alternative to comparison group designs in OD evaluations: The abbreviated time series design. *Academy of Management Journal, 21*, 499-507.

Bartunek, J.M., & Franzak, F.J. (1988). The effects of organizational restructuring on frames of reference and cooperation. *Journal of Management, 14*(4), 579-592.

Bedeian, A.G., Armenakis, A.A., & Gibson, R.W. (1980). The measurement and control of beta change. *Academy of Management Review, 5*, 561-566.

Bentler, P.M. & Bonnett, D.G. (1980). Significance tests and goodness of fit in the analysis of covariance structures. *Psychological Bulletin, 88*, 588-606

Bernardin, H.J. (1978). Effects of rater training on leniency and halo errors in student ratings of instructors. *Journal of Applied Psychology, 63*, 301-308.

Buono, A.F., Bowditch, J. & Lewis, J.W. (1985). When cultures collide: The anatomy of a merger. *Human Relations, 38*(5), 477-500.

Burr, J.A., & Nesselroade, J.R. (1990). Change measurement. In A. von Eye (Ed.), *Statistical methods in longitudinal research* (Vol. 1, pp. 3-34). Boston: Academic Press.

Chan, D. (1998). The conceptualization and analysis of change over time: An integrative approach incorporating longitudinal mean and covariance structures analysis (LMACS) and multiple indicator latent growth modeling(LGM). *Organizational Research Methods, 1,* 421-483.

Chan, D., & Schmitt, N. (2000). Interindividual differences in intraindividual changes in proactivity during organizational entry: A latent growth modeling approach to understanding newcomer adaptation. *Journal of Applied Psychology, 85*(2), 190-210.

Collins, L.M. (1996). Measurement of change in research on aging: Old and new issues from an individual growth perspective. In J.E. Birren & K.W. Schaie (Eds.), *Handbook of psychology and aging* (4th ed., pp. 38-56). San Diego, CA: Academic Press.

Cook, T.D., & Campbell, D.T. (1976). *The design and conduct of quasi-experiments and true experiments in field settings* (pp. 223-326). Chicago: Rand McNally.

Cordery, J.L., Mueller, W.S., & Smith, L.M. (1991). Attitudinal and behavioral effects of autonomous group working: A longitudinal field study. *Academy of Management Journal, 34*(2), 464-476.

Cronbach, L.J., & Furby, L. (1970). How should we measure "change"–Or should we? *Psychological Bulletin, 74,* 68-80.

Dawis, R.V., & Lofquist, L.H. (1993). From TWA to PEC. *Journal of Vocational Behavior, 43*(1), 113-121.

Edwards, J.R. (1994). Regression analysis as an alternative to difference scores. *Journal of Management, 20,* 683-689.

Feldman, D.C. (1976). A practical program for employee socialization. *Organizational Dynamics, 5*(2), 64-80.

Frayne, C.A., & Geringer, J.M. (2000). Self-management training for improving job performance: A field experiment involving salespeople. *Journal of Applied Psychology, 85*(3), 361-372.

Friedman, B.A., & Cornelius, E.T. (1976). Effect of rater participation in scale construction on the psychometric characteristics of two rating scale formats. *Journal of Applied Psychology, 61,* 210-216.

Garst, H., Frese, M., & Molenaar, P.C.M. (2000). The temporal factor of change in stressor-strain relationships: A growth curve model on a longitudinal study in East Germany. *Journal of Applied Psychology, 85*(3), 417-438.

Gavin, J.F., & McPhail, S.M. (1978). Intervention and evaluation: A proactive team approach to OD. *Journal of Applied Behavioral Science, 14*(2), 175-194.

Gavin, J.F., & Montgomery, J.C. (1983). Field study and replication of the survey feedback method. *Academy of Management Proceedings,* 230-234.

Golembiewski, R.T., & Billingsley, K. (1980). Measuring change in OD panel designs: A response to my critics. *Academy of Management Review, 5,* 97-103.

Golembiewski, R.T., Billingsley, K., & Yeager, S. (1976). Measuring change and persistence in human affairs: Types of change generated by OD designs. *Journal of Applied Behavioral Science, 12,* 133-157.

Griffin, R.W. (1981). A longitudinal investigation of task characteristics relationships. *Academy of Management Journal, 24*, 99-113.

Harman, H.H. (1976). *Modern factor analysis* (3rd ed.). Chicago: University of Chicago Press.

Hedge, J.W., & Kavanagh, M.J. (1988). Improving the accuracy of performance evaluations: Comparison of three methods of performance appraiser training. *Journal of Applied Psychology, 73*(1), 68-73.

Hertzog, C. (1996). Research design in studies of aging and cognition. In J.E. Birren & K.W. Schaie (Eds.), *Handbook of psychology and aging* (4th ed., pp. 24-37). San Diego, CA: Academic Press.

Hui, C., Lam, S.S.K., & Law, K.K.S. (2000). Instrumental values of organizational citizenship behavior for promotion: A field quasi-experiment. *Journal of Applied Psychology, 85*(5), 822-828.

Hulin, C. (1991). Adaptation, persistence, and commitment in organizations. In M.D. Dunnette & L.M. Hough (Eds.), *Handbook of industrial and organizational psychology* (Vol. 2, 2nd ed., pp. 445-505). Palo Alto, CA: Consulting Psychologists Press.

Ivancevich, J.M. (1979). Longitudinal study of the effects of rater training on psychometric error in ratings. *Journal of Applied Psychology, 64*(5), 502-508.

Jöreskog, K.G. (1969). A general approach to confirmatory maximum likelihood factor analyses. *Psychometrika, 34*, 183-202.

Kilmann, R.H., & Herden, R.P. (1976). Toward a systematic methodology for evaluating the impact of interventions on organizational effectiveness. *Academy of Management Review, 1*(3), 87-98.

Lance, C.E., Vandenberg, R.J., & Self, R.M. (2000). Latent growth models of individual change: The case of newcomer adjustment. *Organizational Behavior and Human Decision Processes, 83*(1), 107-140.

Lindell, M.K., & Drexler, J.A. (1979). Issues in using survey methods for measuring organizational change. *Academy of Management Review, 4*, 13-19.

Lindell, M.K., & Drexler, J.A. (1980). Equivocality of factor incongruence as an indicator of type of change in OD interventions. *Academy of Management Review, 5*, 105-107.

Louis, M.R. (1980). Surprise and sense-making: What newcomers experience in entering unfamiliar organizational settings. *Administrative Science Quarterly, 25*, 226-251.

Menard, S. (1991). *Longitudinal Research. Sage University Paper Series on Quantitative Applications in the Social Sciences, 07-75*. Newbury Park, CA: Sage.

Meyer, J.P., Bobocel, D.R., & Allen, N.J. (1991). Development of organizational commitment during the first year of employment: A longitudinal study of pre- and post-entry influences. *Journal of Management, 17*(4), 717-733.

Millsap, R.E., & Hartog, S.B. (1988). Alpha, beta, and gamma change in evaluation research: A structural equation approach. *Journal of Applied Psychology, 73*(3), 574-584.

Mowday, R.T., Porter, L.W., & Steers, R.M. (1982). *Employee-organization linkages: The psychology of commitment, absenteeism, and turnover.* New York: Academic Press.

Ogbonna, E., & Harris, L.C. (1998). Managing organizational culture: Compliance or genuine change? *British Journal of Management, 9*, 273-288.

Porras, J.I., & Berg, P.O. (1978). The impact of organization development. *Academy of Management Review, 3*(2), 249-266.

Porras, J.I., & Singh, J.V. (1986). Alpha, beta, and gamma change in modelling-based organization development. *Journal of Occupational Behavior, 7,* 9-24.

Randolph, W.A. (1982). Planned organizational change and its measurement. *Personnel Psychology, 35*(1), 117-139.

Rice, R.E., & Contractor, N.S. (1990). Conceptualizing effects of office information systems: A methodology and application for the study of alpha, beta, and gamma changes. *Decision Sciences, 21*(2), 301-317.

Sauser, W.I., & Pond, S.B. (1981). Effects of rater training and participation on cognitive complexity: An exploration of Schneier's cognitive reinterpretation. *Personnel Psychology, 34,* 563-577.

Schaubroeck, J., & Green, S.G. (1989). Confirmatory factor analytic procedures for assessing change during organizational entry. *Journal of Applied Psychology, 74*(6), 892-900.

Schein, E.H. (1968). Organizational socialization and the profession of management. *Industrial Management Review, 9,* 1-16.

Schmitt, N. (1982). The use of analysis of covariance structures to assess beta and gamma change. *Multivariate Behavioral Research, 17,* 343-358.

Schmitt, N., Pulakos, E.D., & Lieblein, A. (1984). Comparison of three techniques to assess group-level beta and change. *Applied Psychological Measurement, 8,* 249-260.

Schneider, B., Goldstein, H.W., & Smith, D.B. (1995). The ASA framework: An update. *Personnel Psychology, 48*(4), 747-773.

Spector, P.E., Chen, P.Y., & O'Connell, B.J. (2000). A longitudinal study of relations between job stressors and job strains while controlling for prior negative affectivity and strains. *Journal of Applied Psychology, 85*(2), 211-218.

Stamoulis, D.T., & Hauenstein, N.M.A. (1993). Rater training and rating accuracy: Training for dimensional accuracy versus training for ratee differentiation. *Journal of Applied Psychology, 78*(6), 994-1003.

Staw, B.M., Bell, N.E., & Clausen, J.A. (1986). The dispositional approach to job attitudes: A lifetime longitudinal test. *Administrative Science Quarterly, 31,* 56-77.

Tennis, C.N. (1989). Responses to the alpha, beta, gamma change typology. *Group and Organization Studies, 14,* 134-149.

Terborg, J.R, Howard, G.S., & Maxwell, S.E. (1980). Evaluating planned organizational change: A method for assessing alpha, beta, and gamma change. *Academy of Management Review, 5,* 109-121.

Terborg, J.R., Maxwell, S.E., & Howard, G.S. (1982). On the measurement and control of beta change: Problems with the Bedeian, Armenakis, & Gibson technique. *Academy of Management Review, 7,* 292-295.

Thompson, R.C., & Hunt, J.G. 1996. Inside the black box of alpha, beta, and gamma change: Using a cognitive-processing model to assess attitude structure. *Academy of Management Review, 21,* 655-690.

Tisak, J., & Smith, C. S. (1994a). Defending and extending difference score methods. *Journal of Management, 30,* 675-682.

Tisak, J., & Smith, C. S. (1994b). Regression analysis as an alternative to difference scores–Rejoinder. *Journal of Management, 30,* 691-694.

Tucker, L.R. (1951). *A method for synthesis of factor analysis studies* (Report No. 984). Washington, DC: Department of the Army, Personnel Research Section.

Vance, R.J., Winne, P.S., & Wright, E.S. 1983. A longitudinal examination of rater and ratee effects in performance ratings. *Personnel Psychology, 36,* 609-620.

Vandenberg, R.J., & Lance, C.E. (2000). A review and synthesis of the measurement invariance literature: Suggestions, practices, and recommendations for organizational research. *Organizational Research Methods, 2,* 4-69.

Vandenberg, R.J., & Self, R.M. (1993). Assessing newcomers' changing commitments to the organization during the first 6 months of work. *Journal of Applied Psychology, 78*(4), 557-568.

Vandenberg, R.J., Self, R.M., & Seo, J.H. (1994). A critical examination of the internalization, identification, and compliance commitment measures. *Journal of Management, 20*(1), 123-140.

Vandenberg, R.J., & Seo, J.H. (1992). Placing recruiting effectiveness in perspective: A cognitive explication of the job-choice and organizational-entry period. *Human Resource Management Review, 2,* 239-273.

Van De Vliert, E., Huismans, S.E., & Stok, J.J.L. (1985). The criterion approach to unraveling beta and alpha change. *Academy of Management Review, 10,* 269-274.

Wanous, J.P. (1992). Installing a realistic job preview: Ten tough choices. *Personnel Psychology, 42*(1), 117-134.

Weitlauf, J.C., Smith, R.E., & Cervone, D. (2000). Generalization effects of coping-skills training: Influence of self-defense training on women's efficacy beliefs, assertiveness, and aggression. *Journal of Applied Psychology, 85*(4), 625-633.

Zmud, R.W., & Armenakis, A.A. (1978). Understanding the measurement of change. *Academy of Management Review, 3,* 661-669.

APPENDIX

Adam, E.E. (1991). Quality circle performance. *Journal of Management, 17,* 25-39.

Adkins, C. (1995). Previous work experience and organizational socialization: A longitudinal examination. *Academy of Management Journal, 38,* 839-862.

Alie, R.E. (1982). Professionalization in a rationally managed corporate organization. *Journal of Management, 8,* 65-81.

Allen, N.J., & Meyer, J.P. (1990). Organizational socialization tactics: A longitudinal analysis of links to newcomers' commitment and role orientation. *Academy of Management Journal, 33,* 847-858.

Amabile, T.M., & Conti, R. (1999). Changes in the work environment for creativity during downsizing. *Academy of Management Journal, 42,* 630-640.

Ancona, D.G., & Caldwell, D.F. (1992). Building the boundary: External activity and the performance in organizational teams. *Administrative Science Quarterly, 37,* 634-665.

Anderson, C.R. (1977). Locus of control, coping behaviors, and performance in a stress setting: A longitudinal study. *Journal of Applied Psychology, 62,* 446-451.

Andrisani, P.J., & Nestel, G. (1976). Internal-external control as contributor to and outcome of work experience. *Journal of Applied Psychology, 61,* 156-165.

Andrisani, P.J., & Shapiro, M.B. (1978). Women's attitudes toward their jobs: Some longitudinal data on a national sample. *Personnel Psychology, 31,* 15-34.

Armenakis, A., & Smith, L. (1978). A practical alternative to comparison group designs in OD evaluations: The abbreviated time series design. *Academy of Management Journal, 21,* 499-507.

Armenakis, A.A., & Zmud, R.W. (1979). Interpreting the measurement of change in organizational research. *Personnel Psychology, 32*, 709-723.

Arnold, H.J. (1985). Task performance, perceived competence, and attributed causes of performance as determinants of intrinsic motivation. *Academy of Management Journal, 28*, 876-888.

Arvey, R.D., Dewhirst, H.D., & Brown, E.M. (1978). A longitudinal study of the impact of changes in goal setting on employee satisfaction. *Personnel Psychology, 31*, 595-608.

Ashforth, B.E., & Saks, A.M. (1996). Socialization tactics: Longitudinal effects on newcomer adjustment. *Academy of Management Journal, 39*, 149-178.

Atwater, L.E., Waldman, D.A., Atwater, D., & Cartier, P. (2000). An upward feedback field experiment: Supervisors' cynicism, reactions, and commitment to subordinates. *Personnel Psychology, 53*, 275-297.

Barber, A.E., Daly, C.L., Giannantonio, C.M., & Phillips, J.M. (1994). Job search activities: An examination of changes over time. *Personnel Psychology, 47*, 739-766.

Barber, A.E., Dunham, R.B., & Formisano, R.A. (1992). The impact of flexible benefits on employee satisfaction: A field study. *Personnel Psychology, 45*, 55-75.

Barling, J., Weber, T., & Kelloway, E.K. (1996). Effects of transformational leadership training on attitudinal and financial outcomes: A field experiment. *Journal of Applied Psychology, 81*, 827-832.

Bartunek, J.M., & Franzak, F.J. (1988). The effects of organizational restructuring on frames of reference and cooperation. *Journal of Management, 14*, 579-592.

Basadur, M., Graen, G.B., & Scandura, T.A. (1986). Training effects on attitudes toward divergent thinking among manufacturing engineers. *Journal of Applied Psychology, 71*, 612-617.

Bass, B.M., Cascio, W.F., McPherson, J.W., & Tragash, H.J. (1976). PROSPER: Training and research for increasing management awareness of affirmative action in race relations. *Academy of Management Journal, 19*, 353-369.

Bateman, T.S., & Organ, D.W. (1983). Job satisfaction and the good soldier: The relationship between affect and employee "citizenship." *Academy of Management Journal, 26*, 587-595.

Bateman, T.S., & Strasser, S. (1983). A cross-lagged regression test of the relationships between job tension and employee satisfaction. *Journal of Applied Psychology, 68*, 439-445.

Bauer, T.N., & Green, S.G. (1996). Development of leader-member exchange: A longitudinal test. *Academy of Management Journal, 39*, 1538-1567.

Bauer, T.N., & Green, S.G. (1994). Effect of newcomer involvement in work-related activities: A longitudinal study of socialization. *Journal of Applied Psychology, 79*, 211-223.

Bauer, T.N., Maertz, C.P., Dolen, M.R., & Campion, M.A. (1998). Longitudinal assessments of applicant reactions to employment testing and test outcome feedback. *Journal of Applied Psychology, 83*, 892-903.

Beatty, R.W., Schneier, C.E., & Beatty, J.R. (1977). An empirical investigation of perceptions of ratee behavior frequency and ratee behavior change using Behavioral Expectation Scales (BES). *Personnel Psychology, 30*, 647-658.

Bernardin, H.J. (1978). Effects of rater training on leniency and halo errors in student ratings of instructors. *Journal of Applied Psychology, 63*, 301-308.

Billings, R.S., Klimoski, R.J., & Breaugh, J.A. (1977). The impact of change in technology on job characteristics: A quasi experiment. *Administrative Science Quarterly, 22,* 318-339.

Blau, G. (1999). Early-career job factors influencing the professional commitments of medical technologists. *Academy of Management Journal, 42,* 687-695.

Brett, J.M., Feldman, D.C., & Weingart, L.R. (1990). Feedback-seeking behavior of new hires and job changers. *Journal of Management, 16,* 737-749.

Brockner, J., Tyler, T.R., & Cooper-Schneider, R. 1992. The influence of prior commitment to an institution on reactions to perceived unfairness: The higher they are, the harder they fall. *Administrative Science Quarterly, 37,* 241-261.

Brousseau, K.R., & Prince, J.B. (1981). Job-person dynamics: An extension of longitudinal research. *Journal of Applied Psychology, 66,* 59-62.

Brown, K.A., & Mitchell, T.R. (1991). A comparison of just-in-time and batch manufacturing: The role of performance obstacles. *Academy of Management Journal, 34,* 906-917.

Brown, K.A., & Huber, V.L. (1992). Lowering floors and raising ceilings: A longitudinal assessment of the effects of an earnings-at-risk plan on pay satisfaction. *Personnel Psychology, 45,* 279-311.

Buckley, M.R., Fedor, D.B., Veres, J.G., Wiese, D.S., & Carraher, S.M. (1998). Investigating newcomer expectations and job-related outcomes. *Journal of Applied Psychology, 83,* 452-461.

Burkhardt, M.E. (1994). Social interaction effects following a technological change: A longitudinal investigation. *Academy of Management Journal, 37,* 869-898.

Burkhardt, M.E., & Brass, D.J. (1990). Changing patterns or patterns of change: The effects of a change in technology on social network structure and power. *Administrative Science Quarterly, 35,* 104-127.

Callister, R.R., Kramer, M.W., Turban, D.B. Feedback seeking following career transistors. *Academy of Management Journal, 42,* 429-438.

Campion, M.A., & McClelland, C.L. (1993). Follow-up and extension of the interdisciplinary costs and benefits of enlarged jobs. *Journal of Applied Psychology, 78,* 339-351.

Caplan, R.D., Vinokur, A.D., Price, R.H., & Van Ryn, M. (1989). Job seeking, reemployment, and mental health: A randomized field experiment in coping with job loss. *Journal of Applied Psychology, 74,* 759-769.

Carlson, J.R., & Zmud, R.W. (1999). Channel expansion theory and the experiential nature of media richness perceptions. *Academy of Management Journal, 42,* 153-170.

Chacko, T.I. (1983). Job and life satisfactions: A causal analysis of their relationships. *Academy of Management Journal, 26,* 163-169.

Chan, D., & Schmitt, N. (2000). Interindividual differences in intraindividual changes in proactivity during organizational entry: A latent growth modeling approach to understanding newcomer adaptation. *Journal of Applied Psychology, 85,* 190-210.

Chan, D., Schmitt, N., Sacco, J.M., & DeShon, R.P. (1998). Understanding pretest and posttest reactions to cognitive ability and personality tests. *Journal of Applied Psychology, 83,* 471-485.

Chao, G.T., O'Leary-Kelly, A.M., Wolf, S., & Klein, H.J. (1994). Organizational socialization: Its content and consequences. *Journal of Applied Psychology, 79,* 730-743.

Chatman, J.A. (1991). Matching people and organizations: Selection and socialization in public accounting firms. *Administrative Science Quarterly, 36,* 459-484.

Chesney, A.A., & Locke, E.A. (1991). Relationships among goal difficulty, business strategies, and performance on a complex management simulation task. *Academy of Management Journal, 34,* 400-424.

Cohen, S.L., & Turney, J.R. Intervening at the bottom: Organizational development with enlisted personnel in an Army work-setting. *Personnel Psychology, 31,* 715-730.

Cordery, J.L., Mueller, W.S., & Smith, L.M. (1991). Attitudinal and behavioral effects of autonomous group working: A longitudinal field study. *Academy of Management Journal, 34,* 464-476.

Curry, J.P., Wakefield, D.S., Price, J.L., & Mueller, C.W. (1986). On the causal ordering of job satisfaction and organizational commitment. *Academy of Management Journal, 29,* 847-858.

Davidson, M., & Friedman, R.A. (1998). When excuses don't work: The persistent injustice effect among black managers. *Administrative Science Quarterly, 43,* 154-183.

Davy, J.A., & Shipper, F. (1993). Voter behavior in union certification elections: A longitudinal study. *Academy of Management Journal, 36,* 187-199.

Deadrick, D.L., & Madigan, R.M. (1990). Dynamic criteria revisited: A longitudinal study of performance stability and predictive validity. *Personnel Psychology, 43,* 717-744.

Dean, R.A., & Wanous, J.P. (1984). Effects of realistic job previews on hiring bank tellers. *Journal of Applied Psychology, 69,* 61-68.

DeNisi, A.S., Randolph, W.A., & Blencoe, A.G. (1983). Potential problems with peer ratings. *Academy of Management Journal, 26,* 457-464.

Dorfman, P.W., & Stephan, W.G. (1984). The effects of group performance on cognitions, satisfaction, and behavior: A process model. *Journal of Management, 10,* 173-192.

Dormann, C., & Zapf, D. (1999). Social support, social stressors at work, and depressive symptoms: Testing for main and moderating effects with structural equations in a three-wave longitudinal study. *Journal of Applied Psychology, 84,* 874-884.

Druskat, V.U., & Wolff, S.B. (1999). Effects and timing of developmental peer appraisals in self-managing work groups. *Journal of Applied Psychology, 84,* 58-74.

Duchon, D., Green, S.G., & Taber, T.D. (1986). Vertical dyad linkage: A longitudinal assessment of antecedents, measures, and consequences. *Journal of Applied Psychology, 71,* 56-60.

Dunham, R.B., Pierce, J.L., & Castaneda, M.B. (1987). Alternative work schedules: Two field quasi-experiments. *Personnel Psychology, 40,* 215-242.

Dwyer, D.J., & Fox, M.L. (2000). The moderating role of hostility in the relationship between enriched jobs and health. *Academy of Management Journal, 43,* 1086-1096.

Earley, P.C. (1994). Self or group? Cultural effects of training on self-efficacy and performance. *Administrative Science Quarterly, 39,* 89-117.

Early, P.C., & Mosakowski, E. (2000). Creating hybrid team cultures: An empirical test of transnational team functioning. *Academy of Management Journal, 43*, 26-49.

Eden, D., & Aviram, A. (1993). Self-efficacy training to speed reemployement: Helping people to help themselves. *Journal of Applied Psychology, 78*, 352-360.

Eden, D. (1985). Team development: A true field experiment at three levels of rigor. *Journal of Applied Psychology, 70*, 94-100.

Erez, M., Earley, P.C., & Hulin, C.L. (1985). The impact of participation on goal acceptance and performance: A two-step model. *Academy of Management Journal, 28*, 50-66.

Farkas, A.J., & Tetrick, L.E. (1989). A three-wave longitudinal analysis of the causal ordering of satisfaction and commitment on turnover decisions. *Journal of Applied Psychology, 74*, 855-868.

Fields, M.W., & Thacker, J.W. (1992). Influence of quality of work life on company and union commitment. *Academy of Management Journal, 35*, 439-450.

Fisher, C.D. (1985). Social support and adjustment to work: A longitudinal study. *Journal of Management, 11*, 39-53.

Ford, J.K., Smith, E.M., Sego, D.J., & Quinones, M.A. (1993). Impact of task experience on training-emphasis ratings. *Journal of Applied Psychology, 78*, 583-590.

Frayne, C.A., & Geringer, J.M. (2000). Self-management training for improving job performance: A field experiment involving salespeople. *Journal of Applied Psychology, 85*, 361-372.

Friedman, B.A., & Cornelius, E. T. (1976). Effect of rater participation in scale construction on the psychometric characteristics of two rating scale formats. *Journal of Applied Psychology, 61*, 210-216.

Friedman, R.A., & Podolny, J. (1990). Differentiation of boundary spanning roles: Labor negotiations and implications for role conflict. *Administrative Science Quarterly, 37*, 28-47.

Fullagar, C., & Barling, J. (1989). A longitudinal test of a model of the antecedents and consequences of union loyalty. *Journal of Applied Psychology, 74*, 213-227.

Futrell, C.M. (1978). Effects of pay disclosure on satisfaction for sale managers: A longitudinal study. *Academy of Management Journal, 21*, 140-144.

Ganster, D.C., Mayes, B.T., Sime, W.E., & Tharp, G.D. (1982). Managing organizational stress: A field experiment. *Journal of Applied Psychology, 67*, 533-542.

Garst, H. Frese, M., Molenaar, P.C.M. (2000). The temporal factor of change in stressor-strain relationships: A growth curve model on a longitudinal study in East Germany. *Journal of Applied Psychology, 85*, 417-438.

Gerhart, B. (1987). How important are dispositional factors as determinants of job satisfaction? Implications for job design and other personnel programs. *Journal of Applied Psychology, 72*, 366-373.

Gist, M.E., Stevens, C.K., & Bavetta, A.G. (1991). Effects and self-efficacy and post-training intervention on the acquisition and maintenance of complex interpersonal skills. *Personnel Psychology, 44*, 837-861.

Glomb, T.M., Munson, L.J., Hulin, C.L., Bergman, M.E., & Drasgow, F. (1999). Structural equations models of sexual harassment: Longitudinal explorations and cross-sectional generalizations. *Journal of Applied Psychology, 84*, 14-28.

Goktepe, J.R., & Schneier, C.E. (1989). Role of sex, gender roles, and attraction in predicting emergent leaders. *Journal of Applied Psychology, 74*, 165-167.

Goodman, J.S., & Blum, T.C. (1996). Assessing the non-random sampling effects of subject attrition in longitudinal research. *Journal of Management, 22,* 627-652.

Graen, G., & Schiemann, W. (1978). Leader-member agreement: A vertical dyad linkage approach. *Journal of Applied Psychology, 63,* 206-212.

Graen, L., Cashman, J.F., Ginsbury, S., & Scheimann, W. (1977). Effects of linking-pin quality on the quality of working life of low participants. *Administrative Science Quarterly, 22,* 491-504.

Green, S.G., & Bauer, T.N. (1995). Supervisory mentoring by advisers: Relationships with doctoral student potential, productivity, and commitment. *Personnel Psychology, 48,* 537-561.

Greenberg, J. (1990). Employee theft as a reaction to underpayment inequity: The hidden cost of pay cuts. *Journal of Applied Psychology, 75,* 561-568.

Greene, C.N., & Podsakoff, P.M. (1981). Effects of withdrawal of a performance-contingent reward on supervisory influence and power. *Academy of Management Journal, 24,* 527-542.

Greene, C.N., & Schriesheim, C.A. (1980). Leader-group interactions: A longitudinal field investigation. *Journal of Applied Psychology, 65,* 50-59.

Greenhalgh, L., Neslin, S.A., & Gilkey, R.W. (1985). The effects of negotiator preferences, situational power, and negotiator personality on outcomes of business negotiations. *Academy of Management Journal, 28,* 9-33.

Greensberg, J., Scott, K.S., & Welchans, T.D. (2000). The winding road from employee to complainant: Situational and psychological determinants of wrongful-termination claims. *Administrative Science Quarterly, 45,* 557-590.

Griffin, R.W. (1980). Relationships among individual task design, and leader behavior variables. *Academy of Management Journal, 23,* 665-683.

Griffin, R.W. (1981). A longitudinal investigation of task characteristics relationships. *Academy of Management Journal, 24,* 99-113.

Griffin, R.W. (1982). Objective and social sources of information in task redesign: A field experiment. *Administrative Science Quarterly, 28,* 184-200.

Griffin, R.W. (1988). Consequences of quality circles in an industrial setting: A longitudinal assessment. *Academy of Management Journal, 31,* 338-358.

Griffin, R.W. (1991). Effects of work redesign on employee perceptions, attitudes, and behaviors: A long-term investigation. *Academy of Management Journal, 34,* 425-435.

Griffin, R.W., Bateman, T.S., Wayne, S.J., & Head, T.C. (1987). Objective and social factors as determinants of task perceptions and responses: An integrated perspective and empirical investigation. *Academy of Management Journal, 30,* 501-523.

Hackett, R.D., Bycio, P., & Guion, R.M. (1989). Absenteeism among hospital nurses: An idiographic-longitudinal analysis. *Academy of Management Journal, 32,* 424-453.

Hall, D.T., & Foster, L.W. 1977. A psychological cycle and goal setting: Goals, performance, and attitudes. *Academy of Management Journal, 20,* 282-290.

Hall, D.T., Goodale, J.G., Rabinowitz, S., & Morgan, M.A. (1978). Effects of top-down departmental and job change upon perceived employee behavior and attitudes: A natural field experiment. *Journal of Applied Psychology, 63,* 62-72.

Hart, P.M. (1999). Predicting employee life satisfaction: A coherent model of personality, work, and nonwork experiences, and domain satisfactions. *Journal of Applied Psychology, 84,* 564-584.

Hazer, J.T., & Alvares, K.M. (1981). Police work values during organizational entry and assimilation. *Journal of Applied Psychology, 66*, 12-18.

Hedge, J.W., & Kavanagh, M.J. (1988). Improving the accuracy of performance evaluations: Comparison of three methods of performance appraiser training. *Journal of Applied Psychology, 73*, 68-73.

Helmrich, R.L., Swain, L.L., & Carsrud, A.L. (1986). The honeymoon effect in job performance: Temporal increases in the predictive power of achievement motivation. *Journal of Applied Psychology, 71*, 185-188.

Herold, D. (1977). Two-way influence processes in leader-follower dyads. *Academy of Management Journal, 20*, 224-237.

Hom, P.W., & Griffeth, R.W. (1991). Structural equations modeling test of a turn-over theory: Cross-sectional and longitudinal analyses. *Journal of Applied Psychology, 76*, 350-366.

Hom, P.W., DeNisi, A.S., Kinicki, A.J., & Bannister, B.D. (1982). Effectiveness of performance feedback from behaviorally anchored rating scales. *Journal of Applied Psychology, 67*, 568-576.

Howard, G.S., & Dailey, P.R. (1979). Response-shift bias: A source of contamination of self-report measures. *Journal of Applied Psychology, 64*, 144-150.

Hui, C., Lam, S.S.K., & Law, K.K.S. (2000). Instrumental values of organizational citizenship behavior for promotion: A field quasi-experiment. *Journal of Applied Psychology, 85*, 822-828.

Hynes, K., Feldhusen, J.F., & Richardson, W.B. (1978). Application of a three-stage model of instruction to youth leadership training. *Journal of Applied Psychology, 63*, 623-628.

Irving, P.G., & Meyer, J.P. (1994). Reexamination of the met-expectations hypothesis: A longitudinal analysis. *Journal of Applied Psychology, 79*, 937-949.

Ivancevich, J.M. (1977). Different goal setting treatments and their effects on performance and job satisfaction. *Academy of Management Journal, 20*, 406-419.

Ivancevich, J.M. (1979). High and low task stimulation jobs: A causal analysis of performance-satisfaction relationships. *Academy of Management Journal, 22*, 206-222.

Ivancevich, J.M., & McMahon, J.T. (1982). The effects of goal setting, external feedback, and self-generated feedback on outcome variables: A field experiment. *Academy of Management Journal, 25*, 359-372.

Ivancevich, J.M., & Lyon, H.L. (1977). The shortened work week: A field experiment. *Journal of Applied Psychology, 62*, 34-37.

Ivancevich, J.M. (1976). Effects of goal setting on performance and job satisfaction. *Journal of Applied Psychology, 64*, 502-508.

Ivancevich, J.M. (1979). Longitudinal study of the effects of rater training on psychometric error in ratings. *Journal of Applied Psychology, 64*, 502-508.

Ivancevich, J.M. (1980). A longitudinal study of behavioral expectation scales: Attitudes and performance. *Journal of Applied Psychology, 65*, 139-146.

Ivancevich, J.M. (1982). Subordinates' reactions to performance appraisal interviews: A test of feedback and goal-setting techniques. *Journal of Applied Psychology, 67*, 581-587.

Jackson, P.R., Staffors, E.M., Banks, M.H., & Warr, P.B. (1983). Unemployment and psychological distress in young people: The moderating role of employment commitment. *Journal of Applied Psychology, 68*, 525-535.

Jackson, S.E. (1983). Participation in decision making as a strategy for reducing job-related strain. *Journal of Applied Psychology, 68,* 3-19.

Jacobs, R., & Kozlowski, S.W. (1985). A closer look at halo error in performance ratings. *Academy of Management Journal, 28,* 201-212.

Johnson, J.W., & Ferstl, K.L. (1999). The effects of interrater and self-other agreement on performance improvement following upward feedback. *Personnel Psychology, 52,* 271-303.

Johnson, S.M., Smith, P.C., & Tucker, S.M. (1982). Response format of the Job Descriptive Index: Assessment of reliability and validity by the multitrait-multimethod matrix. *Journal of Applied Psychology, 67,* 500-505.

Johnston, M.W., Griffeth, R.W., Burton, S., & Carson, P.P. (1993). An exploratory investigation into the relationship between promotion and turnover: A quasi-experimental longitudinal study. *Journal of Management, 19,* 33-49.

Jordan, P.C. (1986). Effects of extrinsic reward on intrinsic motivation: A field experiment. *Academy of Management Journal, 29,* 405-412.

Joyce, W.F. (1986). Matrix organization: A social experiment. *Academy of Management Journal, 29,* 536-561.

Judge, T.A., & Watanabe, S. (1993). Another look at the job satisfaction-life satidfaction relationship. *Journal of Applied Psychology, 78,* 939-948.

Judge, T.A., & Welbourne, T.M. (1994). A confirmatory investigation of the dimensionality of the Pay Satisfaction Questionnaire. *Journal of Applied Psychology, 79,* 461-466.

Kane, J.S., Bernardin, H.J., Villanova, P., & Peryrefitte, J. (1995). Stability of rater leniency: Three studies. *Academy of Management Journal, 38,* 1036-1051.

Keller, R.T. (1986). Predictors of the performance of project groups in R & D organizations. *Academy of Management Journal, 29,* 715-726.

Keller, R.T. (1994). Technology-information processing fit and the performance of R&D project groups: A test of contingency theory.

Keller, R.T., & Szilagyi, A.D. (1978). A longitudinal study of leader reward behavior, subordinate expectations, and satisfaction. *Personnel Psychology, 31,* 119-129.

Kim, J.S. (1984). Effect of behavior plus outcome goal setting and feedback on employee satisfaction and performance. *Academy of Management Journal, 27,* 139-149.

Kim, J.S., & Hamner, W.C. (1976). Effects of performance feedback and goal setting on productivity and satisfaction in an organizational setting. *Journal of Applied Psychology, 61,* 48-57.

Kinicki, A.J., Prussia, G.E., McKee-Ryan, F.M. (2000). A panel study of coping with involuntary job loss. *Academy of Management Journal, 43,* 90-100.

Klandermans, B. (1986). Perceived costs and benefits of participation in union action. *Personnel Psychology, 39,* 379-397.

Klein, H.J., & Weaver, N.A. (2000). The effectiveness of an organizational-level orientation training program in the socialization of new hires. *Personnel Psychology, 53,* 47-66.

Knapp, R.J., Capel, W.C., & Youngblood, D.A. (1976). Stress in the deep: A study of undersea divers in controlled dangerous situations. *Journal of Applied Psychology, 61,* 507-512.

Kopelman, R.E. (1976). Organizational control system responsiveness, expectancy theory constructs, and work motivation: Some interrelations and causal connections. *Personnel Psychology, 29,* 205-220.

Kopelman, R.W., & Thompson, P.H. (1976). Boundary conditions for expectancy theory predictions of work motivation and job performance. *Academy of Management Journal, 19,* 237-258.

Korsgaard, M.A., Schweiger, D.M., & Sapienza, H.J. (1995). Building commitment, attachment, and trust in strategic decision-making teams: The role of procedural justice. *Academy of Management Journal, 38,* 60-84.

Kossek, E.E., Roberts, K., Fisher, S., & DeMarr, B. (1998). Career self-management: A quasi-experimental assessment of the effects of a training intervention. *Personnel Psychology, 51,* 935-962.

Krackhardt, D., & Porter, L.W. (1985). When friends leave: A structural analysis of the relationship between turnover and stayers' attitudes. *Administrative Science Quarterly, 30,* 242-261.

Lachman, R. (1989). Power from what? A reexamination of its relationships with structural conditions. *Administrative Science Quarterly, 34,* 231-251.

Lam, S.S.K., & Schaubroek, J. (2000). The role of locus of control in reactions to being promoted and to being passed over: A quasi experiment. *Academy of Management Journal, 43,* 66-78.

Latham, G.P., & Yukl, G.A. (1976). Effects of assigned and participative goal setting on performance and job satisfaction. *Journal of Applied Psychology, 61,* 166-171.

Lee, T.W., Ashford, S.J., Walsh, J.P., & Mowday, R.T. (1992). Commitment propensity, organizational commitment, and voluntary turnover: A longitudinal study of organizational entry processes. *Journal of Management, 18,* 15-32.

Leister, A., Borden, D., & Fiedler, F.E. (1977). Validation of contingency model leadership training: Leader match. *Academy of Management Journal, 20,* 464-470.

Liden, R.C., & Graen, G. (1980). Generalizability of the vertical dyad linkage model of leadership. *Academy of Management Journal, 23,* 451-465.

Liden, R.C., Wayne, S.J., & Stilwell, D. (1993). A longitudinal study on the early development of leader-member exchanges. *Journal of Applied Psychology, 78,* 662-674.

Long, R.J. (1979). Desires for an patterns of worker participation in decision making after conversion to employee ownership. *Academy of Management Journal, 22,* 611-617.

Lounsbury, J.W., & Hoopes, L. (1986). A vacation from work: Changes in work and nonwork outcomes. *Journal of Applied Psychology, 71,* 392-401.

Lubinski, D., Benbow, C.P., & Ryan, J. (1995). Stability of vocational interests among the intellectually gifted from adolescence to adulthood: A 15-year longitudinal study. *Journal of Applied Psychology, 80,* 196-200.

Magneau, J.M., Martin, J.E., & Peterson, M.M. (1988). Dual and unilateral commitment among stewards and rank-and-file union members. *Academy of Management Journal, 31,* 359-376.

Major, D.A., Kozlowski, S.W.J., Chao, G.T., & Gardner, P.D. (1995). A longitudinal investigation of newcomer expectations, early socialization outcomes, and the moderating effects of role development factors. *Journal of Applied Psychology, 80,* 418-431.

Manning, M.R. (1989). Work-related consequences of smoking cessation. *Academy of Management Journal, 32,* 606-621.

Mansour-Cole, D.M., & Scott, S.G. (1998). Hearing it through the grapevine: The influence of source, leader-relations, and legitimacy on survivors' fairness perceptions. *Personnel Psychology, 51,* 25-54.

Marks, M.L., Mirvis, P.H., Hackett, E.J., & Grady, J.F. (1986). Employee participation in a Quality Circle program: Impact on quality of work life, productivity, and absenteeism. *Journal of Applied Psychology, 71,* 61-69.

Martin, R., & Wall, T.D. (1989). Attentional demand and cost responsibility as stressors in shopfloor jobs. *Academy of Management Journal, 32,* 69-86.

Martocchio, J.J. (1994). Effects of conceptions of ability on anxiety, self-efficacy, and learning in training. *Journal of Applied Psychology, 79,* 819-825.

Mathieu, J.E., Tannenbaum, S.I., & Salas, E. (1992). Influences of individual and situational characteristics on measures of training effectiveness. *Academy of Management Journal, 35,* 828-847.

Mathieu, J.E., Martineau, J.W., & Tannenbaum, S.I. (1993). Individual and situational influences on the development of self-efficacy: Implications for training effectiveness. *Personnel Psychology, 46,* 125-147.

Mayer, R.C., & Davis, J.H. (1999). The effect of the performance appraisal system on trust for management: A field quasi-experiment. *Journal of Applied Psychology, 84,* 123-136.

McCarty, P.A. (1986). Effects of feedback on the self-confidence of men and women. *Academy of Management Journal, 29,* 840-847.

McCauley, C.D., Lombardo, M.M., & Usher, C.J. (1989). Diagnosing management development needs: An instrument based on how managers develop. *Journal of Management, 15,* 389-403.

Meglino, B.M., DeNisi, A.S., & Ravlin, E.C. (1993). Effects of previous job exposure and subsequent job status on the functioning of a realistic job preview. *Personnel Psychology, 46,* 803-822.

Meglino, B.M., DeNisi, A.S., Youngblood, S.A., & Williams, K.J. (1988). Effects of realistic job previews: A comparison using an enhancement and a reduction preview. *Journal of Applied Psychology, 73,* 259-266.

Meyer, J.P., Allen, N.J., & Gellatly, I.R. (1990). Affective and continuance commitment to the organization: Evaluation of measures and analysis of concurrent and time-lagged relations. *Journal of Applied Psychology, 75,* 710-720.

Meyer, J.P., Bobocel, D.R., & Allen, N.J. (1991). Development of organizational commitment during the first year of employment: A longitudinal study of pre- and post-entry influences. *Journal of Management, 17,* 717-733.

Miner, A.S. (1997). Idiosyncratic jobs in formalized organizations. *Administrative Science Quarterly, 32,* 327-351.

Morrison, E.W. (1993). Newcomer information seeking: Exploring types, modes, sources, and outcomes. *Academy of Management Journal, 36,* 557-589.

Mudd, S., & Pohlman, A. (1976). Sensitivity of image profile and image clarity measures to change: Nixon through Watergate. *Journal of Applied Psychology, 61,* 223-228.

Munson, L.J., Hulin, C., & Drasgow, F. (2000). Longitudinal analysis of dispositional influences and sexual harassment: Effects on job and psychological outcomes. *Personnel Psychology, 53,* 21-46.

Murphy, K.R., & Anhalt, R.L. (1992). Is halo error a property of the rater, ratees, or the specific behaviors observed? *Journal of Applied Psychology, 77,* 494-500.

Nathan, B.R., Mohrman, A.M., Jr., Milliman, J. (1990). Interpersonal relations as a context for the effects of appraisal interview on performance and satisfaction: A longitudinal study. *Academy of Management Journal, 34,* 352-369.

Nelson, D.L., & Sutton, C. (1990). Chronic work stress and coping: A longitudinal study and suggested new directions. *Academy of Management Journal, 33,* 859-869.

Noe, R.A., & Schmitt, N. (1986). The influence of trainee attitudes on training effectiveness: Test of a model. *Personnel Psychology, 39,* 497-523.

Nordholm, L.A., & Westbrook, M.T. (1982). Job attributes preferred by female health professionals, before and after entering the workplace. *Personnel Psychology, 35,* 853-863.

Norton, S.P., Gustafson, D.P., & Foster, C.E. (1977). Assessment for management potential: Scale design and development, Training Effects and Rater/Ratee Sex Effects. *Academy of Management Journal, 20,* 117-131.

O'Brien, G.E., & Plooij, D. (1977). Comparison of programmed and prose culture training upon attitudes and knowledge. *Journal of Applied Psychology, 62,* 499-505.

O'Reilly, C.A., III. (1980). Individuals and information overload in organizations: Is more necessarily better?

Oldahm, G.R. (1988). Effects of changes in workspace partitions and spatial density on employee reactions: A quasi-experiment. *Journal of Applied Psychology, 73,* 253-258.

Oldham, G.R., & Brass, D.J. (1979). Employee reactions to an open-plan office: A naturally occurring quasi-experiment. *Administrative Science Quarterly, 24,* 267-284.

Oldham, G.R., Cummings, A., Mischel, L.J., & Schmidtke, J.M. (1995). Listen while you work? Quasi-experimental relations between personal-stereo headset use and employee work responses. *Journal of Applied Psychology, 80,* 547-564.

Orpen, C. (1978). Work and nonwork satisfaction: A causal-correlational analysis. *Journal of Applied Psychology, 63,* 530-532.

Orpen, C. (1981). Effect of flexible working hours on employee satisfaction and performance: A field experiment. *Journal of Applied Psychology, 66,* 113-115.

Ostroff, C., & Kozlowski, S.W. (1992). Organizational socialization as a learning process: The role of information acquisition. *Personnel Psychology, 45,* 849-874.

Parker, S.K., Wall, T.D., & Jackson, P.R. (1997). "That's not my job": Developing flexible employee work orientations. *Academy of Management Journal, 40,* 899-929.

Pearce, J.L., & Porter, L.W. (1986). Employee responses to formal performance appraisal feedback. *Journal of Applied Psychology, 71,* 211-218.

Pierce, J.L., & Dunham, R.B. (1987). Organizational commitment: Pre-employment propensity and initial work experience. *Journal of Management, 13,* 163-178.

Pierce, J.L., & Dunham, R.B. (1992). The 12-hour work day: A 48-hour, eight-day week. *Academy of Management Journal, 35,* 1086-1098.

Ployhart, R.E., & Ryan, A.M. (1998). Applicants' reactions to the fairness of selection procedures: The effects of positive rule violations and time of measurement. *Journal of Applied Psychology, 83,* 3-16.

Powell, G.N. (1991). Applicant reactions to the initial employment interview: Exploring theoretical and methodological issues. *Personnel Psychology, 44,* 67-83.

Pulakos, E.D., & Schmitt, N. (1983). A longitudinal study of a valence model approach for the prediction of job satisfaction of new employees. *Journal of Applied Psychology, 68,* 307-312.

Quick, J.C. (1979). Dyadic goal setting and role stress: A field study. *Academy of Management Journal, 22,* 241-252.

Rabinowitz, S., Hall, D.T., & Goodale, J.G. (1977). Job scope and individual differences as predictors of job involvement: Independent or interactive? *Academy of Management Journal, 20,* 273-281.

Randolph, W.A., & Elloy, D.F. (1989). How can OD consultants and researchers assess gamma change? A comparison of two analytical procedures. *Journal of Management, 15,* 633-648.

Randolph, W.A. (1982). Planned organizational change and its measurement. *Personnel Psychology, 35,* 117-139.

Rauchenberger, J., Schmitt, N., & Hunter, J.E. (1980). A Test of the need hierarchy concept by a Markov model of change in need strength. *Administrative Science Quarterly, 25,* 654-670.

Reilly, R.R., Smither, J.W., & Vasilopoulos, N.L. (1996). A longitudinal study of upward feedback. *Personnel Psychology, 49,* 599-612.

Rentsch, J.R., & Steel, R.P. (1998). Testing the durability of job characteristics as predictors of absenteeism over a six-year period. *Personnel Psychology, 51,* 165-190.

Robinson, S.L. (1996). Trust and breach of the psychological contract. *Administrative Science Quarterly, 41,* 574-599.

Robinson, S.L., Kraatz, M.S., & Rousseau, D.M. (1994). Changing obligations and the psychological contract: A longitudinal study. *Academy of Management Journal, 37,* 137-152.

Romzek, B.S. (1989). Personal consequences of employee commitment. *Academy of Management Journal, 32,* 649-661.

Roos, L.L., Jr. (1978). Institutional changes, career mobility, and job satisfaction. *Administrative Science Quarterly, 23,* 318-330.

Rose, R.L. (1984). Assessing the sustained effects of a stress management intervention on anxiety and locus of control. *Academy of Management Journal, 27,* 190-198.

Rosen, N., Billings, R., & Tierney, J. (1976). The emergence and allocation of leadership resources. *Academy of Management Journal, 19,* 165-183.

Rusbult, C.E., & Farrell, D. (1983). A longitudinal test of the investment model: The impact on job satisfaction, job commitment, and turnover of variations in rewards, costs, alternatives, and investments. *Journal of Applied Psychology, 68,* 429-438.

Russell, J.S., Wexley, K.N., & Hunter, J.E. (1984). Questioning the effectiveness of behavior modeling training in an industrial setting. *Personnel Psychology, 37,* 465-481.

Ryan, A.M., Schmit, M.J., & Johnson, R. (1996). Attitudes and effectiveness: Examining relations at an organizational level. *Personnel Psychology, 49,* 853-882.

Saks, A.M., & Ashforth, B.E. (1997). A longitudinal investigation of the relationships between job ninformation sources, applicant perceptions of fit, and work outcomes. *Personnel Psychology, 50,* 395-426.

Saks, A.M. (1995). Longitudinal field investigation of the moderating and mediating effects of self-efficacy on the relationship between training and newcomer adjustment. *Journal of Applied Psychology, 80,* 211-225.

Samoulis, D.T., & Hauenstein, N.M. (1993). Rater training and rating accuracy: Training for dimensional accuracy versus training for ratee differentiation. *Journal of Applied Psychology, 78*, 994-1003.

Sanchez, R.J., Truxillo, D.M., & Bauer, T.N. (2000). Development and examination of an expectancy-based measure of test-taking motivation. *Journal of Applied Psychology, 85*, 739-750.

Sauser, W.I., & Pond, S.B. Effects of rater training and participation on cognitive complexity: An exploration of Schneier's cognitive reinterpretation. *Personnel Psychology, 34*, 563-577.

Scarpello, V., & Vandenberg, R.J. (1987). The Satisfaction With My Supervisor Scale: Its utility for research and practical applications. *Journal of Management, 13*, 447-466.

Schaubroeck, J., & Green, S.G. (1989). Confirmatory factor analytic procedures for assessing change during organizational entry. *Journal of Applied Psychology, 74*, 892-900.

Schaubroeck, J., Ganster, D.C., Sime, W.E., & Ditman, D. (1993). A field experiment testing supervisory role clarification. *Personnel Psychology, 46*, 1-25.

Schneider, B., Ashworth, S.D., Higgs, A.C., & Carr, L. (1996). Design, validity, and use of strategically focused employee attitude surveys. *Personnel Psychology, 49*, 695-705.

Schriesheim, C.A., Hinkin, T.R., & Podsakoff, P.M. (1991). Can ipsative and single-item measures produce erroneous results in field studies of French and Raven's (1959) five bases of power? An empirical investigation. *Journal of Applied Psychology, 76*, 106-114.

Sherrid, S.D., & Beech, R.P. (1976). Self-dissatisfaction as a determinant of change in police values. *Journal of Applied Psychology, 61*, 273-278.

Smither, J.W., London, M., Vasilopoulos, N.L., & Reilly, R.R. (1995). An examination of the effects of an upward feedback program over time. *Personnel Psychology, 48*, 1-34.

Sorcher, M., & Spence, R. (1982). The InterFace Project: Behavior modeling as social technology in South Africa. *Personnel Psychology, 35*, 557-581.

Spector, P.E., Chen, P.Y., & O'Connell, B.J. (2000). A longitudinal study of relations between job stressors and job strains while controlling for prior negative affectivity and strains. *Journal of Applied Psychology, 85*, 211-218.

Sprangers, M., & Hoogstraten, J. (1989). Pretesting effects in retrospective pretest-posttest designs. *Journal of Applied Psychology, 74*, 265-272.

Spreitzer, G.M. (1995). Psychological empowerment in the workplace: Dimensions, measurement, and validation. *Academy of Management Journal, 38*, 1442-1465.

Stamoulis, D.T., & Hauenstein, N.M. (1993). Rater training and rating accuracy: Training for dimensional accuracy versus training for ratee differentiation. *Journal of Applied Psychology, 786*, 994-1003.

Staw, B. M., Bell, N.E., & Clausen, J.A. (1986). The dispositional approach to job attitudes: A lifetime longitudinal test. *Administrative Science Quarterly, 31*, 56-77.

Staw, B.M., & Ross, J. (1985). Stability in the midst of change: A dispositional approach to job attitudes. *Journal of Applied Psychology, 70*, 469-480.

Steel, R.P., & Rentsch, J.R. (1997). The dispositional model of job attitudes revisited: Findings of a 10-year study. *Journal of Applied Psychology, 82*, 873-879.

Steel, R.P. (1985). Factors influencing the success and failure of two quality circle programs. *Journal of Management, 11*, 99-119.

Stevens, C.K. (1997). Effects of preinterview beliefs on applicants' reactions to campus interviews. *Academy of Management Journal, 40,* 947-966.

Stevens, C.K., & Gist, M.E. (1997). Effects of self-efficacy and goal-orientation training on negotiation skill maintenance: What are the mechanisms? *Personnel Psychology, 50,* 955-978.

Szilagyi, A.D. (1977). An empirical test of causal inference between role perceptions, satisfaction with work, performance and organizational level. *Personnel Psychology, 30,* 375-388.

Tannenbaum, S.I., Mathieu, J.E., Salas, E., & Cannon-Bowers, J.A. (1991). Meeting trainees' expectations: The influence of training fulfillment on the development of commitment, self-efficacy, and motivation. *Journal of Applied Psychology, 76,* 759-769.

Taylor, M.S., Masterson, S.S., Renard, M.K., & Tracy, K.B. (1998). Managers' reactions to procedurally just performance management systems. *Academy of Management Journal, 41,* 568-579.

Taylor, M.S., Tracy, K.B., Renard, M.K., Harrison, J.K., Carroll, S.J. (1995). Due process in performance appraisal: A quasi-experiment in procedural justice. *Administrative Science Quarterly, 40,* 495-523.

Taylor, M.S., & Bergmann, T.J. (1987). Organizational recruitment activities and applicants' reactions at different stages of the recruitment process. *Personnel Psychology, 40,* 261-285.

Tetrick, L.E., Thacker, J.W., Fields, M.W. (1989). Evidence for the stability of the four dimensions of the Commitment to the Union Scale. *Journal of Applied Psychology, 74,* 819-822.

Thacker, J.W., & Fields, M.W. Union involvement in quality-of-worklife efforts: A longitudinal investigation. *Personnel Psychology, 40,* 97-111.

Tharenou, P., & Harker, P. (1984). Moderating influence of self-esteem on relationships between job complexity, performance, and satisfaction. *Journal of Applied Psychology, 69,* 623-632.

Toffler, B.L. (1981). Occupational role development: The changing determinants of outcomes for the individual. *Administrative Science Quarterly, 26,* 396-418.

Tosi, H., Hunter, J., Chesser, R., Tarter, I.R., & Carroll, S. (1976). How real are changed induced by management by objectives. *Administrative Science Quarterly, 21,* 276-306.

Tsui, A.S., & Gutek, B.A. (1984). A role set analysis of gender differences in performance, affective relationships, and career success of managers. *Academy of Management Journal, 27,* 619-635.

Umstot, D.D., Bell, C.H., & Mitchell, T.R. (1976). Effects of job enrichment and task goals on satisfaction and productivity: Implications for job design. *Journal of Applied Psychology, 61,* 379-394.

Van Dierendonck, D., Schaufeli, W.B., & Buunk, B.P. (1998). The evaluation of an individual burnout intervention program: The role of inequity and social support. *Journal of Applied Psychology, 83,* 392-407.

Van Dyne, L., & Le Pine, J. (1998). Helping and voice in extra-role behaviors: Evidence of construct and predictive validity. *Academy of Management Journal, 41,* 108-119.

Van Maanen, J., & Katz, R. (1976). Individuals and their careers: Some temporal considerations for work satisfaction. *Personnel Psychology, 29,* 601-616.

Vance, R.J., Winne, P.S., & Wright, E.S. (1983). A longitudinal examination of rater and ratee effects in performance ratings. *Personnel Psychology, 36,* 609-620.

Vancouver, J.B. (1997). The application of HLM to the analysis of the dynamic interaction of environment, person, and behavior. *Journal of Management, 23,* 795-818.

Vandenberg, R.J., & Lance, C.E. (1992). Examining the causal order of job satisfaction and organizational commitment. *Journal of Management, 18,* 153-167.

Vandenberg, R.J., & Self, R.M. (1993). Assessing newcomers' changing commitments to the organization during the first 6 months of work. *Journal of Applied Psychology, 78,* 557-568.

Vandenberg, R.J., Self, R.M., & Seo, J.H. (1994). A critical examination of the internalization, identification, and compliance commitment measures. *Journal of Management, 20,* 123-140.

Vanderplas, J.M. (1976). Boolean analysis of awareness training. *Journal of Applied Psychology, 61,* 658-662.

Wagemen, R. (1995). Interdependence and group effectiveness. *Administrative Science Quarterly, 40,* 145-180.

Walker, A.G., & Smither, J.W. (1999). A five-year study of upward feedback: What managers do with their results matter. *Personnel Psychology, 52,* 393-423.

Wall, T.D., Kemp, N.J., Jackson, P.R., & Clegg, C.W. (1986). Outcomes of autonomous workgroups a long-term field experiment. *Academy of Management Journal, 29,* 280-304.

Watson, W.E., Kumar, K., & Michaelsen, L.K. (1993). Cultural diversity's impact on interaction process and performance: Comparing homogenous and diverse task groups. *Academy of Management Journal, 36,* 590-602.

Weitlauf, J.C., Smith, R.E., & Cervone, D. (2000). Generalization effects of coping-skills training: Influence of self-defense training on women's efficacy beliefs, assertiveness, and aggression. *Journal of Applied Psychology, 854,* 625-633.

Wexley, K.N., & Baldwin, T.T. (1986). Posttraining strategies for facilitating positive transfer: An empirical examination. *Academy of Management Journal, 29,* 503-520.

Williams, K., & Alliger, G.M. (1994). Role stressors, mood spillover, and perceptions of work-family conflict in employed parents. *Academy of Management Journal, 37,* 837-868.

Winefield, A.H., & Tiggemann, M. (1990). Employment status and psychological well-being: A longitudinal study. *Journal of Applied Psychology, 75,* 455-459.

Winefield, A.H., Winefield, H.R., Tiggemann, M., & Goldney, R.D. (1991). A longitudinal study of the psychological effects of unemployment and unsatisfactory employment on young adults. *Journal of Applied Psychology, 76,* 424-431.

Youngblood, S.A., Mobley, W.H., & Meglino, B.M. (1983). A longitudinal analysis of the turnover process. *Journal of Applied Psychology, 68,* 507-516.

Zalesny, M.D., & Farace, R.V. (1987). Traditional versus open offices: A comparison of sociotechnical, social relations, and symbolic meaning perspectives. *Academy of Management Journal, 30,* 240-259.

CHAPTER 5

MEASURING INVARIANCE USING CONFIRMATORY FACTOR ANALYSIS AND ITEM RESPONSE THEORY
Perceptions of Organizational Politics in the United States and the Middle East

Terri A. Scandura, Ethlyn A. Williams, and Betti A. Hamilton

Abstract: The use of western-based measures of organizational phenomena in cross-cultural research is now widespread. Yet, an exportation of the "Western" value system, reflected in these measures, may present limitations when applied to different cultures. Measurement invariance of the general political behavior dimension of the perceptions of organizational politics (POPS) scale in two cultures was evaluated using confirmatory factor analytic (CFA) and item response theory (IRT) techniques. Items tapping general political behavior were administered to respondents from the United States (U.S.) and Middle East. This allowed for the examination of item invariance and measurement equivalence. An interpretation of the findings, and implications for the future use of the general political behavior measure and possibly other U.S.-based measures across cultures are discussed.

INTRODUCTION

Research on cross-cultural issues has expanded in the past two decades (Cheung & Rensvold, 1999). Work examining various cultures has uncovered many methodological issues. One concern is the extent to which researchers test the "stability and transferability of organizational measures between groups in cross-cultural research" (Riordan & Vandenberg, 1994, p. 643). Since "Western" (e.g., the United States and England) value systems have been the basis for the development of many management approaches aimed at increasing organizational effectiveness, the question of "what is being measured?" needs to be addressed when measures based on the culture of the United States (for example) are applied to other cultures.

Hofstede (1980b), has questioned the validity of transferring what is learned or developed in one culture to another. Local conditions, societal norms, and cultural traditions may reflect differences that present barriers when exporting Western-based ideologies to other cultures (Newman & Nollen, 1996). Therefore, the equivalence or transferability of the measures employed in international research is a critical issue (Riordan & Vandenberg, 1994). Hulin, Drasgow, and Parsons label this phenomenon the "equivalence of meaning vis-à-vis a network of relations" (1983, p. 189) and further clarify the importance of the equivalence of measures:

> The fidelity of a psychological instrument translation is judged ultimately by the fit of measures of constructs in the target culture and language into networks of relations. The fit of the target language construct into its own network must be the same as the fit of the original language construct into its own network. The goal of translation is equivalence of meaning vis-à-vis a network of relations. The analysis of the degree of equivalence is ultimately determined by the extent of convergence of network relations. This assumes that commonality exists between and among different cultures in the world. (p. 189)

The purpose of this study is to provide a substantive investigation of the extent to which a psychological measure of general political behavior elicits equivalent responses for samples from the United States and the Middle East. Measurement equivalence is examined using two approaches: "Confirmatory Factor Analysis" (CFA) and "Item Response Theory" (IRT). IRT is utilized as an objective means for confirming the results obtained using the CFA approach. Reise, Widaman, and Pugh (1993) utilized a similar approach to explore measurement invariance using a five-item measure of negative affect for Chinese and U.S. samples. Convergence of the results of both approaches indicates support for either measurement equivalence and/or the identification of items that do not attain invariance across cultures. While demonstrating the similarities and differences between the

CFA and IRT approaches, Reise et al. did not discuss the reasons underlying their results (i.e., no explanation was provided of why certain items might be noninvariant across their samples). We employ the approach used by Reise et al. and extend their work by examining some of the cultural explanations and implications underlying our findings. It can be expected that political behavior may be viewed differently in the United States and the Middle East.

General political behavior involves the behaviors of individuals acting in a self-serving manner to obtain valued outcomes (Kacmar & Carlson, 1997), and is measured by the "perceptions of organizational politics" (POPS) scale. The majority of the studies involving perceptions of organizational politics have not compared perceptions across cultures (Cropanzano, Howes, Grandey, & Toth, 1997; Ferris & Kacmar, 1992; Madison, Allen, Porter, Renwick, & Mayes, 1980). A few studies have employed samples from other countries. Kumar and Ghadially (1989), for example, examined organizational politics and its effects on a sample of Indian managers. Drory and Romm (1988) compared Canada and Israel and found that Canadians perceived the various elements of the scale administered as more political, less moral, and less prevalent in their organization than the Israeli sample. Both samples considered political behavior (nonsanctioned influence attempts or informal ones) as less desirable than the use of formal channels. The measures in that study however, appear to have been administered in English and developed using respondents from only one culture (the country was not identified).

Research that attempts to establish measurement equivalence is still not very prevalent, and research comparing the United States and Middle East exists in very small numbers (Scandura, Pillai, & Williams, 1998). The most wide scale study of culture to date is that of Hofstede (1980a). There is also emerging work that examines national culture (Trompenaars, 1994) with the general conclusion that culture varies across nations. Hofstede (1980a) did not examine a wide range of Middle Eastern cultures but the findings for Iran can be used to illustrate Middle Eastern cultures. Hofstede's research as well as Badawy's (1980) suggests that there are significant differences between Middle Eastern and western managers. Badawy (1980) and Elsayed-Ekhouly and Buda (1996) assert that the Middle Eastern styles are consistent from country to country (in reference to Arab/Middle Eastern countries). Ali (1999) considers Middle Eastern/Arab states to be: Algeria, Kuwait, Oman, Qatar, Saudi Arabia, United Arab Emirates, Egypt, Jordan, Lebanon, Mauritania, Morocco, Sudan, Tunisia, and Djibouti.

Boyacigiller and Adler notes that cultural values of the United States have fundamentally framed management research, "...thus imbuing organizational science with implicit, yet inappropriate, universalism" (1991, p. 262). Hofstede (1980a) ranked the United States highest on the dimension of individualism indicating the tendency to be self-oriented and emotionally independent with the emphasis placed on individual initiative, right to privacy, autonomy, and individual decisions (Elsayed-Ekhouly & Buda, 1996). Boyacigiller and Adler (1991) suggest that many organizational theories reflect the individualist bias of the U.S. culture. Thus, as noted by Allen, Miller, and Nath (1988), in countries where individualism dominates, the relationship with the organization may be viewed as a calculative one (determining the value of outcomes resulting from the exertion of effort relative to the costs of maintaining effort or severing ties). The implication for the study of perceptions of organizational politics is that political behavior may be very prevalent in the United States since the goal of the individual is self-interest. In fact, this behavior may be regulated by organizational policies. Self-interest necessitates identifying conflict situations in which political behavior might influence the final outcome for the individual. In the Middle East (specifically Iran), Hofstede (1980b) found high levels of collectivism. Thus, the relationship between the organization and the individual may be more symbiotic. As noted by Elsayed-Ekhouly and Buda (1996), the Middle Eastern employee is emotionally dependent on their organization and the private life of the individual may be subordinated to the organization (or clan) one belongs to in return for the provision of expertise, order, and security. In Middle Eastern culture, behaviors demonstrating self-interest are not reflective of the norms of society so perceptions of politics may vary according to the cultural context. Also, since there is a larger power differential between supervisors and subordinates in Middle East nations it may be perceived in a different manner than in the United States.

HOW PERCEPTIONS OF ORGANIZATIONAL POLITICS MIGHT VARY ACROSS CULTURES

The literature on organizational politics suggests that political behavior will increase where there are few rules and regulations to guide action (Fandt & Ferris, 1990; Tushman, 1977), where there is uncertainty in decision making (Drory & Romm, 1990), and where there is a highly competitive environment within the organization (Farrell & Peterson, 1982). Organizational politics refers to the intentional use of influence processes to maximize self or group interests (Gray & Ariss, 1985; Madison, Allen, Porter, Renwick, & Mayes, 1980). How employees perceive decision-making events may cause them to form cognitive conclusions about the meaning of these events and discern power motives. Perceptions of organizational politics (POPS) refers to employees' evaluations of the extent to which processes in the organization are likely to involve political behavior. This political behavior may involve actions aimed at obtaining sanctioned ends through the use of nonsanctioned influence means. With respect to policy implementation, perceptions of politics may influence employee attitudes and behavior since employees often respond and react to perceived cues in the environment (Ferris & Kacmar, 1992).

Research suggests that perceptions of organizational politics might be a source of stress and may result in dysfunctional outcomes such as absenteeism and turnover (Gandz & Murray, 1980; Gilmore, Ferris, Dulebohn, & Harrell-Cook, 1996). Drory (1993) for example, found strong associations between political climate and negative job attitudes. These relationships were stronger at lower levels in the organizations than at higher levels (Gandz & Murray, 1980; Madison et al., 1980).

Cross-cultural research on organizational politics conducted thus far (e.g., India and Israel) presents similar findings to those reported in U.S. samples with politics viewed in a negative light and negatively affecting job attitudes (Drory, 1993; Drory & Romm, 1988; Ferris & Kacmar, 1992; Kumar & Ghadially, 1989; Parker, Dipboye, & Jackson, 1995). Employees in one culture may perceive some situations as more highly political than employees in other cultures. This might reflect cultural norms. Similarly, perceptions of organizational politics may be affected by an employee's relationship with their supervisor. Also, individuals in different cultures may have very different values. The items in the perceptions of organizational politics scale (labeled as POPS1 to POPS6: Table 1) will next be examined according to the four cultural dimensions posited by Hofstede (1980a): power distance, uncertainty avoidance, masculinity/femininity, and individualism/collectivism.

Power distance represents the extent to which the society accepts the fact that power in institutions is distributed unequally (Hofstede, 1980b). Badawy (1980) presents a comparison of the Middle Eastern and western

Table 1.   Perceptions of Organizational Politics: General Political Behavior Scale[a]

Items	
POPS1.	Favoritism rather than merit determines who gets ahead around here.
POPS2.	There has always been an influential group in this department that no one ever crosses.
POPS3.	People here don't speak up for fear of retaliation by others.
POPS4.	People in this organization attempt to build themselves up by tearing others down.
POPS5.	I have seen changes made in policies here that only serve the purposes of a few individuals, not the work unit or the organization.
POPS6.	There is a group of people in my department who always get things their way because no one wants to challenge them.

Note: [a]Taken from Ferris and Kacmar (1991).

cultures, noting that they are products of their different political, historical, and regional socioeconomic features. Organization design in the Middle East was found to reflect the high levels of power distance that exist in the society. Wright (1981) notes that higher-level Moslem managers desire power and openly exercise influence. This also reflects the ownership patterns of organizations in the region. For example, there are few publicly traded firms (Ali, 1999). Public institutions have a strong link to rulers and ruling families and private organizations tend to be held by a few well connected and established business partners (Ali, 1999). This contributes to autocratic behaviors with concentrated power. Thus, organizations in the Middle East are highly bureaucratic (many rules and regulations) with centralized power and authority at the top. In the western system, the opposite is found with low power distance and decentralized power and authority relationships. Thus, responses to items measuring political behaviors may be interpreted according to Middle Eastern or western standards (e.g., POPS2: "there has always been an influential group in this department that no one ever crosses") and response patterns may differ based on the manner in which the item is worded. This may affect the interpretation of the item. For instance the word "cross" in POPS2 has the definition "intersect," "cancel," "contrary," or "annoyed" (Mirriam-Webster, 1995). The idea of "crossing" someone as related in the POPS scale may not exist in the Arabic culture and may be difficult to translate in a way that differentiates it from the more straightforward translation of "challenge." Thus, the way the item is interpreted in both cultures may result in different response patterns. In the United States, the influence that various individuals have over others may be monitored and regulations may exist to regulate power relationships. Certain groups having influence over others may be perceived as a common occurrence in the Middle East, whereas in the United States this type of behavior may be perceived as less common since power distance is perceived to be lower (Hofstede, 1980a).

Badawy (1980) also notes that in the Middle East decisions are made at the highest levels, coupled with an unwillingness to take risks; reflecting the high level of uncertainty avoidance found by Hofstede (1980a). The United States, in comparison, uses sophisticated planning techniques and decision makers are less risk averse. Thus, in examining an item that involves decision making (e.g., POPS3 "people here don't speak up for fear of retaliation by others" and POPS6: "there is a group of people in my department who always get their way because no one wants to challenge them") the extent to which a behavior is perceived may be determined by the extent to which individuals have decision making authority or decision influence. The items in the POPS scale that relate to challenging decisions made (POPS3 and POPS6) appear straightforward and it may not be difficult to convey their meanings in an Arabic translation. However, the way that the phrases "get their way" and "speak up" are translated and interpreted might change as these might not be as straightforward as the phrases "succeed in influencing decisions" and "speak assertively" appear to be. In the United States, the influence that employees at all levels have may be stronger than in the Middle East where top level managers make decisions and lower level employees do not have the power to challenge them.

With respect to relationships, Badawy (1980) notes that in Middle Eastern cultures friendships are binding and intense with hiring based on personal contacts and there is the lack of a vigorous performance evaluation system (Pezeshkpur, 1978). This reflects the feminine culture that values nurturing relationships. In the United States, relationships are less intense and people relate to each other in a more distant manner with candidate selection based on qualifications and formal performance appraisal systems (reflecting the masculine culture that places more emphasis on performance). The extent to which relationships versus performance are valued in a culture also affects the salience of "favoritism." Thus, reports on favoritism (e.g., POPS1: "favoritism rather than merit determines who gets ahead around here"), the wording of the POPS1 item appears straightforward. However, on closer examination the phrase "get ahead" might be ambiguous. A more straightforward way of presenting this idea might involve using the word "succeed" or phrase "receives promotions" in its place. Having a select group of individuals who have the favor of top managers may be less common in the United States than the Middle East since merit is the intended basis for promotions in the United States while the relationship with the supervisor may be the determining factor in the Middle East.

Kacmar and Carlson (1997) note that conflict is consistently related to organizational politics and according to Drory and Romm (1990) is an underlying element to political behavior. While there is virtually no published work that examines perceptions of organizational politics in Middle East countries (Scandura et al., 1998) there is some work that examines conflict resolution styles in the Middle East. Elsayed-Ekhouly and Buda (1996) compared the United States and the Middle East on conflict styles and found that Middle Eastern managers used more avoiding styles than U.S. managers. They concluded that this reflects the different values of collectivism and individualism in each culture. It therefore appears that in the United States, competitive behavior may be more readily addressed on an individual level while in the Middle East such individualistic behavior is not reinforced and may not be openly addressed. Badawy (1980) notes that group solidarity is a characteristic of Middle Eastern society. Wright (1981) also states that "only authoritarian groups may be expected to function with any potency" (1981, p. 92). Thus, behaviors that are motivated by self-interest may be more readily noticed and more residual in the Middle East (e.g., POPS4: "people in this organization attempt to build themselves up by tearing others down"). The idea of "tearing others down" for example connotes "separation" but also connotes "destruction." If not carefully interpreted, the meaning could be misconstrued in Arabic. The idea of "tearing others down" might be more easily interpreted from the phrase "destroying others" or "defeating others."

The orientation toward taking advantage of others may carry over to the way organizational policies are interpreted (e.g., POPS5: "I have seen changes in policies here that only serve the purposes of a few individuals, not the work unit or the organization"). The idea of a policy serving only a few rather than everyone appears straightforward. Other alternative ways of presenting this idea might include "benefit only a few individuals" or "profit only a few individuals." Middle Eastern employees may be more sensitive if policies are perceived as benefitting only select individuals rather than the organization. Thus, political issues may be salient for both cultures with the way questions are constructed having an effect on the response patterns in both cultures. The issues that are tapped may influence the way items are interpreted and the responses that are generated in various cultures.

ESTABLISHING THE EQUIVALENCE OF MEASURES

Traditionally, psychological instruments have been ethnographically translated. The meaning and cultural content of the source language are translated into the target language and then back translated into the original language to test for the integrity of the translation (Brislin, 1980). However, even with the best of translations and manipulations of words to produce the naturalness of the language in all contexts, there are still semantic differences that may obscure real differences in meaning of the construct (Hulin & Mayer, 1986; Rensvold & Cheung, 1998). Therefore, translation alone cannot be relied upon to provide similarity of relations between measures operationalizing the constructs (item responses) and an underlying trait (Hulin, Drasgow, & Parsons, 1983; Riordan & Vandenberg, 1994). To achieve the goal of equivalence, both substantive and measurement theories should be readily transferred with confidence (Riordan & Vandenberg, 1994). There are many methods available to measure the level of equivalence obtained (Cheung & Rensvold, 1999; Ironson & Subkoviak, 1979). These methods attempt to measure response consistency (or lack thereof) between groups by making sure the psychological measurements are on the same scale. This occurs when the empirical relations between the trait indicators and the trait of interest are invariant across groups (Reise et al., 1993; Rensvold & Cheung, 1998; Riordan & Vandenberg, 1994).

We first use a covariance analytic approach as the primary test for the equivalence of measures across cultures. The covariance analytic approach is applied using confirmatory factor analysis (CFA). Lytle et al. (1995) note that multisample analysis of the measurement model in latent structural equation modeling (SEM) is an alternative technique for examining the cross-cultural validity of a construct. This tests the construct validity across groups and the CFA approach is more user friendly and simpler than other approaches (Reise et al., 1993). The covariance structure approach allows the researcher to take into account the measurement error present in the latent construct by including error terms (Bollen, 1989). A fundamental approach to addressing measurement invariance involves studying the covariance patterns of item-factor relations and comparing results across cultures. Windle, Iwawaki and Lerner (1988) note that in many cases the primary approach to examining measurement equivalence involves examining these covariation patterns. We apply the linear CFA approach since it allows us to test the conceptual and true-score equivalency. The multiple-group CFA analysis is the modeling technique applied for testing measurement equivalence across cultures. This technique is well established (Jöreskog & Sörbom, 1993a). Thus, we will cover the CFA approach in less detail than the second approach (IRT) since there is a great deal of literature available that explains how to conduct CFA and interpret the results (Bollen, 1989; Medsker, Williams, & Holahan, 1994).

When invariance is not established, the items show differential functioning on some level based on group specific response patterns. This may reflect the difficulty of the item, the discriminating power of the item, or the ability to "guess" at the item. Based on these differences, Ironson and Subkoviak (1979) outlined four basic methods for determining the differences between the groups: (1) *The Bias Method Based on Transformed Difficulty:* This method compares an item to other items on a test and measures its relative difficulty for one group versus another. Group differences are compared and deviations measured; the smaller the magnitude of the deviations, the better chance of achieving equivalency. (2) *Biased Method Based on Item Discrimination:* This method uses the item discrimination index to measure bias. The goal is to have items fall on the same range of discriminating power for both groups. (3) *The Chi-Square Method:* This method compares the entire distribution of responses for the two groups in question and is similar to conducting proportion correct analyses. (4) *The Item Characteristic Curve Method:* This method relates performance between an individual's ability level to the abilities measured by the items in the test. This relationship is captured in mathematical expressions relating probability of success on an item to the ability measured by the test. The resultant graphed function should be comparable for the two groups. Ironson and Subkoviak (1979) deemed the item characteristic curve method, which is based on item response theory, to be the superior of the four methods. Others have joined in that assessment because unlike classical test theory, item response theory is sample invariant (Hambleton, Swaminathan, & Rogers, 1991), relies on stringent assumptions such as assuming the tests measures a single common trait or ability (Hambleton & Jones,

1993), and links item performance and ability on the same scale (Hamble-ton & Jones, 1993; Harvey & Hammer, 1999).

Item response theory is applied here as the second approach to test measurement equivalence since it provides the general framework which subsumes many models and techniques. This approach goes beyond CFA techniques by allowing the researcher to go beyond the identification of the noninvariant items to examine the extent of differential functioning of each item. The strength of item response theory lies in its properties that provide a strong rationale for cross-cultural research applications (Lytle, Brett, Barsness, Tinsley, & Janssens, 1995). The sample independence nature of the IRT breaks the circular cycle of classical test theory whereby true score (which can be used to express a person's ability) is dependent on the test instrument. Because true score is dependent on the observed score (Observed Score = True Score + Error), persons taking a relatively more difficult test will have lower true scores than those taking a relatively easy test. However their real ability will be constant regardless of the level of difficulty of the test (Hambleton & Jones, 1993). To break that cycle, Lord (1952) focused on mathematical models that are not group depen-dent. Sample independence thus provides the capability to compare groups regardless of the dissimilarity of the examinees or the test (Hamble-ton, Swaminathan, & Rogers, 1991). Additionally, other classical test theory assumptions regarding error (true and error scores are uncorrelated), reli-ability (inextricably tied to the test using parallel forms, and assuming equal errors of measurement for all examinees), and focusing on the test as the point of reference (inability of item level analysis) are all addressed in IRT (Hambleton & Jones, 1993; Hambleton, Swaminathan, & Rogers, 1991; Hulin, Drasgow, & Parsons, 1983). These properties make IRT ideal for determining invariance in cross-cultural comparisons.

METHOD

Samples

The questionnaire was administered to 445 respondents residing in the United States. These respondents were students in an executive Masters of Business Administration program in the southeastern United States. After accounting for missing data the final sample size was 396. The Middle East-ern sample included 219 respondents from Jordan and Saudi Arabia who were employed in a variety of organizations. The final sample included 186 respondents after accounting for missing data (68 Jordanians, 118 Saudi Arabians). For the Middle East, two Arabic males who were visiting Jordan and Saudi Arabia administered the surveys. The two Arabic males who col-lected the data translated the survey from English into Arabic; another

Arab performed the back translation (from Arabic into English). The use of translators native to these foreign countries was employed with the aim of maintaining equivalence in the meaning of the items presented. The Saudi and Jordanian samples were combined. Independent samples t-tests revealed no differences in the demographic variables of age, work experience, education, employment and level in the organization. However, there was a significant difference for sex. The Jordanian sample had equal proportions of male and female respondents while more than 90 %of the Saudi respondents were male. Badawy (1980) supports the combination of Middle East samples, noting that these nations share cultural characteristics and work values.

For both samples, all respondents were professionals employed in service and manufacturing organizations located in major cities. The average age across both samples was 31 years with more than 59 %male in the U.S. sample and 74 %male in the Middle Eastern sample. For both cultures respondents had more than 6 years work experience (10 years for the United States and 6 for the Middle East) and over 60 %were at the supervisory level and above. For the U.S. sample 33 %were at middle management and above while in the Middle East 38.9 %were at middle management and above. More than 90 %reported having education beyond the high school level in both samples, with the U.S. sample having 62 %of respondents with bachelors' degrees and 33.2 %with masters degrees; in the Middle Eastern sample 63.6 %had bachelors degrees and 32.7 %masters degrees. For both samples more than 70 %were employed on a full-time basis.

Measure

Perceptions of Politics (POPS). The scale developed by Kacmar and Ferris (1991) was used to measure perceptions of organizational politics (POPS). The factor that represents general political behavior was employed (6 items) (Kacmar & Ferris, 1991). A five-point Likert-type scale was used with responses ranging from 1 (*strongly disagree*) to 5 (*strongly agree*). The coefficient alpha reliability for the measure was .84 for the U.S. sample and .78 for the Middle East sample. Measurement invariance was tested on this 6-item measure.

Conducting CFA and IRT to Test Measurement Equivalence

The following sections provide detailed descriptions of the application of confirmatory factor analysis (CFA) and item response theory (IRT) for testing measurement equivalence, determining invariance, and comparing results from the two methods. Reise et al. (1993) conducted one of the few analyses directly comparing CFA and IRT on attitudinal data (mood adjective ratings) using the graded response model (Samejima, 1969) to capture response categories of a Likert-type scale. The objective of the paper was to illustrate this type of analysis on cross-cultural behavioral studies and to provide a methodological framework for using CFA and IRT. Prior to their study, most research dealing with item response theory analyzed or applied logistic models (Fan, 1998; Hambleton & Jones, 1993).

Item response theory has been employed for almost 50 years (Hambleton & Jones, 1993). Yet, unlike confirmatory factor analytic (CFA) techniques that have been well developed in the literature, IRT techniques are still in the process of improvement (Hambleton & Jones, 1993; Reise et al., 1993; Reise & Yu, 1990; Rensvold & Cheung, 1998). The complex mathematical models used in the treatment of item response models have not been very popular in the application of attitudinal measurement data (Hambleton & Jones, 1993; Harvey & Hammer, 1999). Additional issues involve development of computerized models to facilitate analysis and establishment of indices that can be readily compared to CFA (Reise & Yu, 1990). From their comparative analysis, Reise et al. (1993) facilitated the use of graded response models for behavioral-type scales in cross-cultural studies. Thus, Reise et al. (1993) focused their attention on model fit issues, not substantive analysis of theoretical concepts of the measure of mood they employed. This point was underscored in their call for "further exploration of the relations between CFA and IRT models and their differential utility for representing data and testing theoretical hypotheses" (p. 565).

In the current study, we apply the analytical approach developed by Reise et al. (1993) to evaluate the POPS scale with the goal of discerning implications for theory. We attempt to extend the work of Reise et al. (1993) by evaluating a behavioral scale for invariance (across two cultures) to interpret substantive implications for both groups. In this cross-cultural study, the value-added by examining both CFA and IRT approaches are in concert with calls to add rigor to cross-cultural research by "establishing conceptual and metric equivalences" (Sin, Cheung, & Lee 1999; p. 91) and to develop meaningful discourse on the issue (Cheung & Rensvold, 1999; Reise et al., 1993; Riordan & Vandenberg, 1994). Thus, results obtained from CFA and IRT will be compared. There is a large body of literature supporting factor analytic techniques (Riordan & Vandenberg, 1994; Rensvold & Cheung, 1998). In comparison, studies involving the graded response model are much fewer (Hambleton & Jones, 1993; Reise et al., 1993).

CFA Models

Model construction using the multiple-group CFA approach was employed (Jöreskog & Sörbom, 1993b). Details on the CFA technique can be found in Riordan and Vandenberg (1994) and Reise et al. (1993). The evaluations of CFA models are more straightforward than IRT techniques with the availability of fit indices for interpreting results. Using CFA analysis, baseline, full invariance, and partial invariance models must be compared. Normally, these nested CFA models may be compared using the chi-square statistic (χ^2) (Rensvold & Cheung, 1998). Additionally, the following fit indices are used: Root Mean Square Error of Approximation (RMSEA), Non-Normed Fit Index (NNFI), the Comparative Fit Index (CFI), and the Goodness of Fit Index (GFI) (Bollen, 1989; Kline, 1998).

A baseline model is first estimated with the factor variance (Φ_{11}) (covariance of the first factor with itself) fixed at 1.0 for the U.S. sample and the corresponding parameter estimated in the Middle East sample relating to the unit variance in the first group (United States). Reise et al. (1993) note that constraining the first factor loading is sufficient to identify all remaining parameter estimates in the second group (by fixing the variance in the first). This model serves as a baseline against which the fit of the full measurement invariance and partial measurement invariance models are compared.

In the full measurement invariance model all the factor loading parameters are constrained to be invariant across groups. This model is nested within the baseline model. A nonsignificant increase in chi-square indicates that the hypothesis of full measurement invariance is tenable (Reise et al., 1993). Next, partial measurement invariance models are tested. The requirement to compare groups on a latent variable is that partial measurement invariance be established (Byrne, Shavelson, & Muthén, 1989). Partial invariance occurs if some (not all) of the nonfixed values of item loadings on the factor are invariant across groups. These invariant loadings then define the latent metric. If the full invariance model is rejected (significant change from baseline to full measurement model) then based on the modification indices, the model can be used to determine the noninvariant items. Large modification indices indicate that the factor loading for the item cannot be equated across samples (Reise et al., 1993). Testing for partial invariance then requires respecifying the full measurement model, except that the factor loading for parameters associated with statistically significant (large) modification indices are freely estimated for each group. This model is then compared with the baseline model. A partial measurement invariance model that does not differ statistically from the baseline model indicates that partial measurement invariance is supported.

IRT Models

Model Choice

IRT is a "test theory" (Hambleton & Jones, 1993). As such, it provides a philosophical system encompassing a variety of models. Data and supportable assumptions thus drive model selection. The two general categories of IRT models are logistic models (dealing with dichotomous response data) and graded response models (dealing with polychotomous response data) (Hambleton et al., 1991; Hambleton & Jones, 1993; Thissen, 1991). The main assumptions are: (1) unidimensionality of the scale and (2) local independence (Hambleton et al., 1991). From our preliminary analyses, the POPS general political behavior scale was shown to support the assumption of unidimensionality. With respect to the second assumption, local independence, meeting the unidimensionality criteria usually suffices in order to assume local independence (Hambleton et al., 1991; Hulin, Drasgow, & Parson, 1983). Local independence in IRT means that when there is a homogenous subpopulation with a particular level of ability, ability is partialled out and individual responses to the items are likely to be independent (the reader is referred to Hambleton et al., 1991 for a complete mathematical explanation of this property). The POPS scale is based on a Likert-type response model with five response categories (i.e., polytomous). The most appropriate IRT model for use with this type of data is the graded response model (GRM) first proposed by Samejima (1969) (Thissen, 1991). While there are many computer packages that may be used to run IRT the analyses, we selected the MULTILOG version 6.0 statistical package as an efficient and effective estimation program for testing graded response models as recommended by Reise and Yu's (1990) review of IRT statistical packages.

Model Estimation

IRT models account for examinee item responses (Hulin et al., 1983; Reise et al., 1993; Thissen, 1991) and provide a method of distinguishing between group differences and accounting for test bias (Thissen, Steinberg, & Gerrard, 1986). To accomplish this, IRT models the relationships between item responses and the trait being measured. In this study, the latent variable was general political behavior, labeled theta (θ) (Thissen, 1991). IRT models imply particular distributions of item responses, conditional on theta level (cf. Hambleton et al., 1991; Reise et al., 1993; Thissen, 1991; Van de Rijt, Van Luit, & Pennings, 1999). The basic equation for the graded response IRT model is (Reise et al., 1993):

$$P(x = k|\theta) = [1 + \exp(-a(\theta - b_{j-1}))]^{-1} - [1 + \exp(-a(\theta - b_j))]^{-1}$$

Each respondent's score is thus represented as a value reflecting his or her general political behavior based on the response patterns. This specifies the conditional probability of a person responding in a particular category, (k), given a general political behavior score (theta level). The boundaries between the response categories (ranging from 1 = *strongly disagree*, to 5 = *strongly agree*) are represented by *j*. The item response function

(IRF) results from this mathematical equation. The IRF accounts for the relationship between examinee level on general political behavior and the probability of a particular item response. The a parameter is the item discrimination and its value is proportional to the slope of the IRFs. The steeper the slope, the more discriminating the item (the more strongly responses on an item are related to general political behavior (theta), the larger the corresponding a parameters for the IRFs). The b parameter is the inflection point on the general political behavior (theta scale) at which the probability of success is 50% on that item. The difficulty values are generally represented by z-scores on the same plane with respondent ability level (values range from easy, –3, to difficult, +3). This converts item responses to an estimate of general political behavior (theta values) while also examining the property of the items. The slope of this function reflects the rate at which the probability of endorsement changes as general political behavior increases.

The parameters, as noted above, can be estimated for each item independent of other scale items. Using the IRFs, and any value of theta, the GRM equation above may be used to compute expected response probabilities in each of the five response categories for the item. The resultant curve is the item characteristic curve (ICC) (Hambleton et al., 1991). This is the property of IRT that enables the parameter estimates to be compared meaningfully across cultures when standardized to a common metric, thereby facilitating the establishment of invariance (Reise et al., 1993).

Assessing Fit

Three basic steps were taken to assess model fit. In the first step, the baseline IRT/GRM model is created by freely estimating all parameters. In the second step, the IRT/GRM fully constrained model is estimated. The third step involves comparing the varying degrees of constraint models to the baseline model. Using this nested model fit approach is consistent with procedures by Reise et al. (1993) and allows for comparison of IRT results to CFA results.

Baseline Model

In a multiple group situation, as in this study, the goal is to have the latent variable (general political behavior) be common across both groups such that item parameters can be estimated with respect to this common scale and then tested for invariance. If items for each group were independently calibrated, the issue of noncomparability will arise (Reise et al., 1993; Riordan & Vandenberg, 1994). The baseline model then serves two purposes: (1) creating the common scale through concurrent calibration (Hambleton et al., 1991; Reise et al., 1993), and (2) serving as the unconstrained model for comparing nested models.

Concurrent calibration is a procedure that allows the placement of "item parameter estimates and ability parameter estimates on a common scale without the need for a separate linking and scaling step" (Hambleton et al., 1991, p. 135). This procedure treats the data as if all 582 respondents had taken a 12-item test (because the POPS scale includes 6 items) thereby placing respondent general political behavior on the same scale. In this baseline model, the theta metric is not identified between groups because there are no anchor items (Reise et al., 1993). However, the fit of this model serves as a baseline for judging subsequent models in which invariance is investigated across groups of item parameters. In all, 61 item parameters are estimated in the baseline model.

Full Invariance Model

To test for full invariance, the items are calibrated concurrently using the same procedure as under the baseline model. In this case, all item parameters are constrained to equality across groups creating a six-item anchor test. This is the most restricted model (Reise et al., 1993). To calculate the chi-square difference between the full invariance model and the baseline models, the likelihood function generated by MUTILOG ($G^2 = -2$ * log of the likelihood function) is compared to the value for the baseline model. The G^2 statistic under certain conditions is distributed as a chi-square value with degrees of freedom equal to the number of response patterns minus the number of estimates made in the model and reflects the degree of lack of invariance (Reise et al., 1993; Thissen et al., 1986). This is analogous to comparing nested CFA models using the chi-square statistic (Rensvold & Cheung, 1998).

Partial Invariance Models

Rejecting full invariance does not end the process. The objective is to find at least one invariant item across the groups such that it can be used as an anchor to estimate the latent trait values (theta) with both groups on a common scale (Hambleton et al., 1991; Reise et al., 1993; Thissen et al., 1988). Therefore, when items function differentially across the groups, they can be analyzed within the proper context because of the placement on a common scale (Hambleton et al., 1991). The procedures for testing partial invariance models involved an iterative process based on equating related items with the remaining parameters freely estimated. This is repeated for all six pairs of items, comparing each nested model to the baseline model and testing for invariance. Items found to be invariant are retained and tested again (Reise et al., 1993). A partial invariance model is accepted when the change in G^2 from the baseline model is not statistically significant.

RESULTS

The two samples (the United States and Middle East) were examined to see how the means differed by group. It appears, that in general, there were higher levels of perceptions of organizational politics for the Middle East sample than the U.S. sample. For items 1, 2, 3, and 6 the means were 2.86, 2.94, 2.77, and 2.79 for the United States and 3.17, 3.39, 3.09, and 3.06 for the Middle East sample. The differences in means were statistically significant at the $p < .01$ levels. For item 4 the means were 2.60 for the United States and 2.80 for the Middle East with $p < .10$. For item 5 there was no difference between the means (2.79 for both samples).

CFA

The results of the CFA modeling are presented in Table 2. Results indicate that the chi-square difference between the baseline model and the full measurement invariance model is significant and there is an apparent decrease in model fit. Also, differences in the fit statistics between the models were greater than .01 (Widaman, 1985). Thus, full measurement invariance is not evident.

Based on the rejection of the full invariance model, the modification indices were examined and the index for POPS2 was statistically significant. Based on these results a partial measurement invariance model was tested with the factor loading for this parameter freely estimated for each group (otherwise the specifications were the same as for the full measurement invariance model). The difference between this partial invariance model and the baseline model was not significant. All estimated parameters for the partial measurement model (except for POPS2 for the Middle East sample) were statistically significant ($p < .05$). Thus, support was found for partial measurement invariance.

IRT

IRT graded response model analytical techniques were conducted to evaluate the behavior of the POPS general political behavior scale across the United States and the Middle East. IRT analysis assumes the underlying assessment is the presumed measurement of a single unobservable latent variable, theta, (representing general political behavior) (Reise et al., 1993; Thissen, 1991). The item characteristic curves then summarize the performance of the items in the POPS scale (Thissen et al., 1986). The ref-

Table 2. Estimated Parameter Matrices and Fit Statistics for Baseline, Full Measurement, and Partial Measurement Invariance Confirmatory Factory Analysis Models

Parameter	Baseline		Full Invariance		Partial Invariance	
	U.S.	M.E.	U.S.	M.E.	U.S.	M.E.
λ_{11}	0.78		0.76		0.75	
λ_{21}	0.65	0.16	0.52		0.64	0.15
λ_{31}	0.82	0.94	0.84		0.82	
λ_{41}	0.83	0.96	0.84		0.83	
λ_{51}	0.75	0.99	0.80		0.79	
λ_{61}	0.82	0.91	0.82		0.81	
ϕ_{11}	1.00[a]	1.00	1.00[a]	1.00	1.00[a]	1.00
χ^2	103.55		132.08		107.65	
df	18		23		22	
χ^2 change	—		28.53		4.10	
df change	—		5		4	
Root Mean Square Error of Approx.	0.05		0.15		0.06	
Non-Normed Fit Index	0.92		0.89		0.92	
Comparative Fit Index	0.93		0.92		0.93	
Goodness of Fit Index	0.93		0.90		0.92	

Notes: Parameter estimates centered between the U.S. and Middle East (M.E.) represent parameters constrained to equality across samples.

[a] Parameters fixed at 1.0 to identify each model.

erent group for the POPS scale is the United States since it represents the culture from which the test was originally developed (Ellis & Kimmel, 1992). Analysis of the results centers on how similar or different the curves and corresponding parameters are between the two groups.

In the baseline and full invariance IRT graded response models (see Table 3), item parameters for the United States and the Middle East can be compared. The statistically significant full invariance model indicates that items are functioning differently across the groups and there was no perfect fit of the model to the population. The change in G^2 (from the baseline model) was statistically significant $[G^2(30, N = 582) = 183.8, p < .001]$ indicating that full invariance was not found (Hambleton et al., 1991; Reise et al., 1993). Partial invariance analyses were then conducted on all POPS items. None of the partial invariance models were supported, thus indicating no items to anchor the scale. The lack of an anchor means that the scores for the groups cannot be equated on the same theta scale (Reise et

Table 3.   IRT Item Parameters

Item	Parameter	Baseline U.S.	Baseline M.E.	Full Invariance U.S.	Full Invariance M.E.	Partial Invariance[a] U.S.	Partial Invariance[a] M.E.
POPS1	a	1.81	1.71	1.79		1.81	
	b1	-1.93	-1.00	-1.55		-1.54	
	b2	-0.71	-0.26	-0.57		-0.56	
	b3	0.22	0.15	0.18		0.18	
	b4	1.59	1.40	1.49		1.50	
POPS2	a	1.44	0.34	1.06		1.55	0.31
	b1	-2.23	-5.76	-2.50		-2.02	-6.46
	b2	-0.72	0.46	-0.54		-0.63	0.42
	b3	0.41	3.27	0.66		0.41	3.50
	b4	2.06	9.93	2.69		1.94	10.85
POPS3	a	2.32	2.41	2.38		2.39	
	b1	-1.86	1.02	-1.53		-1.52	
	b2	-0.70	-0.29	-0.57		-0.57	
	b3	-0.02	0.10	0.00		0.00	
	b4	1.51	1.24	1.39		1.40	
POPS4	a	2.19	3.41	2.44		2.44	
	b1	-1.97	-1.14	-1.68		-1.67	
	b2	-0.94	-0.46	-0.77		-0.76	
	b3	-0.11	-0.09	-0.11		-0.11	
	b4	1.16	0.78	1.02		1.03	
POPS5	a	2.13	3.37	2.33		2.32	
	b1	-2.12	-1.20	-1.80		-1.79	
	b2	-0.74	-0.49	-0.67		-0.66	
	b3	0.13	-0.17	0.01		0.02	
	b4	1.53	1.00	1.34		1.36	
POPS6	a	2.35	2.20	2.35		2.36	
	b1	-1.81	-1.38	-1.65		-1.64	
	b2	-0.70	-0.25	-0.55		-0.55	
	b3	0.07	0.18	0.08		0.09	
	b4	1.42	1.30	1.34		1.35	
	Mu	0.00	-0.07	0.00	-0.22	0.00	-0.19
	Sigma	1.00	0.82	1.00	0.82	1.00	0.82
	G-sq change	N/A	N/A	183.8*		125.9*	
	df change	N/A	N/A	30		25	

Notes: Due to space restrictions, we have the shown parameters used in illustrations.

[a]Using IRT item results that are in common with CFA.

*p < .005

al., 1993). Next, the two data sets (United States and Middle East) were analyzed separately to examine the behavior of POPS within each culture.

Analysis of the U.S. data partial invariance model revealed normally functioning item characteristic curves with nonsignificance achieved when POPS2 is freed [$G^2(25, N = 582) = 36.9$, n.s.] corresponding to the CFA results. However, similar analysis of the Middle East data indicated a significant change in G^2 from the baseline model [$G^2(25, N=582) = 86.1$, $p < .001$]. In all of the sub-model analyses, the Middle East data approached, but never reached nonsignificance. Visual inspection of the item parameters presented in Table 3 revealed that POPS2 ("There has always been an influential group in this department that no one ever crosses") is more discriminating (performs more consistently) for the U.S. group than for the Middle Eastern group (the a parameter is higher for United States than Middle East). This is reflected in the ICC curves for POPS2 presented based on the results of the baseline model for the United States and the Middle East (Figure 1). Each curve represents the response "k" according to the Likert scale with k(U.S.) = 1 representing "strongly disagree" to

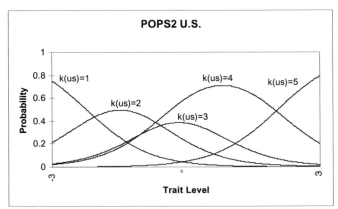

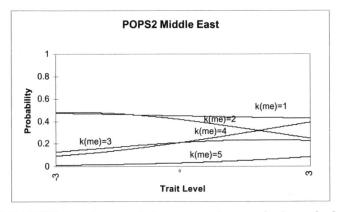

Figure 1. POPS2 Item characteristic curves using results from the baseline model (using IRT)

k(U.S.) = 5 representing "strongly agree" (the same is indicated for the Middle East curves). The U.S. ICC curve reflects the characteristic monotonously increasing function (Hambleton et al., 1991). However, the ICC curve for the Middle East depicts a more linear function. This indicates that the model may not adequately explain the data (Hambleton et al., 1991). The very different respondent response patterns found are reflected in the item characteristic curves and indicate that POPS2 is not behaving similarly in both groups (Thissen et al., 1986). In addition, the graph of the response pattern for an item (the item parameters) also illustrates the differences in behavior of that item across the groups.

In contrast, the remaining items have closely matching item curves across both groups. This is illustrated using POPS6 ("There is a group of people in my department who always get things their way because no one wants to challenge them"), which clearly has closely matching item curves across both groups (see Figure 2). The IRT graded response model takes into account the discrimination index of an item (a parameter) as well as its difficulty level (b parameter). The level of endorsement of that item (a

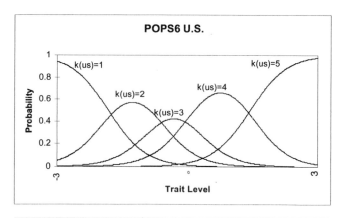

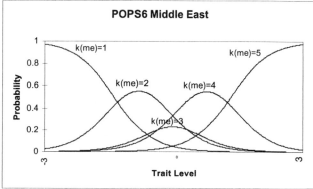

Figure 2. POPS6 item characteristic curves using results from the baseline model (using IRT)

parameter) across both groups is similar. The b parameter is a reflection of the level of ability needed to endorse 50% of the item; the higher the b parameter, the harder it is to endorse (thus requiring a higher standing on that general perception of politics; in an objective test it would be the level needed to have a 50% chance of answering the item correctly, with harder items requiring higher ability) (Hambleton et al., 1991). Partial invariance was not attained (i.e., none of the items were invariant). Thus, while POPS2 shows the most differential item functioning across the two groups, the behavior of the remaining items was not close enough to establish partial measurement invariance. Thus IRT analysis indicated that the scale and its items are noninvariant across cultures.

DISCUSSION

The primary goal of this paper was to evaluate the behavior of the POPS general political behavior scale across the two cultures of the United States and the Middle East. CFA was first employed to establish the presence of measurement invariance. Next, invariance analysis was undertaken with IRT as a comparison with CFA. The concern with measurement invariance is important because it is a basic prerequisite for studying group differences using statistical models (Riordan & Vandenberg, 1994). Once invariance is established, other theoretically important questions may be addressed (Cheung & Rensvold, 1999). CFA results supported one invariant item across the two groups. This result, however, is different from the IRT conclusions. IRT results indicate that the POPS scale functions differentially across the U.S. and Middle Eastern groups. Thus, membership in a group (in this case, the U.S. or the Middle East) may affect the response patterns to the POPS. The difference detected by IRT limit the comparison of the general political behavior scale across these groups since the scale could not be placed on a common metric (Hambleton et al., 1991; Reise et al., 1993).

Given our findings, the general conclusion from IRT is that the scale does not attain measurement equivalence across both groups. There are many reasons why this might be the case. The IRT model specification may need refinement, the choice of IRT model might be problematic, and a larger item pool might be needed. There might be problems with the translation or different interpretations of the items based on culture. It therefore appears that with the different results obtained based on the CFA and IRT approaches, we cannot recommend application of the Middle Eastern translation of the POPS general political behavior measure for cross-cultural comparisons. An examination of the ICC's, however, suggests that (as found through CFA analyses), POPS2 shows the worst differential item functioning.

Implications of the CFA and IRT Results

Confirmatory factor analytic approaches may be less stringent than IRT approaches given that the CFA model does not account for difficulty parameters. A unit of measurement must be assigned to the latent variable using a standardization procedure when conducting CFA and this implies an assumption of invariance. If the item used for standardization is actually noninvariant then problems may arise (Cheung & Rensvold, 1999). Modification indices, however, from a full invariance model do indicate the likely change in model fit that freeing constrained items would yield. This is not the case with IRT, where all variations of the full invariance model (freeing one item at a time) must be tested to yield a final partial invariance model. The results from CFA analyses essentially indicate statistical and practical indices of fit and calculate accurate estimates of the chi-square model fit and its associated degrees of freedom (Reise et al., 1993). The CFA approach also accounts for the measurement error found in latent constructs (Bollen, 1989) and can allow for hypothesis testing since it directly tests assumptions of conceptual and true score equivalency (Riordan & Vandenberg, 1994).

Item response theory, as the name implies, focuses on the item level, not the test (or scale) level. As such, it may pick up smaller differences at the item level that may yield variance across the groups. Thissen et al. (1986) highlights this finer grained analysis by noting that "item bias may not be due to identifiable other traits in one or the other group. Biased items may show a type of multidimensionality that involves different small, unique effects on items in one or both groups. These unique items may be present even if the test appears unidimensional within each group" (p. 119). Additionally, unidimensionality as an imposed constraint is very rigid and may not ever be met as respondents vary along many cognitive factors that influence response patterns (Hambleton et al., 1991; Harvey & Hammer, 1999). As such, a scale that may appear to be unidimensional may contain unique effects, which in this case was accentuated in our group comparisons. Based on previous research, however, the general political behavior subscale of the POPS measure has been shown to be unidimensional (Kacmar & Ferris, 1991) and CFAs conducted on the U.S. and Middle Eastern samples for this study supported the unidimensionality of the scale within culture.

The results of both CFA and IRT analyses, while different, highlight where improvements can be made before applying the POPS (general political behavior) scale across cultures. Rather than throwing out all the items, CFA suggests that POPS2 is noninvariant across groups and this is supported by the IRT analyses and the item characteristic curve for POPS2. This reveals that the item is not measuring similarly in both groups while the remaining items appear to have the potential to measure similarly across groups. In spite of this potential, the groups essentially differ on overall perceptions of organizational politics (general political behavior).

The results of the current study indicate that further work is needed on the Middle Eastern (Arabic) translation of the POPS scale and that 5 of the 6 items examined here might be applied to the Middle East if refined. The manner in which items are constructed in English can facilitate ease in translation. If the same meaning or behavior can be tapped from one culture to another then it is reasonable to assume that we can compare responses. The levels of perceptions and the saliency of the concept, while important, do not preclude comparisons since these differences help to elucidate the meaning of our results. Researchers who are able to establish measurement equivalence may be able to eliminate the alternative explanations and limitations with respect to their results and can have more confidence that the same concept was tapped in the cultures examined.

Given the results of our study and our review of the cultural dimensions, the following changes are recommended to refine the POPS scale for translation into another language. The scale might be refined as follows. POPS1: Favoritism rather than merit determines who succeeds in this organization; POPS3: People in this organization don't speak assertively or reveal their honest opinion for fear of retaliation by others; POPS4: People in this organization attempt to gain recognition by destroying others; POPS5: I have seen changes in the policies here that benefit only a few individuals and not the work unit or the organization; and POPS6: There is a group of people in my department who always succeed in influencing decisions because no one wants to challenge them. It is also important to note that there are variations of the measure utilized here, with the most recent version published found in Kacmar and Carlson (1997). As researchers continue to refine their measures in one culture they may also create measures that are more stable when applied to other cultures. The way a measure is developed and validated may also indicate whether it is intended for use in other cultures.

Cross-Cultural Issues

An important issue in cross-cultural studies is overcoming differences in language as well as cultural interpretations. Factors such as translation error, differences in cultural experience or knowledge, or a combination (Ellis & Kimmel, 1992) may be plausible explanations for differences in response patterns. In this study, care was taken to translate and back-translate the questionnaire. However, Hulin et al. (1983) views this method as having "serious roadblocks to progress in cross-cultural and international organizational research" (p. 185). Other factors that may have influenced the results in this particular case may involve the samples or the scale used. The sample demographics with respect to education, level in the organization, and employment status were similar for both the United States and the Middle East. Management practices may have been yet another factor that affected perceptions. The types of organizations and the way they are managed may vary based on culture and work values, resulting in differential responses to survey instruments.

A closer look at the CFA results shows items that are found to be invariant in the perceptions of general political behavior tend to have face validity. Statements in these items appear to be straightforward and might be translated without having much change to the underlying meaning such as POPS6 (Table 1). POPS2, which involved translating a word that has different meanings in different contexts ("crosses") into an item that could be easily understood in Arabic, elicited different response patterns by culture. It also interesting to note that the mean scores on the items measuring political behavior tended to be higher for the Middle Eastern sample, indicating that they perceived higher levels of political behavior overall than did respondents from the United States.

The scale in this study measures general political behavior, and additional cultural differences that might play an important role may not have been adequately captured. The cultural norm in the Middle East is that managers have greater power than subordinates and very different managerial values may exist with respect to decision making, relationships with co-workers, and loyalty to the organization. The traditional methodology for conducting survey research in which organizational politics is measured may also be a factor (Kabanoff, 1997) since the underlying assumption is that the organizational values are captured in the individual's values. Kabanoff points out that this is problematic and suggests that a better approach may be "studying organizations' justice characters through the values that organizations themselves espouse" (1997, p. 693). Since U.S.-based measures assume that self-interest is the main concern of organizational members and policies exist in most organizations to minimize this behavior, the levels of organizational politics observed might reflect the extent to which an individual's interests are being served over those of the organization. For the Middle East, organizational values are expected to be those that preserve status and hierarchy. Yet, individuals might still be able to objectively observe influence attempts as political (even if culturally expected and accepted). Thus, reports on political behaviors observed may reflect the values of the organization. Consideration of these cultural factors may be needed to reduce differential item functioning and improve the validity of measurement with respect to perceptions of politics in non-U.S. samples.

Study Limitations

One limitation of this study is the lack of other culture specific measures that might have captured the underlying principles or given clues to aid in the explanation of noninvariant items between the United States and the Middle East. Nonetheless, this study joins a mere handful of studies on the Middle East. Additionally, the attempt to establish equivalency through rigorous means prior to making substantive statements, places it among the 11.53% of the 53 cross-cultural studies reviewed by Sin and Cheung (1999).

In this study, the dissimilarity of the results underscores differences in the type of information provided by CFA versus IRT. Cheung and Rensvold (1999) and Riordan and Vandenberg (1994) both proposed testing the factorial invariance across the groups as evidence of equivalence. However, this process still does not account for the circular dependence found in classical test theory. CFA is based on classical test theory and as such item statistics are sample dependent creating theoretical issues in measuring invariance across groups (Fan, 1998). Thus, even though statistical procedures have been developed to account for factor scores, theoretically, the focus of CFA is still essentially scale-level information.

The graded response IRT model used does have limitations in addressing practical fit indices (specifically, lack of practical fit indices comparable to those established for CFA) (Reise et al., 1993). Additionally, the model specifications may lack refinement. The choice of IRT model employed may also be an issue. In the examination of Likert-type scale, it is assumed that the response categories can be ordered. In such an instance, the goal is to move beyond correct or incorrect answers to assess the level of discrimination, difficulty, and information provided by each item. Since POPS is a behaviorally anchored scale, there was no "guessing" allowed as might occur in objective tests. These factors supported the use of the graded response model (Samejima, 1969) as used in Reise et al. (1993). However, GRM model fitting techniques are not as refined as those in CFA, relying on heuristic measures and input from other preliminary analyses (Hambleton et al., 1991; Reise et al., 1993; Reise & Yu, 1990). Additionally, IRT is a large sample methodology and requires a large item pool (Harvey & Hammer, 1999). The combined sample size is 582 for this study. A larger Middle Eastern sample might have yielded improved results.

In spite of the limitations presented, CFA provides statistics on model fit and accounts for measurement error, while IRT takes into account item difficulty and makes full use of the data. Thus, IRT may provide additional information for assessing differential item functioning and bias across cultures. Increasing applications of IRT to cross-cultural survey type research can add rigor in testing the validity of measures in different cultural contexts, and may also resolve some of the methodological issues as the use of IRT models in behavioral research increases.

Implications for Practice

We recommend that future research test for measurement equivalence using multiple techniques since the convergence or nonconvergence of results can more fully inform our practice of employing measures developed in one culture to another. CFA modeling is quite popular and relatively simple to use and provides practical and statistical assessment of measurement equivalence. IRT models, on the other hand, have been developed in the context of a long history of psychometric theory that examines the processes involved when people answer questions (Thissen & Steinberg, 1988). The soundly developed theory behind IRT makes it a powerful tool, but it has not been completely translated from educational testing into the management research arena. As revealed in our literature review, our analyses are only one of a handful of studies that apply IRT modeling techniques. Within that set, this study joins a very short list of studies that have applied the graded response model for Likert-type response analysis. Needless to say, more studies employing techniques similar to those used here would be helpful in establishing IRT as a more viable methodology in behavioral, management, and cross-cultural research.

Part of the reason for lack of use of IRT has to do with the available parametrization programs that use the graded response model (Reise & Yu, 1990). Present computational programs, though much improved from past years, are still cumbersome to use and interpret. The lack of practical fit indices similar to those available in CFA (Reise et al., 1993) make interpretation of the IRT graded response models difficult as well. For example, in this paper, the G^2 statistic was used. The MULTILOG program for IRT reports this statistic as default. This statistic facilitates comparison between CFA and IRT modeling (Hambleton et al., 1991; Reise et al., 1993). However, there are many other statistics and techniques that could be used to establish equivalence in measurement but they do not facilitate comparison as is possible with the G^2 statistic (Reise et al., 1993; Thissen et al., 1986). IRT may become easier to implement and interpret when generally accepted fit indices and improved computer software are developed.

Discussion on the meaningful interpretation of research findings across cultures is more meaningful once measurement invariance is achieved. Therefore, establishing measurement invariance is an essential initial step in any cross-cultural comparison (Riordan & Vandenberg, 1994). The groundwork for equivalency of measurement lies in the analysis of the invariance of items as applied to culturally diverse groups. If items are found to be noninvariant across groups, the researcher may then choose to delete those items or retain them and interpret them in cultural context (Cheung & Rensvold, 1999).

Substantively, our results suggest that since relationships with supervisors in the United States may be characterized by more equality than those in the Middle East, political behavior may be less prevalent in the United States (or perceived as less). It is also important to note that behavior that might be characterized as political in the United States may be also be considered political in the Middle East, but there may be different levels of sensitivity to such issues. This has an important implication for the way that political behavior is perceived and described in either culture. Another factor that must be taken into account is the way that items are constructed in English or Arabic. Items developed in the United States may take into consideration the vernacular language practices and include slang terms or wording that may not easily be translated. The impact that the wording of items has on results discussed in cross-cultural research is important since it may be difficult to convey the same meaning once items are translated. Behaviors may occur within a different context or be perceived quite differently. Thus, it appears that the item discrimination bias between the United States and Middle East might be large. We might therefore expect that the application of a complete measure developed in the United States may contain items that may be equivalent (invariant) across cultures and others that are not. Thus, full measurement invariance may be very elusive in cross-cultural research.

It appears that through the use of CFA and IRT it is possible to identify measures that do not fulfill the requirements of full measurement invariance. Through further analyses, subscales that might be applied across cultures may be identified. The perceptions of organizational politics measure presented here, general political behavior, was assessed in two very different cultures, and, as expected could not be applied to individuals in those cultures without considering the underlying norms of the culture. We hope that by presenting the performance of one measure across these divergent cultures we have provided some insight on the differences that might exist. The findings presented here can be also applied to research that compares similar cultures. For example, researchers have described the U.S., British, and Australian cultures as similar with respect to managerial values (Clark & McCabe, 1970; Hofstede, 1980a). The results of this study imply that measures that are developed based on U.S values should not be assumed to be fully transferable to any other culture. Similarly, research suggests that the Middle East, India, and some Latin American cultures may be similar with respect to values such as equality in the work place (supervisor-subordinate interaction), risk avoidance, and collectivism (Scandura et al., 1998). Yet, in each case, a finer grained analysis (such as IRT) may suggest that the invariant items identified across cultures may not always be applied to other cultures without similar detailed analyses.

Establishing measurement equivalence is no longer an option. As shown here, based on CFA analysis alone, the POPS scale was shown to include an item that was noninvariant. Additionally, the information captured and used in CFA and IRT analyses are different and have serious implications for researchers involved in cross-cultural research. Thus, the application of both techniques is recommended as suggested by Reise et al. (1993). Conclusions drawn from cross-cultural research must be well informed and add to the knowledge and practice of management. However, the establishment of measurement equivalence is an important first step to establish meaningful cross-cultural comparisons.

AUTHOR NOTE

Correspondence should be addressed to the first author at: Management Department, School of Business Administration, University of Miami, 414D Jenkins Building, Coral Gables, FL 33124-9145. Tel.: (305) 284-3746, fax: (305) 284-3655, e-mail: scandura@miami.edu.

REFERENCES

Ali, A. (1999). Middle East competitiveness in the 21st century's global market. *Academy of Management Executive, 13,* 102-108.

Allen, D.B., Miller, E.D., & Nath, R. (1988). North America. In R. Nath (Ed.), *Comparative Management* (pp. 23-54). Cambridge, MA: Ballinger.

Badawy, M.K. (1980). Styles of Mideastern managers. *California Management Review, 22,* 51-58.

Bollen, K. (1989). *Structural equations with latent variables.* New York: Wiley & Sons.

Boyacigiller, N.A., & Adler, N.J. (1991). The parochial dinosaur: Organizational science in a global context. *Academy of Management Review, 16,* 262-290.

Brislin, R. (1980). Translation and content analysis of oral and written materials. In H.C. Triandis & J.W. Berry (Eds.), *Handbook of cross-cultural psychology: Methodology* (Vol. 2, pp. 389-444). Boston, MA: Allyn and Bacon.

Byrne, B.M., Shavelson, R.J., & Muthén, B. (1989). Testing for the equivalence of factor covariance and mean structures: The issue of partial measurement invariance. *Psychological Bulletin, 105,* 456-466.

Cheung, G.W., & Rensvold, R.B. (1999). Testing factorial invariance across groups: A reconceptualization and proposed new method. *Journal of Management, 25,* 1-27.

Clark, A., & McCabe, S. (1970). Leadership beliefs of Australian managers. *Journal of Applied Psychology, 54,* 1-6.

Cropanzano, R., Howes, J.C., Grandey, A.A., & Toth, P. (1997). The relationship of organizational politics and support to work behaviors, attitudes, and stress. *Journal of Organizational Behavior, 18,* 159-180.

Drory, A. (1993). Perceived political climate and job attitudes. *Organization Studies, 14,* 59-71.

Drory, A., & Romm, D. (1988). Politics in organization and its perception within the organization. *Organization Studies, 9,* 165-179.

Ellis, B.B., & Kimmel. H.D. (1992). Identification of unique cultural response patterns by means of item response theory. *Journal of Applied Psychology, 77,* 177-184.

Elsayed-Ekhouly, S.M., & Buda, R. (1996). Organizational conflict: A comparative analysis of conflict styles across cultures. *International Journal of Conflict Management, 7,* 71-81.

Fan, X. (1998). Item response theory and classical test theory: an empirical comparison of their item/person statistics. *Educational and Psychological Measurement, 58,* 357-381.

Fandt, P.M., & Ferris, G.R. (1990). The management of information and impressions: When employees behave opportunistically. *Organizational Behavior and Human Decision Processes, 45,* 140-158.

Farrell, D., & Peterson, J.C. (1982). Patterns of political behavior in organizations. *Academy of Management Review, 45,* 403-412.

Ferris, G., & Kacmar, K.M. (1992). Perceptions of organizational politics. *Journal of Management, 18,* 93-116.

Gandz, J., & Murray, V. (1980). The experience of workplace politics. *Academy of Management Journal, 23,* 237-251.

Gilmore, D.C., Ferris, G.F., Duhlebohn, J.H., & Harrell-Cook, G. (1996). Organizational politics and employee attendance. *Group and Organizational Management, 21,* 481-494.

Gray, B., & Ariss, S. (1985). Politics and strategic change across organizational life cycles. *Academy of Management Review, 10,* 707-723.

Hambleton, R.K., & Jones, R.W. (1993). Comparison of classical test theory and item response theory and their applications to test development. *Educational Measurement Issues and Practice, 12,* 38-47.

Hambleton, R.K., Swaminathan, H., & Rogers, H.J. (1991). *Fundamentals of item response theory.* Newbury Park, CA: Sage.

Harvey, R.J., & Hammer, A.L. (1999). Item response theory. *The Counseling Psychologist, 27,* 353-383.

Hofstede, G. (1980a). *Culture's consequences.* Beverly Hills, CA: Sage.

Hofstede, G. (1980b). Motivation, leadership, and organization: Do American theories apply abroad? *Organizational Dynamics, 8,* 42-63.

Hulin, C.L., Drasgow, F., & Parsons, C.K. (1983). *Item response theory application to psychological measurement.* Homewood, IL: Dow Jones-Irwin.

Hulin, C.L., & Mayer, L.J. (1986). Psychometric equivalence of a translation of the job descriptive index into Hebrew. *Journal of Applied Psychology, 71,* 83-94.

Ironson, G.H., & Subkoviak, M.J. (1979). A comparison of several methods of assessing item bias. *Journal of Educational Measurement, 16,* 209-225.

Jöreskog, K.G., & Sörbom, D. (1993a). *LISREL 8: User's reference guide.* Chicago: Scientific Software International.

Jöreskog, K.G., & Sörbom, D. (1993b). *LISREL 8: Structural equation modeling with the SIMPLIS command language.* Hillsdale, NJ: Erlbaum.

Kabanoff, B. (1997). Organizational justice across cultures: integrating organization-level and culture-level perspectives. In P.C. Earley & M. Erez (Eds.), *New perspectives on international/organizational psychology* (pp. 676-712). San Francisco: The New Lexington Press.

Kacmar, K.M., & Carlson, D.S. (1997). Further validation of the perceptions of politics scale (POPS): A multiple sample investigation. *Journal of Management, 23,* 627-658.

Kacmar, K.M., & Ferris, G. (1991). Perceptions of organizational politics scale (POPS): Development and construct validation. *Educational and Psychological Measurement, 51,* 193-205.

Kline, R. (1998). *Principles and practice of structural equation modeling.* New York: Guilford Press.

Kumar, P., & Ghadially, R. (1989). Organizational politics and its effects on members of organizations. *Human Relations, 42,* 305-314.

Lazarsfeld, P.F. (1950). The logical and mathematical foundation of latent structure analysis. In S.A. Stouffeer, L. Guttman, E.A. Suchman, P.F. Lazarsfeld, S.A. Star, & J.A. Clausen (Eds.), *Measurement and prediction* (pp. 362-472). New York: Wiley.

Lord, F.M. 1952. A theory of test scores. *Psychometric Monograph, No. 7.*

Lytle, A.L., Brett, J.M., Barsness, Z.I., Tinsley, C.H., & Janssens, M. (1995). A paradigm for confirmatory cross-cultural research in organizational behavior. In B.M. Staw & L.L. Cummings (Ed.), *Research in organizational behavior* (Vol. 17, pp. 167-214). Greenwich, CT: JAI Press.

Madison, D., Allen, R., Porter, L., Renwick, P., Mayes, B. (1980). Organizational politics: An exploration of managers' perceptions. *Human Relations, 33,* 79-100.

Medsker, G.J., Williams, L.J., & Holahan, P.J. (1994). A review of current practices for evaluating causal models in organizational behavior. *Journal of Management, 20,* 439-464.

Mirriam-Webster. (1995). *Mirriam-Webster's pocket dictionary.* Springfield, MA: Merriam-Webster, Incorporated.

Newman, K., & Nollen, S. (1996). Culture and congruence: The fit between management practices and national. culture. *Journal of International Business Studies, 27,* 753-779.

Parker, C., Dipboye, R., & Jackson, S. (1995). Perceptions of organizational politics: An investigation of antecedents and consequences. *Journal of Management, 21,* 891-912.

Pezeshkpur, C. (1978). Challenges to management in the Arab world. *Business Horizons, 21,* 47-55.

Reise, S.P., Widaman, K.F., & Pugh R.H. (1993). Confirmatory factor analysis and item response theory: Two approaches for exploring measurement invariance. *Psychological Bulletin, 114,* 552-566.

Reise, S.P., & Yu, J. (1990). Parameter recovery in the graded response model using MULTILOG. *Journal of Educational Measurement, 27,* 133-144.

Rensvold, R.B., & Cheung, G.W. (1998). Testing measurement models for factorial invariance: A systematic approach. *Educational and Psychological Measurement, 58,* 1017-1034.

Riordan, C.M., & Vandenberg R.J. (1994). A central question in cross-cultural research: Do employees of different cultures interpret work-related measures in an equivalent manner? *Journal of Management, 20,* 643-671.

Samejima, F. (1969). Estimation of latent ability using a response pattern of graded scores. *Psychometric Monograph, No. 17.*

Scandura, T.A., Williams, E.A., & Pillai, R. (1998). *Relationship between perceptions of organizational politics and procedural justice and job satisfaction in the U.S., Australia, India, Colombia and the Middle East* (pp. 80-82). Southern Management Association Proceedings. Atlanta, GA.

Sin, L.Y.M., Cheung, G.W.H., & Lee, R. (1999). Methodology in cross-cultural consumer research: A review and critical assessment. *Journal of International Consumer Marketing, 11*, 75-96.

Thissen, D. (1991). *MULTILOG: A User's Guide.* Mooresville, IN: Scientific Software Inc.

Thissen, D., & Steinberg, L. (1988). Data analysis using item response theory. *Psychological Bulletin, 104*, 385-395.

Thissen, D., Steinberg, L., & Gerrard, M. (1986). Beyond group mean differences: The concept of item bias. *Psychological Bulletin, 99*, 118-128.

Thissen, D., Steinberg, L., & Wainer, H. (1988). Use of item response theory in the study of group differences in trace lines. In H. Wainer & H.I. Braun (Eds.), *Test validity* (pp. 147-169). Hillsdale, NJ: Lawrence Erlbaum Associates

Trompenaars, F. (1994). *Riding the waves of culture: Understanding cultural diversity in business.* New York: Irwin.

Tushman, M.E. (1977). A political approach to organization: A review and rationale. *Academy of Management Review, 2*, 206-216.

Van de Rijt, B.A.M., Van Luit, J.E.H., & Pennings, A.H. (1999). The construction of the Utrecht early mathematical competence scales. *Educational and Psychological Measurement, 59*, 289-309.

Widaman, K.F. (1985). Hierarchically nested covariance structure models for multitrait multimethod data. *Applied Psychological Measurement, 9*, 1-26.

Windle, M., Iwawaki, S., & Lerner, R.M. (1988). Cross-cultural comparability or temperament among Japanese and American preschool children. *International Journal of Psychology, 23*, 547-567.

Wright, P. (1981). Organizational behavior in Islamic firms. *Management International Review, 21*, 86-94.

CHAPTER 6

IDENTIFYING THE SOURCES OF NONEQUIVALENCE IN MEASURES OF JOB SATISFACTION

Vida Scarpello and James C. Hayton

Abstract. The general purpose of this study is to identify the sources of non-equivalence in measures of job satisfaction. We examine the extent to which six popular measures of job satisfaction (*Job Descriptive Index; Short-form Minnesota Satisfaction Questionnaire; Hoppock Job Satisfaction Blank; Brayfield-Rothe Index of Job Satisfaction; Job In General Scale;* and a single-item, global measure) measure the same thing, and test three dominant explanations for the non-equivalence of measures: "time-frame orientation"; "alternative combinatory models"; and "omitted facets." Subjects are 579 employees of a regional healthcare organization in the United Kingdom. Statistical analysis reveals that occupation- and career-related considerations are included within general measures of satisfaction to a greater extent than within the facet-based measures, supporting the "omitted facets" explanation for nonequivalence. Implications for research are discussed.

INTRODUCTION

Since the earliest investigations in the 1920s, job satisfaction has perhaps become the most widely studied variable in Industrial/Organizational Psychology (Balzer & Smith, 1990). In 1976, Locke estimated that some 3,350 articles and dissertations had been written on the subject. A review of a database of psychological and sociological literature (PsycLit) since 1976 found a further 4,512 articles and dissertations referring to job satisfaction, giving a current estimate of approximately 8,000 published works referencing the subject. Job satisfaction has been studied as a dependent, independent, and moderator variable. It has been shown to be significantly related to life and family satisfaction (e.g., Frone, Russell, & Cooper, 1994; Brayfield, Wells, & Strate, 1957; Judge, Boudreau, & Bretz, 1994), job stress (e.g., Ironson, 1992), turnover (e.g., Mobley, 1977; Porter, Steers, Mowday, & Boulian, 1974; Schneider & Snyder, 1975), attendance (e.g., Scott & Taylor, 1985), propensity to vote for a union (e.g., Hamner & Smith, 1978; Schriesheim, 1978), organizational citizenship behaviors (e.g., Bateman & Organ, 1983; Moorman, 1993; Smith, Organ, & Near, 1983), and organizational commitment (e.g., O'Reilly & Caldwell, 1981). Roznowski and Hulin (1992) suggest that job satisfaction occupies a place in organizational behavior research similar to that of general intelligence, or "g," in general psychological research. While g influences what people are *able* to do, job satisfaction influences what people *choose* to do. Therefore, the usefulness of measures of g prior to organizational entry is paralleled by the usefulness of valid measures of job satisfaction after organizational entry (Roznowski & Hulin, 1992).

There are a number of definitions of the job satisfaction construct which, taken together, generally suggest that it is a pleasurable affective response to a match between the preferences for job rewards (called needs) (Weiss, Dawis, England, & Lofquist, 1967), values (Locke, 1976), and goals (Smith, Kendall, & Hulin, 1969) of an individual and the job reinforcers present in the work environment (Dawis, & Lofquist, 1984; Scarpello, 1980). Yet, despite these definitions, the concept of job satisfaction remains ambiguous (Landy, 1989; Tenopyr, 1993).

Possibly as a consequence of conceptual ambiguity a large number of measures of job satisfaction exist. One compendium of work related measures lists 17 measures of overall job satisfaction and a further 29 measures of work-facet satisfactions (Cook, Hepworth, Wall, & Warr, 1981). The large number of alternative measures has met criticism as a leading reason for a number of inconsistent results in the research literature (Kalleberg, 1974; O'Connor, Peters, & Gordon, 1978; Wanous & Lawler, 1972). There are also three general forms of job satisfaction measures: facet-based multi-item measures; multi-item measures of global job satisfaction; and single-item measures of global job satisfaction. Researchers interested in measuring job satisfaction must choose between one or some combination of these three forms. Complicating this choice is empirical evidence of the nonequivalence of the three forms of measures (e.g., Aldag & Brief, 1978; Brayfield, Wells, & Strate, 1957; Ferratt, 1981; Hoppock, 1935; Ironson et al., 1989; Kalleberg, 1974; Scarpello & Campbell, 1983a; Wanous & Lawler, 1972).

In the present study we (a) review exemplars of the three forms of job satisfaction measures, (b) describe and critique the dominant explanations for the nonequivalence of these measures, (c) examine the extent to which the most widely used job satisfaction measures are measuring the same thing, and (d) provide empirical evidence for the sources of their non-equivalence. Our review focuses on two multi-item facet-based measures, three multi-item global measures and one single-item global measure of job satisfaction. The specific instruments were selected according to both the frequency with which they are cited in a database of psychological and sociological literature (PsycLit) and the representativeness of their format. The two facet-based measures are the *Job Descriptive Index* (JDI: 274 references) (Smith, Kendall, & Hulin, 1969), and the *Minnesota Satisfaction Questionnaire* (MSQ: 127 references) (Weiss et al., 1967). The three multi-item measures of global job satisfaction are the *Hoppock Job Satisfaction Blank* ("Hoppock scale": 5 references) (Hoppock, 1935), the *Brayfield-Rothe Index of Job Satisfaction* ("B-R Index": 15 references) (Brayfield & Rothe, 1951) and the *Job in General Scale* (JIG: 1 reference) (Ironson et al., 1989). The single-item global measure is that used by Scarpello and Campbell (1983a, b). A review of the PsycLit database for the use of single-item global measures of job satisfaction revealed 11 references. Following a review of these measures we discuss the alternative explanations for nonequivalence that have been proposed and the evidence which supports these explanations.

THREE FORMS OF JOB SATISFACTION MEASURES

Facet-Based Job Satisfaction Scales

Facet-based scales such as the JDI (Smith et al., 1969) and MSQ (Weiss et al., 1967) attempt to measure satisfaction with specific aspects of the job such as supervision, pay, and co-workers. The rationale for using the sum of facet-based scales as a measure of overall job satisfaction is that "overall job satisfaction is the sum of the evaluations of the discriminable elements of which the job is composed" (Locke, 1969, p. 330).

The JDI has 72 items divided into 5 subscales (Work Itself—18 items; Pay—9 items; Supervision—18 items; Opportunities for Promotion—items; and Co-workers—18 items). The format is a list of adjectives with a three-point response scale of "yes," "no," or "undecided" for each item. Examples of items from the Work Itself subscale are "fascinating" and "routine."

In the field of organization behavior, researchers have credited the JDI with being the most carefully developed of the job satisfaction measures (Locke, 1976). It is also the most widely used measure (Yeager, 1981). Nevertheless, there has been some variation in the reported factorial structure of this measure. Although Smith et al. (1969) specified five factors, Smith, Smith, and Rollo (1974) found seven and Yeager (1981) reports nine factors. Drasgow and Miller (1982) and Hayton and Scarpello (1997) found that when five factors were specified, a number of items in the Work Itself subscale (frustrating, endless, hot, on your feet, and healthful) had near zero loadings on all factors. Drasgow and Miller (1982) also report that the Work Itself subscale is more highly correlated with organizational commitment, work-role centrality and overall satisfaction measured by a single-item global measure of job satisfaction (the G.M. Faces Scale; Kunin, 1955), than are the other four subscales. Ironson et al. (1989) report a correlation ($r = .79$) between the JDI-Work Itself subscale and the B-R Index, which is consistent with Drasgow and Miller's (1982) findings.

Of the six job satisfaction measures included in the present study, only the MSQ (Weiss et al., 1967) is grounded in a theory of job satisfaction. The Theory of Work Adjustment (TWA) proposes that job satisfaction is the result of a correspondence between preferences for job rewards (called needs) and the perceived availability of those job rewards. Minnesota Work Adjustment Project (MWAP) researchers developed instruments to measure the individual's job satisfaction (MSQ) (Weiss et al., 1967), preferences for job rewards (*Minnesota Importance Questionnaire*; MIQ) (Gay, Weiss, Hendel, Dawis, & Lofquist, 1971), and perceptions of available job rewards (*Minnesota Job Description Questionnaire*; MJDQ) (Borgen, Weiss, Tinsley, Dawis, & Lofquist, 1968). All three instruments (MIQ, MJDQ, MSQ) sample identical areas of worker concerns with respect to work preferences (needs), work reinforcers, and job satisfaction. The MSQ comes in two versions. The long form contains 20 scales, which sample 20 areas of worker satisfaction. The short form contains 20 items (one from each of the twenty scales). The short-form MSQ is typically used in job satisfaction research. The short-form MSQ usually factors into two factors: intrinsic and extrinsic (e.g., Bledsoe & Baber, 1979; Hauber & Bruininks, 1986), although other solutions have also been obtained. The items are anchored with a 1-5 Likert-like response format ranging from very dissatisfied to very satisfied. Responses on the items are summed to reflect general job satisfaction.

General Job Satisfaction Scales

General, or overall job satisfaction scales attempt to elicit overall feelings about the job. The Hoppock scale (Hoppock, 1935) is one of the oldest and best-known scales of general job satisfaction. The four items in the scale require the respondent to consider: (1) how well one likes the job; (2) how much of the time one feels satisfied with the job; (3) feelings about changing one's job and/or occupation; and (4) how one compares with others in liking/disliking the present job. The response format requires respondents to select one statement from a list of seven alternatives for each item. Hoppock (1935) reported a corrected split-half reliability of .93 and a correlation of .67 between the four item index and an aggregate score from a scale of approximately 200 specific items related to job satisfaction. McNichols, Stahl, and Manley (1978) found that the Hoppock scale exhibited high internal consistency (coefficient alpha ranged from .76 to .89), and loaded on a single underlying factor.

The B-R index (Brayfield & Rothe, 1951) contains 18 statements concerning feelings about one's work (e.g., "My job is like a hobby to me") anchored with a 1-5 strongly agree-strongly disagree response format. Validity of the B-R Index was inferred from the convergent correlation ($r =$ .92) between the B-R Index and the Hoppock scale.

The JIG scale (Ironson et al., 1989) uses an 18-item list of adjectives with a three-point categorical response format of yes, no, or undecided. Examples of adjectives included in the list are "pleasant" and "waste of time." The convergent validity of the JIG scale was assessed against the B-R Index ($r = .80$), the Faces scale (Kunin, 1955) ($r = .75$), an adjectival scale (adjectives which are prescaled for favorableness) (Ironson & Smith, 1981) ($r = .76$) and a numerical rating scale (-100 to $+100$) ($r = .67$).

Single-Item Global Measures of Job Satisfaction

Single-item global measures have been used infrequently in job satisfaction research (see Highhouse & Becker, 1993). These measures have typically been avoided for three reasons. The first is the traditional assumption that single-item measures are unreliable (e.g., Wanous & Lawler, 1972). Second, some researchers have argued that single-item measures of job satisfaction are too stable (Staines & Quinn, 1979; Weaver, 1980). These researchers note that results of a series of national surveys indicate little change in job satisfaction of American workers when measured by single-item questions of general job satisfaction. Third, it has been argued that single-item and scale measures of job satisfaction are inherently nonequivalent (Ironson et al., 1989; Smith et al., 1969; Smith, 1992) due to differences in the frame of reference used when responding to the single-item global measure and to the facet-based measure. Although there is consistent empirical support for nonequivalence of single-item and facet measures of satisfaction (Aldag & Brief, 1978; Ferratt, 1981; Highhouse & Becker, 1993; Ironson et al., 1989; Kalleberg, 1974; Scarpello & Campbell,

1983a), there is also evidence that multi-item measures of general satisfaction and facet-based measures are nonequivalent (Ash, 1954; Brayfield, Wells, & Strate, 1957; Ferratt, 1981; Hoppock, 1935; Ironson et al., 1989). Furthermore, the Minnesota TWA researchers have also encountered a large number of anomalous cases where people have either higher or lower job satisfaction (as measured by the sum of MSQ items and by single-item global measures of overall job satisfaction) than predicted by the match between their expressed reward preferences and perceptions of rewards available in their job environment (Rounds, Sloan, Dawis, & Lofquist, 1976; Scarpello, 1980; Scarpello & Campbell, 1983b). Nevertheless, in the majority of cases studied, the Minnesota researchers have been able to predict general job satisfaction from the degree of match between the individual's MIQ and MJDQ responses (Rounds et al., 1976; Scarpello, 1980). Thus, although the nonequivalence of the different forms of measures of job satisfaction has been demonstrated, there is no a priori reason to reject the use of single-item global measures of job satisfaction (Scarpello & Campbell, 1983a). The question to answer is "why are the different forms of job satisfaction measures not equivalent measures of the construct?"

CRITIQUE OF EXPLANATIONS FOR THE NONEQUIVALENCE BETWEEN MEASURES OF JOB SATISFACTION AND FACET-BASED MEASURES

Five explanations have been offered for the observed nonequivalence among job satisfaction measures. With respect to the observed nonequivalence of general scales of job satisfaction and facet-based scales, Ironson et al. (1989) suggest that general scales allow respondents to combine relevant aspects of the situation in whatever manner they choose. However, empirical evidence shows that alternative methods of combining facets mathematically make little or no difference in predictive power (Aldag & Brief, 1978; Ferratt, 1981). Aldag and Brief (1978) and Ferratt (1981) compared three alternative methods of combining job satisfaction facets: compensatory; conjunctive; and disjunctive. The compensatory model is the typical linear model, where a high score on one facet compensates for a low score on another. The nonlinear conjunctive model is a "multiple-hurdle" evaluation of satisfaction where a high score on all facets is needed for high overall job satisfaction. The nonlinear "disjunctive model" allows a high score on one facet to outweigh low scores on all other facets. Aldag and Brief (1978) concluded that the three models were equivalent. Ferratt (1981) reported marginal support for the linear compensatory model. Therefore, the facet combination explanation proposed by Ironson et al. (1989) does not seem to be supported by research.

Four explanations have been offered for the observed nonequivalence of single-item global measures of job satisfaction and facet-based measures: (a) the single-item measure is unreliable; (b) the single-item measure is insensitive to change; (c) the single-item measure is inherently nonequivalent to facet-based measures of job satisfaction because of frame-of-reference differences; and (d) facet-based measures of job satisfaction omit variables that comprise job satisfaction assessments and therefore are content deficient in measurement of the construct. These explanations are either no longer viable or have not been empirically examined.

First, the unreliability assumption for the single-item global measure has not been supported by empirical research (Aldag & Brief, 1978; Davis, 1987; Ferratt, 1981; Scarpello & Campbell, 1983a; Wanous et al., 1997). Furthermore, a 1997 meta-analysis of correlations between single-item global measures of job satisfaction and scale measures, estimates that the *minimum* reliability of single-item global measures is close to .70 (Wanous et al., 1997, p. 250).

Second, single-item global measures of job satisfaction have been shown to be relatively stable but not too stable (Wanous et al., 1997). We suggest that some stability for the measures is desirable, as these measures have been found to be more inclusive measures of the construct's content domain (Scarpello & Campbell, 1983a) than are summations of many facet satisfactions. In addition, stability in single-item measures of global job satisfaction may be expected if variability in work-facet satisfactions is masked by the compensatory combination of facets in evaluations of overall satisfaction.

Third, JDI researchers have suggested that single-item and scale measures of job satisfaction are inherently nonequivalent because they evoke a different frame of reference (Smith, 1992; Ironson et al., 1989; Smith et al., 1969; Ryan & Smith, 1954, p. 409). Specifically, Ironson et al. (1989, p .5) have suggested that the JIG scale is explicitly "intended to differ from the JDI in three important respects: more global, more evaluative and longer in time frame" (Ironson et al., 1989, p. 195). In 1998, however, Smith and Stanton retracted this position. They note that "although psychologists can define description and evaluation as different response modes, for the purposes of measuring job satisfaction, respondents make no such separation. Most adjectives seem to contain an inherent evaluative component, and those few that are truly 'neutral' are not very useful for assessing individual differences" (Smith & Stanton, 1998, p. 374). Consequently, although individuals use a frame of reference when responding to job satisfaction questionnaires, Smith and Stanton (1998) acknowledge that the evaluative or descriptive format is not the cause of the observed nonequivalence between single-item and scale measures of general job satisfaction and facet-based measures of the construct. The JDI researchers, however, have not retracted their position that facet-based measures evoke a short time-frame orientation and global measures evoke a longer time-frame orientation in assessments of job satisfaction. This explanation for nonequivalence has not been empirically examined.

Fourth, Scarpello (1980) suggested that the nonequivalence between the single-item global measures and facet-based measures of job satisfaction may be due to the omission of occupational and career concerns in facet-based measures, as these variables may be partly responsible for subjects' assessments of how well the job and job situation fulfills their work-related desires, goals, and values. In a series of studies involving highly diverse samples of subjects, Scarpello and her colleagues attempted to determine whether occupational and career perceptions explain the reasons for the nonequivalence of facet-based and global measures of job satisfaction (Scarpello, 1980; Scarpello & Campbell, 1983a, b; Davis, 1987; Scarpello & Vandenberg, 1992). They found that individuals' views about their occupations and careers explained job satisfaction above and beyond that explained by a match between expressed preferences for job rewards and perceptions of available rewards. They also found that occupational and career views explained job satisfaction above and beyond that explained by the sum of the 20 MSQ facet satisfactions. Specifically, using a sample of highly educated industrial research and development scientists and engineers, Scarpello and Campbell (1983b) found that primary motivation for occupational entry (individuals have numerous motivations for occupational entry), psychological attachment (commitment) to one's occupational choice, type of perceived barrier to occupational change, perceived rate of career progress relative to one's own goal for progress, and satisfaction with career progress differentiated individuals into four quadrants. Quadrant (1) individuals were satisfied with their jobs when their expressed needs matched perceptions of available rewards. Quadrant (2) individuals were satisfied with their jobs when their expressed needs did not match perceptions of available rewards. Quadrant (3) individuals were dissatisfied with their jobs when their expressed needs matched perceptions of available rewards. Quadrant (4) individuals were dissatisfied with their jobs when their expressed needs did not match perceptions of available rewards. Moreover, individuals whose expressed needs matched their perceptions of available rewards (Quadrants 1 & 3) indicated that their primary motivation for occupational entry was interest in the work itself; they were psychologically committed to their occupational choices; and they had no barriers to occupational change. In contrast, individuals whose expressed needs did not match their perceptions of available rewards (Quadrants 2 & 4) indicated that their primary motivation for occupational entry was extrinsic (pay, ease of entry, influence of significant others); they were not psychologically committed to their occupational choices; and perceived a variety of personal and societal barriers to occupational change. Furthermore, individuals who were satisfied with their jobs (Quadrants 1 & 2) perceived their careers to be progressing at rates consistent with their personal goals for progress and were satisfied with career progress, whereas the dissatisfied (Quadrants 3 & 4) indicated slower career progress than their personal goals for progress and were dissatisfied with career progress. A constructive replication study with manufacturing plant employees (Scarpello & Vandenberg, 1992) confirmed the Scarpello and Campbell (1983b) findings.

Scarpello and Campbell (1983a) also showed that predispositions toward the occupation and career contributed to variance explained in overall job satisfaction, as measured by the one-item measure of global satisfaction, "In general, how satisfied are you with your job?" Davis (1987) showed that this single-item measure of job satisfaction correlates more strongly with general measures of job satisfaction and measures of occupational and career perceptions than it does with the short-form MSQ facet-based measure of job satisfaction.

Other researchers also have noted that general measures of job satisfaction allow respondents to consider factors not included in facet-based scales (e.g., Ferratt, 1981; Highhouse & Becker, 1993; Hoppock, 1935; Ironson et al., 1989; Schneider, Gunnarson, & Wheeler, 1992; Smith et al., 1969; Smith, 1992). As early as 1935, Hoppock suggested that factors extraneous to the job may be fundamental causes of job satisfaction, arguing that the "mere summation of satisfaction with various aspects of the job is not equivalent with satisfaction with the job as a whole" (1935, p. 274). In support of this argument Hoppock noted the moderate correlation ($r = .67$) between an inductively derived scale of specific satisfactions and his four item *Job Satisfaction Blank.* Indeed, the principal developer of the JDI (Smith, 1992) recognizes that general satisfaction measures include considerations that are not under the organization's control. Smith (1992, p. 5) notes "general job satisfaction involves components not caused by the immediate job situation." Furthermore, the JDI developers intentionally constructed the JDI scale to focus only on those aspects of the job situation which "help target the kinds of changes needed in particular situations and provides the ability to evaluate the success of interventions designed to improve satisfaction" (Smith, 1992, p. 7). Thus, nonequivalence between the single-item global measure of job satisfaction and the JDI facet-based measure was produced intentionally.

Except for the work-itself scale, the intention to use the JDI solely as diagnostic tool for organization-based interventions restricted the measurement of the construct to dimensions under the control of management. The fact that the JDI intentionally assesses only a portion of the construct of job satisfaction is not obvious from writings by JDI researchers or by the overwhelmingly accepted definition of job satisfaction proposed by Smith's student Edwin Locke. Specifically, Locke (1969, p. 316) defined job satisfaction as the *"pleasurable emotional state resulting from the appraisal of one's job as achieving or facilitating the achievement of one's job values. Job dissatisfaction is the unpleasurable emotional state resulting from the appraisal of one's job as frustrating or blocking the attainment of one's job values or as entailing disval-*

ues. Job satisfaction and dissatisfaction are a function of the perceived relationship between what one wants from one's job and what one perceives it as offering or entailing" (emphasis added). This definition of job satisfaction suggests a proactive rather than a reactive assessment of the job and one's job situation. It implies that the individual considers the job within the context of his/her personal values (or preferences, in the Theory of Work Adjustment).

Scarpello and colleagues (Scarpello, 1980; Scarpello & Campbell, 1983a, b; Davis, 1987; Scarpello & Vandenberg, 1992) suggested that two important work values, not explicitly measured by facet-based job satisfaction scales (although they may be captured to varying degrees in facet-based measures) (see Scarpello & Campbell, 1983a) are motivations for occupational choices and career aspirations. Their findings that, in addition to job-related facets, predispositions toward the occupation and career influence assessments of overall job satisfaction are consistent with research by Kalleberg (1974), Graen, Orris, and Johnson (1973), and Petty, McGee, and Cavender (1984). Kalleberg (1974) found that in addition to loading on the job satisfaction factor, a single-item measure of job satisfaction also loaded significantly on occupational status and educational attainment. Although Kalleberg interpreted this as a sign of invalidity for the single-item measure (1974, p. 317), an alternative explanation is that individual predispositions toward occupation and career are included within the set of variables considered in evaluations of overall job satisfaction. In support of this alternative explanation, Graen et al. (1973) present evidence that role orientation, the extent to which an individual feels the job to be relevant to his or her career, is significantly related to global job satisfaction and job performance.

The idea that occupation and career variables influence assessments of overall job satisfaction is also supported by the observed correlations among the general job satisfaction scales and the behavior of the JDI Work Itself scale and the JIG scale. Specifically, The JDI Work Itself scale correlates strongly with the JIG scale ($r = .78$) (Ironson et al., 1989), which also correlates strongly with the Hoppock scale ($r = .73$) (McNichols et al., 1978). In the Hoppock scale, the alternative responses in the third item explicitly differentiate between occupational and job change considerations: "I would like to change *both* my job and occupation" and "I would like to exchange my present job for another *in the same line of work*" (emphasis added). The JDI Work Itself scale focused on the nature of work performed (e.g., work on the present job is: fascinating; boring; respected; useful) and therefore appears to measure intrinsic occupational preferences (needs in Theory of Work Adjustment). Similarly, the Brayfield-Rothe Index (B-R Index) was validated on night-school students of personnel management. Brayfield and Rothe (1951) hypothesized that the night-school students of personnel management who also worked in that *occupation* would have higher job satisfaction than those students who did not work in that *occupation*. Their hypothesis was supported, which suggests that the B-R Index captures the measurement of *occupational* concerns. Given that the B-R Index appears to measure occupational concerns, the observed correlation between the B-R Index and the JIG scale ($r = .80$) (Ironson et al., 1989) further suggests that occupational considerations may be reflected in the JIG scale.

Finally, in a meta-analytic study of the relationship between individual job satisfaction and performance, Petty et al. (1984) report stronger correlations between global job satisfaction measures and performance than between facet-based measures and performance. If the thesis is correct that assessments of overall job satisfaction include occupation- and career-related considerations, and that the relationship between satisfaction and performance is dependent upon occupational and career considerations (Graen et al., 1973), then the stronger correlation found by Petty et al. (1984) may be explained by the inclusion of these considerations in assessments of general job satisfaction as measured by one-item global measures of the construct.

THIS STUDY'S PURPOSE AND QUESTIONS

The general purpose of this study is to identify the sources of nonequivalence of measures of job satisfaction and the extent to which the six measures reviewed here measure the same thing. Our specific research questions directly address three alternative explanations for the observed nonequivalence of job satisfaction measures. The reliability of single-item global measures of job satisfaction is already supported by empirical research and the stability issue has been dealt with logically and empirically. Thus, this investigation focuses on (a) the time-frame orientation explanation for nonequivalence, (b) a further examination of the facet combination evidence and the omitted variable evidence, and (c) the extent to which failure to measure occupational and career concerns contributes to the observed nonequivalence of job satisfaction measures.

> **Question 1.** Does the pattern of correlations among the six job satisfaction measures support the time-frame orientation explanation for nonequivalence?

The time-frame orientation argument proposes that individuals respond differently to facet-based measures than they do to general measures of job satisfaction because the former evoke a shorter time-frame orientation and the latter a longer time-frame orientation (Ironson et al., 1989; Smith et al., 1969). If this is correct, then we can expect the correlation between the JDI and the MSQ to be stronger than the correlations between these measures and the four general job satisfaction measures (JIG, B-R Index, Hoppock scale, and single-item global measure).

Question 2. Do different methods of combining facets (compensatory; conjunctive; disjunctive) influence the ability of facet-based measures (JDI and MSQ) to predict general job satisfaction measured by the single-item, the Hoppock scale, the B-R Index and the JIG scale?

If one of the nonlinear models of combining job satisfaction facets accounts for more variance in overall job satisfaction than the compensatory model typically used, this would reflect a superior paramorphic representation of the underlying cognitive process. If no method is significantly better at predicting overall satisfaction, then an alternative explanation for nonequivalence must be sought.

The third explanation for nonequivalence proposes that facet-based measures omit important considerations that are included in evaluations of overall job satisfaction. Based on our review, this study investigates whether or not a major cause of nonequivalence among measures of job satisfaction is the extent to which they are influenced by predispositions toward occupation- and career-related variables. This leads us to two questions.

Question 3. Do the job satisfaction measures exhibit convergent and discriminant validity when compared with occupation- and career-related variables?

This question is important for two reasons. First, to the extent that the job satisfaction measures include similar content they will exhibit satisfactory convergent validity among themselves. Second, to the extent that occupational and career-related considerations are included in some of these measures of job satisfaction, the satisfaction measures will be correlated with the measures of these non-job variables, and will therefore fail to exhibit satisfactory discriminant validity.

Question 4. Which of the job satisfaction scales is most content valid— as demonstrated by predicting job satisfaction measured by the single-item general measure of job satisfaction?

If job satisfaction includes considerations of occupation and career views, then measures that include these considerations will be more content valid than measures that do not. One way to assess the content validity of an attitudinal measure is to compare it with another measure of the same construct. Because the ultimate criterion for an attitudinal measure is "present attitude," both content and predictive validity can be established simultaneously by using a criterion-related validation strategy and regression analysis (see the method used by Scarpello & Vandenberg, 1987, in the development of the satisfaction with the supervisor scale). In this approach the single-item global measure of the construct is used as the criterion variable and the scales are used as predictors. In contrast with scale measures, the use of a single-item, global measure of the job satisfaction criterion assumes that the respondent knows the relevant components and their relative importance in evaluating his or her overall attitude toward the job. Given the difficulty of determining, a priori, the content domain of job satisfaction, single-item global measures of job satisfaction provide a useful criterion against which to evaluate the content validity of multiple-item scales. To the extent that occupation- and career-related variables contribute to the variance explained in the single-item measure of job satisfaction over and above that accounted for by a scale measure of job satisfaction, we can conclude that these considerations are not already included within that scale. Furthermore, we can infer that the frame of reference the individual uses in assessing job satisfaction is the extent to which the job and job situation fulfill the individual's occupational and career desires, values, and goals.

METHOD

Subjects

Subjects are 579 (20%) employees of a publicly funded regional health-care organization in Southeast England. The organization has thirteen "directorates" ranging from critical care to facilities maintenance. Sample demographics were as follows: 81% female; median age 37 years; 40% employed more than 30 hours/week. The sample demographics are representative of the population, which was 87% female, median age between 35 and 44 years, and 47% employed more than 30 hours/week.

Procedure

The organization distributed 2,000 questionnaires via interoffice mail to randomly selected employees across the 13 directorates. Random selection, across directorates, was the preferred sampling approach of the organization, which selected the sample and sent the questionnaires to the employees. Cover letters from both the Human Resources Department of the organization and the researchers assured respondents of confidentiality and encouraged them to complete the questionnaire. Completed questionnaires were returned in sealed envelopes via interoffice mail to a central hospital location where they were collected and sent to the researchers.

Measures

The constructs measured in this study were job satisfaction, occupational identification, motivation for occupational choice, perceived barriers to occupational change, occupational commitment, and perceptions of career progress.

As stated, job satisfaction was measured by one single-item global measure, three multi-item general scales and two facet-based scales. The single-item global measure of job satisfaction was "How satisfied are you with your job *in general?*" (Highhouse & Becker, 1993; Scarpello & Campbell, 1983a). This item was anchored with a 1-5 Likert-like rating scale ranging from very dissatisfied to very satisfied. The three general job satisfaction scales were the *Hoppock Job Satisfaction Blank* (Hoppock, 1935), the *Brayfield-Rothe Index of Job Satisfaction* (Brayfield & Rothe, 1951), and the *Job In General* scale (Ironson et al., 1989). The two facet-based job satisfaction measures were the *Job Descriptive Index* (Smith et al., 1969) and the short-form *Minnesota Satisfaction Questionnaire* (Weiss et al., 1967).

Occupational views were measured by one single-item and three scale measures. The single-item measure required respondents to indicate their occupational identification by choosing one of three response categories: (1) this is the best possible occupation for me; (2) this is my preferred occupation; or (3) this is not my preferred occupation (Scarpello & Campbell, 1983a; Davis, 1987; Scarpello & Vandenberg, 1992). The three scale measures assessed motivations for occupational choice, barriers to occupational change, and occupational commitment.

The *Motivation for Occupational Choice* scale (MOC)(Davis, 1987) is a 29-item scale which is concerned with the perceived reasons for choosing the occupation. The response format is a five-point Likert-like scale indicating agreement with each item from "not at all" to "to a large extent." The scale includes both extrinsic motives (e.g., I chose this occupation because I needed to make money), and intrinsic motives (e.g., I thought this occupation would allow me to work independently).

The *Barriers to Occupational Change* scale (BOC) (Davis, 1987; Scarpello & Vandenberg, 1992) is an 11-item scale with five-point response format reflecting degree of agreement with each item. The scale measures the attributions an individual makes about perceived barriers to occupational change. These include internal barriers (e.g., I'm too old to change now), external personal barriers (e.g., I have too many family commitments to change now), societal barriers (e.g., I can't change because it's not what you do but what education or training you have that counts) and no barriers (e.g., I love the kind of work I do).

Occupational commitment was measured using a modified version of the nine item *Organizational Commitment Questionnaire* (OCQ) (Mowday, Steers, & Porter, 1979). The original items were altered by substituting the term "occupation" for the term "organization" (Scarpello & Vandenberg, 1992). The seven-point Likert scale response format ranged from "strongly disagree" to "strongly agree."

Influences on career satisfaction were measured by the *Perceptions of Career* scale (POC) (Davis, 1987). This is a 26-item scale which measures influences on career satisfaction. The response format reflects agreement with each statement in a five-point Likert-like rating format. Five subscales measure the different influences on career satisfaction: supervisor influence; societal equity comparisons; company facilitation; status/influence comparisons; occupational equity comparisons. These subscales each use one of two sets of anchors: from "not at all" to "a very large extent," and from "never" to "always." Examples of items are "When evaluating my career progress, I compare my pay to the pay of others in different occupations" and "When evaluating my career progress, I compare myself to others in the same type of job."

Statistical Analyses

Zero order correlations were computed for each of the study's variables. Cronbach's (1951) coefficient alpha internal consistency reliability was calculated for responses to each scale.

Exploratory factor analysis was conducted to verify each scale's factor structure. Confirmatory factor analysis was not used due to either limited evidence or evidence for inconsistent factor structures for some of the measures used in this study. Specifically, the Hoppock scale and the B-R Index have very limited evidence for their structures. The MSQ is relatively stable in terms of prior work, finding 2 factors (but even this is not unanimous). The JDI has had very diverse results, ranging from 5 to 9 factors (see Yeager, 1981). The dimensionality of each scale was examined using both principal components and principal axis analysis. Although traditionally the "mineigen greater than one rule" (Guttman, 1954; Kaiser, 1960) has been used as a factor retention criterion, it has been consistently found to overestimate the number of factors to retain (e.g., Zwick & Velicer, 1982, 1986). Therefore, the scree test (Catell, 1960; Cattell & Jaspers, 1967) was used to identify the number of factors to retain. The resulting components were subjected to oblique (Oblimin) rotation (SPSS default delta value of zero) and examined for simple structure (Thurstone, 1947).

The results of both factor analysis were very nearly identical. The Hoppock scale was found to be unidimensional. Although the B-R Index and the JIG scale were initially found to have two factors, examination of the items in the two factors revealed that these reflected positive and negative item wording and a near simple structure was obtained for a unidimensional solution. The MSQ was found to possess two factors (Intrinsic Satisfaction, $\alpha = .84$ and Extrinsic Satisfaction, $\alpha = .78$). The JDI was found to exhibit five factors Work Itself = .78; Coworkers, $\alpha = .87$; Pay, $\alpha = .81$; Promotions, $\alpha = .80$; Supervision, $\alpha = .89$) as suggested by Smith et al. (1969).

For the remaining measures, factor analysis revealed five factors for the *Motivation for Occupational Choice* scale (Intrinsic Motivations, $\alpha = .89$; Knowledge of the Occupation, $\alpha = .82$; Ease of Entry, $\alpha = .70$; Flexibility, $\alpha = .71$; and Family and Social Influences, $\alpha = .62$); five factors, relating to sources of information about career progress (Supervisor Influence, $\alpha = .89$; Company Facilitation, $\alpha = .88$; Societal Equity Comparisons, $\alpha = .90$; Equity-Within-Occupations, $\alpha = .90$; Status and Influence, $\alpha = .86$) were also found for the *Perceptions of Career* scale; and four factors were found for the *Barriers to Occupational Change* scale (Societal Barriers, $\alpha = .81$; External Personal Barriers, $\alpha = .66$; No Perceived Barriers, $\alpha = .78$; and Internal Personal Barriers, $\alpha = .77$). Overall, the obtained factor structures of all measures reflected those suggested by prior research and theory (Brayfield & Rothe, 1951; Davis, 1987; Hoppock, 1935; Ironson et al., 1989; Scarpello & Vandenberg, 1992; Smith et al., 1969; Weiss et al., 1967). Furthermore, all items were retained on the scales. These data provide evidence that this study's measures are applicable to subjects in England as they are to subjects in the United States.

Total scale scores were used for all measures except barriers to occupational change (which consists of two scales: barriers to occupational change and no barrier). Summation of composite scores measuring a single underling construct is an acceptable and common research practice. Although it would have been interesting to assess the dimensions of Motivation for Occupational Choice and Perception of Career scales individually, this could not be done due to sample size limitations (with the cross-validation strategy employed). Given that these scales are multidimensional, using summation scores is likely to produce lower correlations between them and the other measures in the study. However, summation scores are equivalent to using unit weights and these replicate better in multiple regression analyses than do fractional weights.

The three alternative methods of combining the facets of the MSQ and JDI, examined by Aldag and Brief (1978), were compared: (1) the linear compensatory model, which represents overall job satisfaction as the weighted sum of facet scores; (2) the nonlinear conjunctive model (Einhorn, 1970), which reflects a "multiple hurdles" approach where low satisfaction on any facet results in low overall job satisfaction; and (3) the nonlinear disjunctive model, in which high satisfaction on one facet may offset low satisfaction on other facets. The three facet combination models were compared using multiple regression. The facet scores from each facet-based scale were used as independent variables. Each of the four measures of general job satisfaction were used as the dependent variable in these models.

The convergent and discriminant validities of the total scores on each of the six job satisfaction measures (four general and two facet-based measures) were assessed against each other and against six occupational and career concerns (occupational commitment, occupational identification, motivation for occupational choice, perceptions of career, barriers to occupational change and no barriers to occupational change). Convergent and discriminant validities were assessed by using Campbell and Fiske's (1959) multitrait-multimethod (MTMM) procedure and by calculating fidelity coefficients (Drasgow & Miller, 1982). The original correlational approach to MTMM has been criticized for the lack of quantitative criteria for the acceptable level of convergent validity and its inability to detect common method variance (Cote, Buckley, & Best, 1987; Schmitt, Coyle, & Saari, 1977). A solution to this involves computing the fidelity coefficient r for each scale (where r is the correlation between the scale's items and the scale factor structure). Computation of fidelity coefficients followed the model and procedures outlined by Drasgow and Miller (1982). Specifically, items on each measure were analyzed by principal-axis factor analysis. The factor structure matrix, a diagonal matrix of item standard deviations, and an n x 1 vector of ones and zeros (one for each factor and its items) was used to obtain fidelity coefficients for each factor. The magnitude of this coefficient reflects the influence of random measurement error, item specific variance, and scale items which load on factors other than that which the scale is attempting to measure. To the extent that these effects are present the fidelity coefficient is reduced. Drasgow and Miller (1982) suggest that a fidelity coefficient value of equal to or greater than .90 indicates convergent validity. The range of minimum acceptable convergent validity coefficients was computed as to $2r^2 - 1$, where r is the obtained fidelity coefficient. Fidelity coefficients were computed for each job satisfaction measure. The modeling of common method variance can only be overcome using alternative approaches such as analysis of variance (ANOVA) (Kavanagh, McKinney, & Wolins, 1971) and confirmatory factor analysis (CFA) (e.g., Widaman, 1985). This was not feasible because multiple measures were not available for constructs other than job satisfaction.

Full and reduced regression analysis was used to determine the extent to which the job satisfaction measures already include occupation- and career-related considerations. A full model was constructed for each job satisfaction measure and included the occupation- and career-related variables. Reduced models excluded each of these variables in turn. Unique variance contributed by the occupational and career variables was indicated by the change in R^2. Prior to the analysis, the sample was randomly split into two groups of size $n_1 = 281$ and $n_2 = 298$ so that the regression models could be cross-validated (Note: the uneven sample sizes are an artifact of the method used by SPSS. When randomly sampling "approximately 50% of cases" SPSS literally gives an approximate rather than an exact split). Result replicability was assessed empirically by use of the Chow test (Chow, 1960). The Chow test is an application of the general linear F-test, which provides a check on the stability of the parameter estimates across samples. A nonsignificant F statistic indicates that the parameter estimates are stable and therefore replicable.

Following the ordinary least squares (OLS) regression analysis the data were checked to ensure that model assumptions were not violated. Commonly known as BLUE (Best Linear Unbiased Estimator) analysis, this involved checking that the studentized residuals are normally distributed, that the predictors are linearly related to the criterion, and that the variance of the residuals is constant. Residual analysis is important from the perspective of testing that the data meet the assumptions of the linear model. The assumptions of the linearity of the relationship between the dependent and independent variables, the normality of the distribution of the dependent variables, homoscedasticity, and independence of the predictor variables must all be met if the model is to provide efficient and unbiased estimates of the parameters of interest. With a discrete polychotomous dependent variable, graphical analysis for constant error variance was impractical. Although White's statistical test for heteroscedasticity (White, 1980) resulted in a failure to reject the null hypothesis of homoscedasticity, this is a weak test (Greene, 1990). A regression of the squared residuals upon the predicted values resulted in a statistically significant prediction of the squared error variance (sample 1: $R^2 = .037$, $p < .01$; sample 2: $R^2 = .047$, $p < .001$), indicating that the error variances were not constant. Violation of this assumption meant that we could not rely upon statistical tests and confidence intervals from OLS, and also that OLS was not the most efficient model for these data.

A common solution to this problem is the application of weighted least squares regression (WLS) (Cohen & Cohen, 1983; Greene, 1990). A two-stage least squares regression model was constructed for the first sample in order to evaluate the most appropriate weight for WLS. The resulting WLS regression model was rechecked to confirm that error variances were now constant ($R^2 = .00$, $F = .01$; n.s.). Application of the same weighting to the second sample also eliminated the heteroscedasticity ($R^2 = .00$, $F = .31$; n.s.). Graphical and statistical analysis (the Kolmogorov-Smirnov test) showed that the standardized residuals were normally distributed in both groups. Graphical analysis of the partial residuals also showed that the relationships between predictors and criterion were linear. None of the variables fell beyond the multicollinearity thresholds for either group. Therefore, we can make reliable inferences about the individual regression coefficients. The results reported below are therefore for the WLS regression models.

RESULTS

Table 1 shows the means, standard deviations and correlations among the study's variables. Coefficient alpha reliabilities for the scores on each scale are shown in the diagonal (subscale score alpha coefficients are noted below).

Results of analysis to answer the study's four questions are presented in Tables 1 through 4.

Question 1 asked whether the time-frame orientation argument for nonequivalence of measures is supported by the pattern of correlations among the six job satisfaction measures. As seen from Table 1, there is no support for the Smith et al. (1969) contention that time-frame orientation influences assessment of job satisfaction and therefore the nonequivalence of general and facet-based measure responses. Although the correlation between the JDI and MSQ (both short-time frame measures) is .67, the correlation between the JIG (a long time-frame measure) and the JDI (a short time-frame measure) is .66. Furthermore, although the correlation between the JIG (long time-frame measure) and MSQ (short time-frame measure) is weaker ($r = .60$) than that the correlation between the JDI and MSQ ($r = .67$), the correlation between the MSQ (short time-frame measure) and the single item global measure (long time-frame measure) is .68. That correlation is stronger than the correlation between the JIG and the single item global measure ($r = .63$) (both long time-frame measures).

Question 2 asked whether different methods of combining facets (compensatory; conjunctive; and disjunctive) influence the ability of facet-based measures (JDI and MSQ) to predict general job satisfaction measured by the single-item, the Hoppock scale, the B-R Index, and the JIG scales. As seen in Table 2, the disjunctive model is inferior to the other two models. In three cases, the regression of the single-item global measure, the regression of the Hoppock scale, and the regression of the B-R Index on the JDI, the conjunctive model explains between 1 and 4% more variance in job satisfaction than explained by the compensatory model. However, even for the JDI, the largest amount of variance explained resulted from regressing the JIG scale on the JDI using the compensatory model. Furthermore, the compensatory model is consistently best for the MSQ. Thus, consistent with Aldag and Brief (1978) and Ferratt (1981) we find no advantage accrues to the conjunctive or disjunctive models over the usual compensatory model.

Question 3 asked whether job satisfaction measures exhibit convergent and discriminant validity, when compared with occupational and career

Table 1.   Means, Standard Deviations and Intrecorrelations Among Variablesa

Scale	M	SD	1	2	3	4	5	6	7	8	9	10	11	12
1. Single-Item Job Satisfaction	3.81	0.88	N/A.b											
2. Hoppock Scale	19.74	3.33	**.69**	.80										
3. Brayfield-Rothe Index	65.70	9.55	**.69**	**.81**	.89									
4. Job in General Scale	40.80	10.43	**.63**	**.69**	**.72**	.89								
5. Job Descriptive Index	130.01	30.47	**.48**	**.47**	**.53**	**.66**	.91							
6. Minnesota Satisfaction Questionnaire	73.39	10.21	**.68**	**.57**	**.63**	**.60**	**.67**	.88						
7. Occupational Commitment	43.14	10.33	*.55*	*.67*	*.69*	*.64*	*.50*	*.56*	.88					
8. Occupational Identification	1.96	0.73	*-.35*	*-.43*	*-.47*	*-.39*	*-.35*	*-.35*	*-.56*	N/A.b				
9. Motivation for Occupational Choice	77.30	15.15	*.26*	*.25*	*.28*	*.27*	*.24*	*.34*	*.38*	*-.26*	.86			
10. Perceptions of Career	66.94	15.95	*.16*	*.09**	*.17*	*.20*	*.31*	*.30*	*.24*	*-.14*	*.28*	.91		
11. Barriers to Occupational Change	15.25	4.89	*-.17*	*-.15*	*-.23*	*-.14*	*-.21*	*-.16*	*-.21*	*.23*	*-.00*	*-.07*	.78	
12. No barriers to Occupational Change	5.41	1.98	*.45*	*.58*	*.56*	*.49*	*.33*	*.42*	*.63*	*-.58*	*.32*	*.13*	*-.10**	.74

Notes: * = p < .05; All other coefficients significant (p < .001). Bold type indicates convergent validity coefficients; italic type indicates discriminant validity coefficients;

aValues in the diagonal are Cronbach's (1951) Coefficient Alpha;

bNo reliability estimate available for single-item measures.

Table 2. R^2 for Linear and Nonlinear Methods of Combining Job Satisfaction Facet Scores

Independent Variables	Single-Item Job Satisfaction	Hoppock Scale	B-R Index	JIG Scale
		Dependent Variables		
Compensatory model				
JDI	.35	.40	.49	.56
MSQ	.48	.34	.42	.38
Conjunctive model				
JDI	.36	.41	.53	.43
MSQ	.44	.32	.39	.28
Disjunctive model				
JDI	.30	.38	.46	.41
MSQ	.42	.32	.39	.27

Note: All coefficients significant ($p < .001$).

variables. The multitrait-multimethod correlation matrix (Table 1) shows that by all four Campbell and Fiske (1959) criteria, the six measures of job satisfaction do not converge with each other. The general measures converge with each other. The MSQ converges with the single-item general measure of job satisfaction and also with the JDI. The JDI converges with the JIG and the MSQ. Although the correlations of the job satisfaction measures are all significantly different from zero, the JDI exhibits the lowest correlations among the job satisfaction measures. The quantitative evidence for convergent validity is shown by the fidelity coefficient and minimum acceptable convergent validity coefficients for each of the study's scale measures in Table 3. As seen from this table, with the exception of the JDI, the job satisfaction scales have good evidence of convergent validity.

Table 3.   Fidelity Coefficients and Minimum Convergent Validity Coefficients for Job Satisfaction Measures

Scale	Fidelity Coefficient (r)	$r_{min} = 2r^2 - 1$
Hoppock JSB	.90	.62
Brayfield-Rothe JSI	.95	.82
Job In General Scale	.94	.78
Minnesota Satisfaction Questionnaire	.95	.80
Job Descriptive Index	.79	.25

Data in Table 1 further show that the correlations between the general job satisfaction measures and the facet-based scales (different methods measuring the same construct) are higher than the correlations between these measures and occupational identification, motivation for occupational choice, and perceptions of career and "external" barriers to occupational change (different methods of measurement were not available for these variables). Additionally, the job satisfaction measures vary in the extent to which they discriminate from occupational commitment and from the measure of "no perceived barriers" to occupational change (which reflects psychological attachment to the occupation due to interest in the work itself). The scale measures of job satisfaction do not show higher correlation values among each other than shown between them and the occupational commitment and the "no barriers" to occupational choice scale measures. As one example, consider the following: the Hoppock scale and the B-R index fail to discriminate from occupational commitment and show stronger correlations with "no barriers" to occupational change than they do with the JDI.

A further criterion for construct validity advocated by Campbell and Fiske (1959) is that the same pattern of trait interrelationships should be observed in all of the heterotrait-monomethod and heterotrait-heteromethod "blocks." As seen in Table 1, with the exception of the JDI (and to some extent the JIG) the pattern of interrelationships among the job satisfaction measures and between these measures and the occupational commitment measure is consistent. With the exception of the JIG, the general measures of job satisfaction tend to correlate more strongly with each other than they do with the JDI. The Hoppock scale and the B-R Index correlate with the MSQ to a lesser extent than MSQ correlates with either the single-item global measure of job satisfaction or the with the JDI. The general satisfaction scales also correlate more strongly with occupational commitment than does the single item global measure of job satisfaction, the JDI or the MSQ. Finally, the Hoppock scale and the B-R Index correlate more strongly with the "no barriers" to occupational change measure than they do with the JDI and MSQ. The JDI and MSQ, however, show moderate correlations with the "no barriers" measure ($r = .33$ and $r = .42$, respectively).

Question 4 asked which of the job satisfaction scales is most valid in predicting job satisfaction by use of the single-item general measure of job satisfaction as the criterion variable. As seen in Table 1, the zero-order correlations between the five multi-item job satisfaction measures and the single-item global measure indicate that there is little difference between the Hoppock scale, the B-R index, and the MSQ, with each accounting for approximately 47% of variance in the single-item measure. The JIG scale is slightly lower (40% of variance explained), and the JDI is by far the least valid when measured against the single-item global measure (23% of variance explained). The extent to which occupation and career-related vari-

Table 4.   Hierarchical Regression of Single-Item Global Measure of Job Satisfaction on Each Job Satisfaction Scale, Occupational and Career Variables[a]

Predictor Variables	β [b]	SE B [b]	ΔR^2 [c]	$F*$ [c, d]	Chow Test [e]
Hoppock Scale	.54	.011	.152***	158.58	.10
All Occupational and Career Measures			.033***	5.72	.17
Full Model R^2 .45***					.14
F 111.69					
Brayfield-Rothe Index	.53	.004	.146***	149.38	.80
All Occupational and Career Measures			.018*	3.00	2.33
Full Model R^2 .44***					1.44
F 64.27					
Job in General Scale	.38	.004	.093***	85.16	22.97***
All Occupational and Career Measures			.059***	9.00	84.02***
Full Model R^2 .37***					20.72***
F 49.45					
Minnesota Satisfaction Questionnaire	.51	.003	.168***	187.85	.62
All Occupational and Career Measures			.061***	11.37	1.40
Full Model R^2 .49***					.42
F 77.78					
Job Descriptive Index	.27	.001	.053***	46.75	23.94***
All Occupational and Career Measures			.147***	21.63	87.12***
Full Model R^2 .35***					20.79***
F 44.20					

Notes: * = p < .05; ** = p < .01; *** = p < .001;

[a]Results reported are for the combined sample;

[b]The standardized regression coefficients and standard errors are from the full regression model;

[c]Change in R and F* are the result of dropping each predictor from the full model and calculating the change in R;

[d]F* is the test statistic for the change in R resulting from removing each predictor from the full model;

εBased on a comparison of results from the two original samples with those of the combined sample.

ables contribute to the variance explained in the single-item measure of job satisfaction over and above that accounted for by a scale measure of job satisfaction is shown for the study's two sub-samples, in Table 4.

As seen from Table 4, occupation- and career-related variables have a significant influence upon R^2 for all job satisfaction measures. Comparison of the F^* statistic for the five scales shows that the influence of these variables is least pronounced for the B-R Index and the Hoppock scale and more pronounced for the JIG scale, JDI and MSQ. It is also worth noting that for the JDI, the effect of omitting occupation- and career-related variables from the full model was greater in terms of the decrease in variance accounted for than the effect of omitting the JDI itself.

Finally, the Chow test for the stability of regression coefficients across samples, shown in Table 4, indicates that for three of the five job satisfaction measures the regression results are not significantly different for the two samples. For the JDI and JIG scales the weights for the WLS regression models are different for the two samples, resulting in a failure to successfully cross-validate our results.

DISCUSSION

The results reported here offer insight into the source of nonequivalence among job satisfaction measures. Of the three proposed explanations for nonequivalence tested here we are able to reject two. The time-frame orientation argument was not supported by the patterns of correlations among the JDI, JIG and other facet-based and general scales even though these scales were explicitly designed to differ in terms of time-frame orientation (Ironson et al., 1989). The alternative combinatorial models argument was once again refuted by the data. Our results are consistent with those of Aldag and Brief (1978) and Ferratt (1981) in finding little support for alternative nonlinear methods of combining facet satisfaction.

In our examination of the omitted variables explanation for nonequivalence we found strong support for the argument that occupation- and career-related considerations are relevant to overall evaluations of job satisfaction. These results are consistent with Scarpello and Campbell's (1983a) findings with a sample of predominately male industrial R&D professionals in the United States, and with Scarpello and Vandenberg's (1992) findings with a sample of predominately male manufacturing plant employees. The present results were obtained from a predominately female sample of hospital employees in the United Kingdom. Three findings seem particularly important to discuss.

First, the general measures of job satisfaction failed to discriminate from the facet-based measures and some occupationally oriented measures. This indicates that, as previous research has suggested, predispositions toward occupation and career are relevant to overall evaluations of job satisfaction. Furthermore, although the general measures include considerations beyond facet-based measures, the pattern of correlations among all six job satisfaction measures and the occupation- and career-related variables was the same, indicating that they are all measuring the same construct.

Second, when using the single-item global measure as a criterion, the Hoppock scale, B-R Index, and MSQ are all equally content valid. The JIG is less content valid and the JDI is the least content valid. The implication here is that the form of measure does not dictate the degree of content validity.

Third, the occupation- and career-related variables improved prediction of the single-item measure of job satisfaction for all scale measures of job satisfaction. These variables made the least additional contribution to variance explained for the general scale measures. This was not surprising since the literature review and the correlation coefficients among the study's variables indicated that, with the exception of the JIG, the other general scale measures already include occupation- and career-related considerations. The greatest impact was seen for the facet-based measures, which is consistent with our expectation that these measures are least influenced by predispositions toward occupation and career. An unexpected result was the great improvement in predictive power that these variables made to the JDI. The fact that occupation- and career-related variables contribute more to the prediction of a single-item global measure of job satisfaction than this facet-based measure suggests that the scope of the JDI is very narrow with respect to the content domain of job satisfaction. As intended (Smith, 1992), the JDI appears to measure the portion of the construct that is directly under the organization's control, and thus, is content deficient in the measurement of the full construct. Although both the JDI and MSQ successfully discriminated from the general job satisfaction measures and the occupation and career related measures, our results show that the MSQ measures a greater portion of the job satisfaction construct (47% of variance explained) than measured by the JDI (23% of variance explained).

Although some readers may suggest that this study lacks direct control for common method variance, this is not a threat to the inferences that we draw from the data. Method variance may have inflated correlations among the variables in the analysis. However, this would not necessarily influence the analysis of patterns of correlations, as has been conducted here. Furthermore, the successful cross-validation of our results using a randomly split-sample reduces the plausibility of an artifact (such as method variance) accounting for the results reported here.

Finally, the stability of the scales' factor structures and the correlational data among the job satisfaction measures is remarkably reproducible across time and across two countries. Specifically, the reported correlation between the JIG and the Hoppock scale in 1978 was .73; it was .69 in this study. The correlation between B-R Index and the Hoppock scale in 1951

(Brayfield & Rothe, 1951) was .92; it was .81 in this study. The correlation between the JIG and the B-R Index in 1989 (Ironson et al., 1989) was .80; it was .72 in this study. The correlation between the JDI and JIG in 1989 (Ironson et al., 1989) was .78; it was .66 in this study. These data strongly support the stability of the scales' psychometric properties and their research use.

In summary, our results indicate that job satisfaction scales are not equivalent in their measurement of the construct's content domain. Those measures which include the measurement of occupational and career considerations appear to be more inclusive measures of the job satisfaction construct than measures that exclude or limit the measurement of those considerations. In this study, career considerations showed weaker relationships to job satisfaction measures than did occupational considerations. This may be due to our use of total scores for the multidimensional career scales. Thus, independent study of the strength of the relationship between career considerations and job satisfaction deserves research attention.

In this study, the *Hoppock Job Satisfaction Blank*, the *Brayfield-Rothe Index of Job Satisfaction*, and the short-form *Minnesota Satisfaction Questionnaire* (two general satisfaction scales and one facet-based scale) explained similar variance in global job satisfaction (as measured by the single-item measure of job satisfaction). The *Job In General* scale and the *Job Descriptive Index* explained the least amount of variance in global job satisfaction (as measured by the single-item measure of job satisfaction). This suggests that the frame of reference individuals use when reacting to job satisfaction questionnaires is the extent to which their jobs fulfill occupational and career aspirations. These results thus suggest fresh directions for researchers interested in developing more construct valid measures of job satisfaction. In the meantime, results also suggest care in selecting the job satisfaction measure appropriate for a specific research project (measurement of the construct as opposed to use of the measure as a diagnostic tool for an organizational development intervention). If the intent is to use the measure to assess the construct either as a dependent, independent, or moderator variable, then the results of the study may be compromised by the use of a measure which is content deficient.

ACKNOWLEDGMENT

The present study was supported in part by funding from the W.T. Beebe Institute of Personnel & Employment Relations, J. Mack Robinson College of Business, Georgia State University, Atlanta, Georgia.

Correspondence concerning this article should be sent to Vida Scarpello, Department of Management, J. Mack Robinson College of Business, Georgia State University, Atlanta, GA 30302-4014. Electronic mail may be sent via the internet to mgtvvs@langate.gsu.edu.

REFERENCES

Aldag, R.J., & Brief, A.P. (1978). Examination of alternative models of job satisfaction. *Human Relations, 31*, 91-98.

Ash, P. (1954). The SRA Employee Inventory–a statistical analysis. *Personnel Psychology, 7*, 337-364.

Balzer, W.K., & Smith, P.K. (with Kravitz, D.A., Lovell, S.E., Paul, K.B., Reilly, B.A., & Reilly, C.E.) (1990). *User's Manual for the Job Descriptive Index (JDI) and the Job In General (JIG) Scales.* Bowling Green University.

Bateman, T.S., & Organ, D.W. (1983). Job satisfaction and the good soldier: The relationship between affect and employee "citizenship." *Academy of Management Journal, 26*, 587-595.

Borgen, F.H., Weiss, D.J., Tinsley, H.E.A., Dawis, R.V., & Lofquist, L.II. (1968). The measurement of occupational reinforcer patterns. *Minnesota Studies in Vocational Rehabilitation, 49.*

Brayfield, A.H., & Rothe, H.F. (1951). An index of job satisfaction. *Journal of Applied Psychology, 35*, 307-311.

Brayfield, A.H., Wells, R.W., & Strate, M.W. (1957). Interrelationships among measures of job satisfaction and general satisfaction. *Journal of Applied Psychology, 41*, 201-205.

Campbell, D.T., & Fiske, D.W. (1959). Convergent and discriminant validation by the multitrait-multimethod matrix. *Psychological Bulletin, 56*, 81-105.

Cattell, R.B. (1960). The scree test for the number of factors. *Multivariate Behavioral Research, 1*, 245-276.

Cattell, R.B., & Jaspers, J. (1967). A general plasmode for factor analytic exercises and research. *Multivariate Behavioral Research Monographs, 3*, 1-212.

Chow, G. (1960). Tests of equality between sets of coefficients in two linear regressions. *Econometrica, 28*, 591-605.

Cohen, J., & Cohen, P. (1983). *Applied multiple regression/correlation analysis for the behavioral sciences* (2nd ed.). Hillsdale, NJ: Lawrence Earlbaum Associates.

Cote, J.A., Buckley, M.R., & Best, R.J. (1987). Combining methodologies in the construct validation process: An empirical illustration. *Journal of Psychology, 121*, 301-309.

Cook, J.D., Hepworth, S.J., Wall, T.D., & Warr, P.B. (1981). *The experience of work.* London: Academic Press.

Cronbach , L.J. (1951). Coefficient alpha and the internal structure of tests. *Psychometrika, 16*, 297-334.

Davis, T.J. (1987). *The development of occupational and career scales for use in identification of antecedents of job satisfaction.* Ph.D. Dissertation, University of Georgia.

Dawis, R.V., & Lofquist, L.H. (1984). *A psychological theory of work adjustment.* Minneapolis: University of Minnesota Press.

Drasgow, F.D., & Miller, H.E. (1982). Psychometric and substantive issues in scale construction and validation. *Journal of Applied Psychology, 67*, 268-279.

Einhorn, H.J. (1970). Use of nonlinear, compensatory models in decision-making. *Psychological Bulletin, 73*, 211-230.

Ferratt, T.W. (1981). Overall job satisfaction: Is it a linear function of facet satisfaction? *Human Relations, 34*, 463-473.

Frone, M.R., Russell, M., & Cooper, M.L. (1994). Relationship between job and family satisfaction: causal or noncausal variation? *Journal of Management, 20,* 565-579.

Gay, F.G., Weiss, D.J., Hendel, D.D., Dawis, R.V., & Lofquist, L.L. (1971). Manualfor the Minnesota Importance Questionnaire. *Minnesota Studies in Vocational Rehabilitation, 28.*

Graen, G.B., Orris, J.B., & Johnson, J.T. (1973). Role assimilation processes in a complex organization. *Journal of Vocational Behavior, 3,* 395-420.

Greene, W.H. (1990). *Econometric analysis.* New York: Macmillan.

Guttman, L. (1954). Some necessary conditions for common factor analysis. *Psychometrika, 19,* 149-162.

Hamner, W.C., & Smith, F.J. (1978). Work attitudes as predictors of unionization activity. *Journal of Applied Psychology, 63,* 415-421.

Hayton, J.C., & Scarpello, V. (1997). A comparison of factor retention rules using five measures of job satisfaction. *Proceedings of the Southern Management Association.*

Highhouse, S., & Becker, A.S. (1993). Facet measures and global job satisfaction. *Journal of Business and Psychology, 8,* 1.

Hoppock, R. (1935). *Job satisfaction.* New York: Harper.

Horn, J.L. (1965). A rationale and test for the number of factors in factor analysis. *Psychometrika, 32,* 179-185.

Ironson, G.H. (1992). Job stress and health. In C.J. Cranny, P.C., Smith, & E.F. Stone (Eds.), *Job Satisfaction: How people feel about their jobs and how it affects their performance* (pp. 219-239). New York: Lexington Books.

Ironson, G.H., & Smith, P.C. (1981). Anchors away–The stability of meaning when their location is changed. *Personnel Pychology, 34,* 249-262.

Ironson, G.H., Smith, P.C., Brannick, M.T., Gibson, W.M., & Paul, K.B. (1989). Construction of a "Job in General" scale: A comparison of global, composite, and specific measures. *Journal of Applied Psychology, 74,* 193-200.

Judge, T.A., Boudreau, J.W., & Bretz, R.D. (1994). Job and life attitudes of male executives. *Journal of Applied Psychology, 79,* 767-782.

Kaiser, H.F. (1960). The application of electronic computers to factor analysis. *Educational and Psychological Measurement, 20,* 141-151.

Kalleberg, A. (1974). A causal approach to the measurement of job satisfaction. *Social Science Research, 3,* 299-322.

Kavanagh, M.J., MacKinney, A.C., & Wolins, L. (1971). Issues in managerial performance: Multitrait-multimethod analysis of ratings. *Psychological Bulletin, 75,* 34-49.

Kunin, T. (1955). The construction of a new type of attitude measure. *Personnel Psychology, 8,* 65-78.

Landy, F. (1989). *The psychology of work behavior* (4th ed.). Monterey, CA: Brooks Cole.

Locke, E.A. (1969). What is job satisfaction? *Organizational Behavior and Human Performance, 4,* 309-336.

Locke, E.A. (1976). The nature and causes of job satisfaction. In M.D. Dunnette (Ed.), *Handbook of industrial and organizational psychology.* Chicago: Rand McNally.

McNichols, C.W., Stahl, M.K., & Manley, T.R. (1978). A validation of Hoppock's job satisfaction measure. *Academy of Management Journal, 21,* 737-742.

Mobley, W.H. (1977). Intermediate linkages in the relationship between job satisfaction and employee turnover. *Journal of Applied Psychology, 62,* 237-240.

Moorman, R.H. (1993). The influence of cognitive and affective based job satisfaction measures on the relationship between job satisfaction and organizational citizenship behavior. *Human Relations, 46,* 759-776.

Mowday, R.T., Steers, R.M., & Porter, L.W. (1979). The measurement of organizational commitment. *Journal of Vocational Behavior, 14,* 224-247.

O'Connor, E.J., Peters, L.H., & Gordon, S.M. (1978). The measurement of job satisfaction: Current practices and future considerations. *Journal of Management, 4,* 17-26.

O'Reilly, C.A., & Caldwell, D.F. (1981). The commitment and job tenure of new employees: Some evidence of postdecisional justification. *Administrative Science Quarterly, 26,* 597-616.

Petty, M. M., McGee, G.W., & Cavender, J.W. (1984). A meta-analysis of the relationships between individual job satisfaction and individual performance. *Academy of Management Review, 9,* 712-721.

Porter, L.W., Steers, R.M., Mowday, R.T., & Boulian, P.V. (1974). Organizational commitment, job satisfaction, and turnover among psychiatric technicians. *Journal of Applied Psychology, 59,* 603-609.

Rounds, J.B., Jr., Sloan, E.B., Dawis, R.V., & Lofquist, L.H. (1976, September). *Work adjustment project follow-up study: Preliminary findings.* Paper presented at the 84th Annual Meeting of the American Psychological Association.

Roznowski, M., & Hulin, C. (1992). The scientific merit of valid measures of general constructs with special reference to job satisfaction. In C.J. Cranny, P.C. Smith, & E.F. Stone (Eds.), *Job Satisfaction: How people feel about their jobs and how it affects their performance* (pp. 123-163). New York: Lexington Books.

Ryan, T.A., & Smith, P.C. (1954). *Principles of industrial psychology.* New York: Ronald.

Scarpello, V. (1980). *Examination of factors influencing discorrespondence between overall jobsatisfaction and need/reinforcer correspondence.* Ph.D. Dissertation, University of Minnesota.

Scarpello, V., & Campbell, J.P. (1983a). Job satisfaction: Are all the parts there? *Personnel Psychology, 36,* 577-600.

Scarpello, V., & Campbell, J.P. (1983b). Job satisfaction and the fit between individual needs and organizational rewards. *Journal of Occupational Psychology, 56,* 315-328.

Scarpello, V., & Vandenberg, R.J. (1987). Multitrait-multimethod validation of the Satisfaction With My Supervisor Scale. *Educational and Psychological Measurement, 52,* 203-212.

Scarpello, V., & Vandenberg, R.J. (1992). Generalizing the importance of occupational and career views to job satisfaction attitudes. *Journal of Organizational Behavior, 13,* 125-140.

Schmitt, N., Coyle, B.W., & Saari, B.B., (1977). A review and critique of analyses of multitrait-multimethod matrices. *Multivariate Behavioral Research, 12,* 447-478.

Schneider, B., Gunnarson, S.K., & Wheeler, J.K. (1992). The role of opportunity in the conceptualization and measurement of job satisfaction. In C.J. Cranny, P.C. Smith, & E.F. Stone (Eds.), *Job Satisfaction: How people feel about their jobs and how it affects their performance* (pp. 53-68). New York: Lexington Books.

Schneider, B., & Snyder, R.A. (1975). Some relationships between job satisfaction and organization climate. *Journal of Applied Psychology, 60,* 318-328.

Schriesheim, C.A. (1978). Job satisfaction, attitudes towards unions, and voting in a union representation election. *Journal of Applied Psychology, 63,* 548-552.

Scott, K.D., & Taylor, G.S. (1985). An examination of conflicting findings on the relationship between job satisfaction and absenteeism: A meta-analysis. *Academy of Management Journal, 28,* 599-612.

Smith, P.C. (1992). In pursuit of happiness: Why study general satisfaction? In C.J. Cranny, P.C., Smith, & E.F. Stone (Eds.), *Job Satisfaction: How people feel about their jobs and how it affects their performance* (pp. 5-19). New York: Lexington Books.

Smith, P.C., Kendall, L.M., & Hulin, C.L. (1969). *The measurement of satisfaction in work and retirement.* Chicago: Rand McNally & Company.

Smith, C.A., Organ, D.W., & Near, J.P. (1983). Organizational citizenship behavior: Its nature and its antecedents. *Journal of Applied Psychology, 68,* 653-663.

Smith, P.C., Smith, O.W., & Rollo, J. (1974). Factor structure for blacks and whites of the Job Descriptive Index and its discrimination of job satisfaction. *Journal of Applied Psychology, 59,* 99-100.

Smith, P.C., & Stanton, J.M. (1998). Perspectives on the measurement of job attitudes: The long view. *Human Resource Management Review, 8,* 367-386.

Staines, G.L., & Quinn, R.P. (1979, January). American workers evaluate the quality of their jobs. *Monthly Labor Review.*

Tenopyr, M. L. (1993). Construct validation needs in vocational behavior theories. *Journal of Vocational Behavior, 43,* 84-89.

Thurstone, L.L. (1947). *Multiple factor analysis.* Chicago: University of Chicago Press.

Wanous, J.P., & Lawler, E.E., III (1972). Measurement and meaning of job satisfaction. *Journal of Applied Psychology, 56,* 95-105.

Wanous, J.P., Reichers, A.E., & Hudy, M.J. (1997). Overall job satisfaction: How good are single-item measures? *Journal of Applied Psychology, 82,* 247-252.

Weaver, C.N. (1980). Job satisfaction in the United States. *Journal of Applied Psychology, 65,* 364-367.

Weiss, D.J., Dawis, R.V., England, G.W. & Lofquist, L.H. (1967). Manual for the Minnesota Satisfaction Questionnaire. *Minnesota Studies in Vocational Rehabilitation, XXII.*

White, H. (1980). A heteroscedasticity-consistent covariance matrix estimator and a direct test for heteroscedasticity. *Econometrica 48,* 817-838.

Widaman, K.F. (1985). Hierarchically nested covariance structure models for multi-trait-multimethod data. *Applied Psychological Measurement, 9,* 1-26.

Yeager, S.J. (1981). Dimensionality of the Job Descriptive Index. *Academy of Management Journal, 24,* 205-212.

Zwick, W.R. & Velicer, W.F. (1986). Factors influencing five rules for determining the number of components to retain. *Psychological Bulletin, 99,* 432-442.

Zwick, W.R., & Velicer, W.F. (1982). Factors influencing four rules for determining the number of components to retain. *Multivariate Behavioral Research, 17,* 253-269.

CHAPTER 7

THE IMPORTANCE OF MEASUREMENT EQUIVALENCE IN TRANSNATIONAL RESEARCH
A Test of Individual-Level Predictions About Culture and The Differential Use of Organizational Influence Tactics, With and Without Measurement Equivalence

Xiaohua (Tracy) Zhou, Chester A. Schriesheim, and
Wolfgang Beck

Abstract: The use of Item Response Theory (IRT) to assess measurement equivalence is briefly presented and then illustrated with survey data from two countries, the United States ($N = 271$) and Germany ($N = 176$). Two individual-level hypotheses are tested about the use of influence tactics (dependence and personal punishment), Hofstede's cultural value of power-distance, and the target of influence (superior, subordinate, or peer). Different results are shown to be possible when analyses use measures that are and are not psychometrically equivalent. Implications and future directions for research are discussed.

INTRODUCTION

Much recent research and debate has been motivated by the question of how one can demonstrate that an instrument or scale measures the same construct, in the same way, when it has been administered to two or more qualitatively distinct groups (e.g., Cheung & Rensvold, 1999). One manner in which this question can be phrased is as follows: Are the scores for individuals who belong to different groups or populations comparable on the same measurement scale (Reise, Widaman, & Pugh, 1993)? To compare groups of individuals with regard to their levels of constructs or with respect to relationships among these constructs, one must assume that the assessment instruments have "measurement equivalence" or "invariance" across groups (Drasgow, 1987). If this is not true, the differences between groups in means or in patterns of correlations are potentially artifactual and may be substantively misleading. Hence, demonstrating measurement equivalence across different groups is crucial to progress in many research domains, perhaps most commonly recognized when cross-cultural research involves translated measurement scales that were developed in one language and culture and used in another (e.g., Drasgow, 1987; Ellis & Kimmel, 1992; Hulin & Mayer, 1986). However, there are certainly other domains where measurement equivalence should probably be assessed. For example, whether men and women interpret and respond to survey measures in the same way warrants investigation (Eagle, Miles, & Icenogle, 2001, this volume), as does the issue of whether leader-member exchange is viewed the same by both the supervisor and the subordinate (Gerstner & Day, 1997).

The question that should be answered in such contexts is: Do the measures elicit psychologically equivalent responses consistently across the samples being studied? Only when subjects from different groupings ascribe essentially the same meanings to the scale items can meaningful across-groups comparisons be conducted (Riordan & Vandenberg, 1994). However, this necessary prerequisite may be hard to achieve in transnational research as even linguistically precise translation may not produce psychometrically equivalent scales due to such things as cultural differences. Culture has long been known to have strong influences on people's beliefs, values, attitudes, and behaviors (Hofstede, 1980, 1991; Triandis, 1996). Therefore, it is very likely that members of culturally diverse groups do not use a common frame of reference to interpret the item stems and/or response categories of a given scale. The cognitive discrepancy induced by cultural differences has been found to be a major cause of Differential Item Functioning (DIF), which precludes measurement equivalence (cf. Drasgow & Hulin, 1990; Ellis, 1989; Thissen, Steinberg, & Gerrard, 1986). DIF refers to differences in the probability of selecting a specific response to an item by individuals who have equal standings on the underlying construct but are sampled from different groups (Drasgow & Hulin, 1990). DIF items constitute a serious threat to the validity of measures used in different groups. These items may simply function differently for respondents drawn from one group or another or they may measure "different things" for members of one group as compared to members of another. Instruments containing such items may have reduced validity for between group comparisons, because their scores may be indicative of a variety of attributes other than those the scales are intended to measure (Thissen, Steinberg, & Wainer, 1988). Consequently, in transnational research, once preliminary linguistic assessments have been satisfied (ensuring a measurement instrument's semantic equivalence by careful back-translation processes), identifying and eliminating DIF items serves as one excellent quantitative method for establishing measurement equivalence (so that possible erroneous study findings may be avoided).

Prior research has applied two major approaches, confirmatory factor analysis (CFA) and item response theory (IRT) to test for measurement equivalence (Drasgow, 1987; Johns & Xie, 1998; Maurer, Raju, & Collins, 1998; Reise et al., 1993; Riordan & Vandenberg, 1994). Because it is less well known and no major treatments of the IRT approach have appeared in the literature of late, the present study will primarily focus on the IRT approach to demonstrate both its use and the importance of measurement equivalence in transnational research. This purpose will be achieved by the following steps. First, some of the essentials of IRT will be introduced. Second, the process of using IRT to identify DIF items will be briefly presented. Third, IRT analysis will be applied to assess the measurement equivalence of two influence tactic measures and one cultural values scale with survey data collected from two countries (the United States and Germany). Fourth, relevant predictions drawn from Yukl and Tracy (1992) about the use of influence tactics and from Hofstede (1980, 1991) about cultural values will be tested in two ways: one using initial scales (which include both equivalent and nonequivalent items) and one in which only the equivalent items identified in the third step are used. This step serves to illustrate the degree to which test results may vary as a function of the equivalence of the measures employed. Finally, the implications of our findings, along with limitations of the present study, will be discussed.

ITEM RESPONSE THEORY (IRT)

The use of IRT (Lord, 1980) to identify test items that function differentially when transported to a cultural-linguistic setting that is different from that in which the test was developed is a well-established technique for ensuring measurement equivalence (Budgell, Raju, & Quartetti, 1995; Candell & Hulin, 1987; Drasgow, 1987; Ellis, 1989; Ellis & Kimmel, 1992;

Maurer, Raju, & Collins, 1998; Thissen et al., 1986). IRT is concerned with the probabilistic relationship between the response to a test item and the attribute of the person that the test item is intended to measure.

The basic assumptions in standard formulations of IRT are unidimensionality and conditional independence (e.g., Drasgow & Hulin, 1990; Reise et al., 1993). Unidimensionality implies that the set of items assesses a single underlying trait dimension; conditional independence means that if the trait level is statistically held constant, the test items are pair wise uncorrelated. Linking the probability of item responses to the attribute assessed by a test or a scale is what differentiates IRT from classical test theory (Drasgow & Hulin, 1990). The unit of analysis for classical test theory is the complete test, while it is the individual item for IRT. Analyzing scales at the level of individual items allows IRT to address problems beyond the scope of classical test theory. Additionally, another advantage of IRT is the property of parameter invariance, which means that the item parameters estimated using IRT models are independent of the trait distribution of the respondents used to calibrate the items (Hambleton, Swaminathan, & Rogers, 1991). This is in contrast to traditional classical test theory, in which item parameters depend almost entirely on the sample.

A variety of IRT models have been developed for different types of scale items (Drasgow & Hulin, 1990; Thissen & Steinberg, 1988). Since the measurement scales that are analyzed in the present study have graded (polytomous) items with five or seven response categories (Likert-type scales), an appropriate model for our observed data is the graded response model (GRM) described by Samejima (1969). The GRM is a two-parameter logistic model for ordinal polytomous responses. The fundamental equation for the GRM is:

$$P(x = k|\theta) = \frac{1}{1 + \exp[-a(\theta - b_{k-1})]} - \frac{1}{1 + \exp[-a(\theta - b_k)]}$$

$$= P^*(k) - P^*(k+1) \tag{1}$$

This equation specifies the conditional probability of a person responding in a particular response category k. $P^*(k)$ is called the item response function (IRF) that shows the probability of an examinee responding in category k or higher, conditional on his or her θ trait level. The trace lines described by the P^*s are called *item-characteristic curves* (ICC). The item discrimination parameter a is proportional to the slope of the ogive trace line at its point of inflection. It represents the degree to which an item discriminates between adjacent levels of θ trait. One assumption made for the graded response model is that the a parameters are constant for each of the response categories within an item and can vary between items. The category difficulty parameter b_{k-1} represents the trait level (θ) necessary to have a 50% chance of responding in category k or higher. The GRM model depicted above requires that, for each test item with k response categories, one a and k-1 b parameters be estimated. Additionally, the equation can be used to compute the expected probabilities of responding in each of the response categories by subtracting the adjacent IRFs. The plots of the probabilities of the response categories ($P[x = k|\theta]$s) are called *optional characteristic curves* (OCCs). Figure 1 provides an example of OCCs for an item with five response categories, with parameter values $a = 2$, $b_1 = -2$, $b_2 = -1$, $b_3 = .5$, and $b_4 = 1.5$.

The fit of IRT models can be assessed statistically (Drasgow, 1987). Typically, the statistical acceptability of an estimated IRT model is contingent on how close the response proportions predicted from the IRFs are to the response proportions observed in the data. Hypothesis testing consists of comparing the response patterns predicted by the model with the observed data, to determine whether the model and data are in agreement (Thissen, Steinberg, & Gerrard, 1986). Several chi square goodness-of-fit tests have been developed to check the accuracy of fitted IRT models (Cohen, Kim, & Baker, 1993; Lord, 1980; Reise et al., 1993). In the present study, we conducted model-fit tests by using the G^2 statistic, which is part of standard output from the IRT computer program that we employ (MULTI-LOG VI; Thissen, 1991). Under certain assumptions, G^2 approximates a chi-square distribution with degrees of freedom equal to the number of

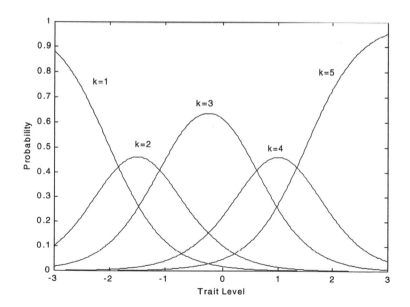

Figure 1. Optional characteristic curves (OCCs) for an item with five response categories with $a = 2$, $b_1 = -2$, $b_2 = -1$, $b_3 = .5$, and $b_4 = 1.5$.

response patterns minus the number of estimates specified in the model (Thissen, 1991). G^2 values reflect the degree of congruence between the frequency of observed response patterns and the frequency of these patterns estimated by the IRT models. High G^2 values imply poor model fit. However, with large item sets (e.g., more than five items) or polytomous item responses, G^2 is not appropriate for judging the fit of IRT models (Thissen, 1991). The required normative base increases very rapidly with the number of parameters that need to be estimated (Nunnally & Bernstein, 1994). Even with a large enough sample size, there will be too many possible response patterns without any observed frequencies and the statistics will have no known reference distribution (Reise et al., 1993). Nevertheless, similar to the chi-square values in CFA, G^2 values can be used to test differences between a more general and a nested model, even in relatively small samples. The G^2 difference between two nested models is itself a G^2 statistic that is more robust with respect to sample size than either of its constituents (Agresti & Yang, 1986). The G^2 difference test indicates whether the constraint(s) imposed on the nested model significantly degraded the fit of the model.

THE USE OF IRT ANALYSIS TO IDENTIFY DIF ITEMS

One central principle for assessing measurement equivalence is that the empirical relations between the trait indicators (e.g., test items) and the trait factors of interest are invariant across groups (Reise et al., 1993). Hui and Triandis (1985, p. 138) stated "an instrument that has similar ICCs across cultures has, at least in part, demonstrated its item equivalence and scalar equivalence." Accordingly, IRT is used to identify differences in the interpretation of test items by comparing the item's ICCs for one group with the ICCs for another group. Specifically, DIF items are identified by determining whether the a and b parameters of item functions are equivalent across two groups. Evidence of differential item functioning exists if the item has different a and b parameters for the two groups (Thissen, Steinberg & Wainer, 1988). In the context of transnational research, DIF analysis generally compares two groups: the focal group, the group to which the test is transported, and the reference group, the standard against which the focal group is compared. The reference group is usually the majority culture or the culture from which the test was originally developed (Ellis & Kimmel, 1992). The DIF tests conducted in this paper evaluated the differences in item response patterns between two cultural groups (U.S. and German samples) and then assessed the equivalence of several translated scales. Items provide equivalent measurement if the a and b parameters are the same for both samples. As one of the features of IRT modeling, the G^2 difference test of nested IRT models was used to assess the equality constraints imposed on the a and b parameters across the samples. More detailed illustration of this IRT analytical procedure will be presented using survey data in the following section.

There are several advantages associated with using the IRT framework to test measurement equivalence (Hambleton et al., 1991; Maurer et al., 1998). First, IRT focuses on the item level of analysis, and the assessment of measurement equivalence is on an item-by-item basis. The calibration and invariance test of each item are independent of other items in the same scale. Second, as indicated above, the IRT item parameters are independent of the attribute distribution of the respondents. Thus, this invariance property allows rigorous comparison of the parameters of an item across samples—regardless of the characteristics of the samples. Third, IRT posits a nonlinear, monotonic relationship between the latent trait (θ) and the probability of a specific item response, which is a less stringent assumption than the linear relationship assumed in both classical test theory and the CFA approach. Fourth, in addition to the a parameter (which is analogous to lambdas or factor loadings in CFA), IRT provides additional useful information about item functioning. The b parameters in IRT models determine how much of the underlying trait being rated is needed for a population of raters to respond at a given level on the rating scale. The only similar counterpart in CFA is the intercept parameter (Vandenberg & Lance, 2000). However, the CFA intercept parameter has not been as well established as the b parameter in IRT. As a result, IRT models are seen by some as imposing a more stringent set of measurement invariance constraints than does CFA (Reise et al., 1993).

THE CURRENT STUDY

Yukl (1998, p. 175) claims that "The essence of leadership is influence over followers." Whether this is true or not, the exercise of influence is commonly seen as a central organizational process (Pfeffer, 1977, 1981). Despite this centrality, however, the scientific study of organizational influence processes is relatively young, although a growing base of research findings is beginning to accumulate (see Yukl, 1998, for a review). In particular, several different influence tactic taxonomies have been developed and, along with each, questionnaire measures to allow their assessment in field studies (e.g., Kipnis, Schmidt, & Wilkinson, 1980; Schriesheim & Hinkin, 1990; Yukl, Lepsinger, & Lucia, 1992).

Regardless of taxonomy or instrument, Kipnis (1984) notes that which influence tactic is employed by an agent depends, in part, upon the target and that more powerful tactics are generally used against weaker targets (and vice versa). Yukl and Tracy (1992) suggest a more complex pattern, with the influence tactic that is employed by an agent being the result of several factors, including the tactic's consistency with prevailing social roles and norms about its use, and the influence target's power and position relative to the agent. Several studies (e.g., Yukl & Falbe, 1990; Yukl & Tracy, 1992) generally support this framework.

Consonant with the Yukl and Tracy (1992) framework, the cultural values to which a person subscribes are generally seen as significantly influencing his/her beliefs, attitudes and cognitions about the acceptability or unacceptability of behaviors (Triandis, 1996). Thus, individuals' beliefs about the appropriateness of different influence tactics in different situations should vary according to their cultural values. In particular, according to Hofstede's (1980) framework, the cultural value of power-distance should affect the use of power and influence tactics in organizations. Power-distance refers to the extent to which the less powerful organization members expect and accept that power is distributed unequally (Hofstede, 1991). Although often seen as a societal attribute that differentiates some countries from others, the power-distance dimension has also been used as a characteristic of individuals (i.e., as an individual difference variable) and consequently it has been used in studies at the individual level of analysis (e.g., Lee, Pillutla, & Law, 2000). This is because people differ in the degree to which they believe in the dominant values associated with their culture.

The influence tactics that a person uses should be consistent with their beliefs and with their expected work roles (Yukl & Tracy, 1992). Consequently, orientations about the appropriate power-distance between supervisors and subordinates should clearly affect people's tendency to use different influence tactics. The evaluation of superiors and subordinates by persons with a high power-distance orientation reflects their beliefs in the legitimacy of power inequality between superiors and subordinates (Hofstede, 1980; Lee, Pillutla, & Law, 2000). Thus, high power-distance individuals would be expected to be more sensitive to the power status of their influence targets and therefore more likely to use strong influence tactics toward subordinates and weak tactics toward superiors. Conversely, persons with a low power-distance orientation should be less sensitive to target status and therefore less likely to vary their use of strong influence tactics according to influence target (Hofstede, 1991). This leads to our hypotheses:

Hypothesis 1. There will be an interaction between influence target and power-distance orientation such that strong influence tactics will be used more frequently against weaker targets by high power-distance persons but not by low power-distance persons (i.e., the use of strong tactics by low power-distance persons will not vary by target; for high power-distance persons stronger tactics will be used more against weaker targets).

Hypothesis 2. There will be an interaction between influence target and power-distance orientation such that weak tactics will be used more frequently against stronger targets by high power-distance persons but not by low power-distance persons (i.e., the use of weak tactics by low power-distance persons will not vary by target; for high power-distance persons weaker tactics will be used more against stronger targets).

These hypotheses are tested using samples from two different cultures (the United States and Germany) that have been identified by Hofstede (1980) as being very close to equal regarding their average power-distance orientations. However, although this might suggest the acceptability of combining the data from both countries to test our hypotheses (particularly since the hypotheses are at the individual—and not organizational or societal—level of analysis), linguistic and cultural differences may preclude such treatment. Thus, we test our hypotheses two ways: First, using measures that have not been refined to ensure measurement equivalence across the two countries, and, second, using measures that have been refined. Due to the reduction of measurement invalidity (caused by various extraneous factors), we expect to obtain stronger support for our hypotheses with the refined measures than with the original unrefined scales.

METHOD

Samples and Procedure

Research data were collected both in the United States and in Germany. The samples consisted of 271 working M.B.A. students enrolled in a medium-sized university in the southeastern United States and 176 working business graduate students enrolled in a similar university in Germany. An anonymous survey was administered by the researchers to students in their courses and was filled out either during normal class time or at home, taking approximately 45 to 60 minutes. Full verbal and written instructions were provided. Participation was voluntary and it was assured that interested respondents would receive a brief summary of final results. A total of 271 out of 300 surveys were returned in the U.S. sample (a 90.3% response rate), while 176 out of 300 surveys were completed by the German sample (a 58.7% response rate, probably a function of the German prohibition against offering extra credit for study participation; see Beck, 1997, for further elaboration). The average age of American respondents was 28.7 years old. Approximately 60.6% of the sample were male. More than two thirds of the respondents surveyed (69.9%) were currently working, the rest of them reported having some prior work experience. The sample worked on average 40.51 hours per week, with an average of 4.67 years work experience; 15.2% of the sample described influence attempts directed toward their subordinates, 47.3% used co-workers as referents, and 29.7% chose their superiors as the target. The average time that the respondents reported knowing their referent was 38.75 months. The German sample consisted of 97 males and 79 females, with an average age of 22.65 years. Almost all the German respondents were currently working (98.9%). They reported working on average 37.70 hours per week, with an average of 1.91 years of work experience; 8.7% of the sample described their subordinates as the referent, 47.1% described peers, 23.8% described superiors, and 20.4% chose to describe how they influence other targets. The average time that the German subjects reported knowing their referents was 16.74 months.

Measures

The measures selected for use in the current investigation were new but very carefully developed to test the research hypotheses stated above. These measures were carefully examined earlier by Beck (1997) for their psychometric quality; in the current study the measures' content adequacy, internal consistency reliability, and appropriateness of factor structure will be further examined below.

The strong and weak influence tactics were measured by an instrument that drew upon earlier work by Kipnis, Schmidt, and Wilkinson (1980), Schriesheim and Hinkin (1990), Tepper (1989), Yukl, Lepsinger, and Lucia (1992), and others. This instrument used as many previously developed items as were believed likely to survive the translation and back translation process. To these were added new items that were developed by a binational (the United States and Germany) research team. This was done to ensure that all of the measures employed in the study applied equally to both Americans and Germans, making the instrument more suitable for the current research than other available scales.

The full instrument that was developed includes 20 tactic subscales that correspond to Tepper's (1989) influence tactics taxonomy. It employs a five-point Likert scale to measure the frequency of using each tactic to influence the referent, ranging from never or almost never use this tactic (1) to always or almost always use this tactic (5). In the current study, only the data on the Dependence and Personal Punishment tactics were used; these subscales were selected because they span the continuum from exceptionally weak (Dependence) to extremely strong (Personal Punishment) influence tactics (Tepper, 1989). Dependence was measured by a 6-item subscale that includes the items, "Get him/her to feel pity for me by expressing a need for help," and "Make him/her want to help me by showing that I depend on his/her help." Two sample items for the 5-item Personal Punishment subscale are, "Punish him/her by ignoring him/her if he/she doesn't do what I want," and "Embarrass him/her in front of co-workers until he/she does what I have requested." The respondents were asked to select an influence target (superior, subordinate, co-worker, or other) and then indicate the degree to which they typically use the approach described by each item to influence that particular target.

The power distance cultural dimension was assessed by an instrument that contains items that measure the original four Hofstede cultural dimensions. Although there are several other cultural measures available (e.g., Hellriegel, Slocum, & Woodman, 1993; Howell, & Dorfmann, 1993), they were developed solely by American researchers, whereas this new instrument was constructed by both American and German researchers. Two sample power distance items are, "By virtue of position, one's supervisor is correct by definition," and "Supervisors should clearly communicate to their employees that subordinates have less power than do their superiors" (response choices are on a 7-point Likert agreement scale).

Test Translation

The research objectives of this study required the collection of data in two cultural settings—the United States and Germany. The measures described above were first developed in English and then translated to German. Since the quality of this translation is considered most crucial for ensuring semantic equivalence (cf. Ellis, 1989; Rioridan & Schaffer, 1999), a prerequisite for establishing measurement equivalence, a multiple-step back translation procedure was applied to deal with linguistic differences (see Brislin, 1980, for a thorough discussion of translation methodologies). This involved the following steps.

1. Translation of the original English (U.S.) questionnaire into German (conducted by W. Beck).
2. Back translation of the German version of the questionnaire into English (conducted by a professional translator).
3. Discussion and resolution of discrepancies by the author of the German version (W. Beck) and the professional translator.
4. Comparison of the original English questionnaire with the back translation by one of its authors (C. Schriesheim).
5. Discussion and resolution of all remaining discrepancies by the original German translator (W. Beck), one of original authors of

the initial English questionnaire (C. Schriesheim), and a German Ph.D. student who had lived for an extensive period of time in the United States.

Any items that were changed or rewritten as a result of this process were subjected to these steps again. Extensive examples of the original items and their translations and back translations are provided in Beck (1997).

Data Analysis

Descriptive Statistics

Means, standard deviations, and coefficient alpha internal consistency reliabilities were computed for U.S. and German samples on each measure.

Item Response Theory (IRT) Analyses

The IRT analyses were conducted to identify the DIF items and to quantitatively establish measurement equivalence for each instrument across the U.S. and German samples. Measurement hypotheses of between-groups equality in item functioning were tested with the multi-group option in MULTILOG VI (Thissen, 1991), implementing a marginal-maximum-likelihood algorithm (Bock & Aitkin, 1981) to estimate parameters. MULTILOG's default estimation method is based on an assumption about the distribution of attributes and then scales item parameters in reference to the distribution, which is specified to have a mean of 0 and a standard deviation of 1. Previous research has supported that MULTILOG is an efficient and effective estimation program for the graded response model (GRM) that was used in the present study (Reise & Yu, 1990).

Before the implementation of the IRT analysis, the basic assumption of unidimensionality, which implies that the set of items assess a single underlying trait dimension, needs to be confirmed. Consequently, this assumption was tested by conducting principal-components analyses by scale and by sample.

Once the unidimensionality assumption was supported, a procedure outlined by Reise et al. (1993) was used to estimate the model parameters and detect DIF items by examining the discrepancy between the baseline model (i.e., in which all the item parameters are freely estimated within each sample) and the partial invariance model for each item (i.e., constraining the parameter estimates for an item to be equal across the two samples). The DIF tests require that estimates of item parameters obtained in different groups be placed on a common metric before the comparisons can be made (Stocking & Lord, 1983). However, if the item parameters are calibrated independently in each group by standardizing the attribute distribution of that group, the obtained parameters across groups are not on a common metric and thus incomparable. Therefore, when implementing the multi-group DIF in MULTILOG, the concurrent item calibration procedure was employed to estimate item and θ parameters based on a common metric (see Hambleton et al., 1991; Kim & Cohen, 1998; Reise et al., 1993). This procedure estimates item parameters simultaneously in a combined data set consisting of both the reference and focal groups and treats items not completed by a particular group as missing. The common metric problem is dealt with by using anchor items, which are constrained to have the same parameters between groups.

Using concurrent calibration, the baseline model was established as follows. Here we use the Dependence tactic data (6 items) for illustration. The input data for MULTILOG were set up as if 447 (271 American and 176 German) respondents had responded to a 12-item scale. Responses to items 1-6 were coded as missing for the 176 German respondents, and responses to items 7-12 were coded as missing for the 271 American respondents. Thus, overall, the baseline model has 12 items and is estimated based on 447 response patterns. The mean and variance on θ for the U.S. (reference) group were set at 0 and 1, respectively, for identification. The mean of the German (focal) group on θ was freely estimated and the variance was set at 1. As a result, 61 parameters were estimated in the baseline model (12 a parameters, 48 b parameters, and the mean parameter for the German sample). The G^2 value of this model serves as a baseline to evaluate subsequent nested models in which equality constraints are imposed on the corresponding item parameters across groups.

Two types of full measurement invariance models were tested to explore whether the Dependence items exhibited significant DIF with respect to a and b parameters. The first type of full invariance model was constructed by constraining all the item parameters in the baseline model to equality across groups. If the G^2 value for this full invariance model is significantly greater than that for baseline model, the null hypothesis of full invariance is rejected and there is at least one DIF item. However, no further nested model comparisons are needed if no significant G^2 difference is detected, and the measurement equivalence of the scale cannot be rejected. The second type of full measurement invariance model constrained only the a parameters to be equal across the groups, leaving the b parameters free. It was used to examine if the discrimination parameters for all the scale items are invariant across groups. It is possible that all the items have invariant a parameters across groups but that some or all of the items still demonstrate DIF because of different b parameters. In such a case, people in different countries have the same probability of a certain item response even when they possess different levels of the latent trait. This test takes advantage of a potentially valuable feature of IRT to detect whether the source of DIF is attributable to differences in a parameters or in b parameters. Additionally, since parameter a is analogous to the lambda (factor loading) in CFA, the full invariance model for a is equivalent to the full factorial invariance model that is usually tested in multi-group CFA models. Therefore, IRT analysis with both a and b parameters takes more information about item functioning into account and makes more accurate conclusions about measurement equivalence than the typical CFA approach.

If the full invariance model for a and b parameters is rejected, we proceed to test for measurement invariance on an item-by-item basis (Reise et al., 1993). Partial measurement invariance is modeled by specifying, one item at a time, the a and four b_j parameters to be invariant across groups. Each partial measurement model is then compared with the baseline model to test the equality hypothesis for each scale item. Because of the iterative nature of this procedure, the significance level is correspondingly adjusted to .01 in order to control for the overall Type I error (cf. Cheung & Rensvold, 1999).

The same IRT analytical procedure was employed with the Personal Punishment scale and the Power-distance scale. However, the Power-distance scale is rated on 7 response categories. Thus, for each item, one a parameter and six b_j parameters were estimated. Another difference was that the significance level was set at .005 for the partial invariance test of the 13-item Power-distance scale (because more comparisons were involved).

Confirmatory Factory Analysis of the Purified Scales

After the DIF items were identified and deleted, confirmatory factor analysis (CFA) was conducted on the combined sample using the maximum likelihood procedure of Lisrel 8 (Jöreskog & Sörbom, 1993) to assess the dimensionality of the remaining items employed to measure the two influence tactics and Power-distance. This was undertaken to increase confidence in the purified scales that we employed for the hypothesis tests. A three-factor model, with two factors representing Dependence and Personal Punishment, respectively, and one factor representing Power-distance, was tested. Each item was specified as loading on only one factor, the errors were specified as uncorrelated among themselves, and the latent trait factor correlations were freely estimated.

Two-way Analysis of Variance (ANOVA)

The tests of our hypotheses were conducted by using two-way ANOVA on the reduced sample ($N = 377$) obtained by excluding those cases that described how they influence referents other than a subordinate, co-worker, or superior. The reduced sample was partitioned by a median split into low- and high-power distance conditions using both the initial and purified scales. For comparison purposes, ANOVAs were conducted for equivalent and nonequivalent measures with subgroups based on (a)

Table 1. Initial Number of Items, Mean, Standard Deviation (SD), and Coefficient Alpha for U.S. and German Samples on the Two Influence Tactics Scales and the Power-Distance Scale

Scale	Initial Number of Items	U.S.			German		
		Mean	SD	α	Mean	SD	α
Dependence	6	16.99	4.18	.79	17.32	3.90	.77
Personal Punishment	5	6.23	1.93	.74	5.98	1.73	.71
Power Distance	13	47.69	10.29	.75	44.12	10.07	.76

high/low Power-distance (initial measure), and (b) high/low Power-distance using the purified scale.

RESULTS

Descriptive Statistics

Means, standard deviations, and coefficient alpha internal consistency reliabilities for U.S. and German samples are presented in Table 1. All the reliability coefficients are greater than .70 and therefore acceptable (Nunnally & Bernstein, 1994), ranging from .71 to .79.

Item Response Theory (IRT) Analyses

Eigenvalues for the first five factors for each scale are reported in Table 2. The pattern of eigenvalues for the two influence tactic scales is support-

Table 2. Eigenvalues for the Initial Two Influence Tactic Scales and the Initial Power-Distance Scale in the U.S. and German Samples

Scales	Eigenvalue				
	1	2	3	4	5
Dependence					
U.S.	2.98	.97	.73	.66	.37
German	2.88	1.01	.77	.64	.35
Personal Punishment					
U.S.	2.39	.87	.76	.58	.41
German	2.57	.86	.75	.44	.38
Power-Distance					
U.S.	3.40	1.72	1.16	1.11	.91
German	3.53	1.74	1.38	1.05	.96

Table 3.   Graded Response Model Fit for Dependence.

Model	Change in G^2	Change in df	p Value
Unconstrained Baseline Model	—	—	—
Full Invariant Model for a & b_j	91.0*	30	< .01
Full Invariant Model for a	3.2	6	ns
Invariant a & b_j for Item 1	22.3*	5	< .01
Invariant a & b_j for Item 2	18.3*	5	< .01
Invariant a & b_j for Item 3	5.3	5	ns
Invariant a & b_j for Item 4	6.9	5	ns
Invariant a & b_j for Item 5	11.8	5	ns
Invariant a & b_j for Item 6	14.8	5	ns

Note: Because the G^2 values for each model are not directly interpretable, these values are not listed. The reported change in G^2 and the corresponding change in degrees of freedom are computed by comparing each model with the baseline model.

*$p < .01$

ive of unidimensionality, but not for the Power-distance measure. However, the IRT literature suggests that a large eigenvalue for the first factor relative to the eigenvalues of the remaining factors is an indication of sufficient unidimensionality, and the graded response model is able to tolerate some violation of the unidimensionality assumption (cf. Drasgow, 1987; Lord, 1980). We thus felt that sufficient unidimensionality supported the use of IRT analyses in the current study.

Results of the DIF analyses for the Dependence, Personal Punishment, and Power-distance scales are shown in Table 3, 4, and 5, respectively. Since the absolute G^2 values for each model are not directly interpretable (Reise et al., 1993), these values are not listed in the tables. As shown in Table 3, the full Dependence invariance model for a and b_j obtained significant changes in G^2 value ($\Delta G^2[30] = 91.0$, $p < .01$). However, constraining only the a parameters to invariance across groups did not result in a significant

Table 4.   Graded Response Model Fit for Personal Punishment

Model	Change in G^2	Change in df	p Value
Unconstrained Baseline Model	—	—	—
Full Invariant Model for a & b_j	27.6	25	ns

Note: Because the G^2 values for each model are not directly interpretable, these values are not listed. The reported change in G^2 and the corresponding change in degrees of freedom are computed by comparing the model with the baseline model.

Table 5.   Graded Response Model Fit for Power-Distance

Model	Change in G^2	Change in df	p Value
Unconstrained Baseline Model	—	—	—
Full Invariant Model for a & b_j	503.0*	91	< .005
Full Invariant Model for a	—[a]	13	—[a]
Invariant a & b_j for Item 1	27.5*	7	< .005
Invariant a & b_j for Item 2	13.5	7	ns
Invariant a & b_j for Item 3	52.0*	7	< .005
Invariant a & b_j for Item 4	41.4*	7	< .005
Invariant a & b_j for Item 5	14.2	7	ns
Invariant a & b_j for Item 6	21.7*	7	< .005
Invariant a & b_j for Item 7	7.6	7	ns
Invariant a & b_j for Item 8	14.1	7	ns
Invariant a & b_j for Item 9	19.0	7	ns
Invariant a & b_j for Item 10	20.0	7	ns
Invariant a & b_j for Item 11	11.7	7	ns
Invariant a & b_j for Item 12	27.0*	7	< .005
Invariant a & b_j for Item 13	39.9*	7	< .005

Note: Because the G2 values for each model are not directly interpretable, these values are not listed. The reported change in G^2 and the corresponding change in degrees of freedom are computed by comparing each model with the baseline model.

a No meaningful results due to a singular matrix error emerging in the computations.

*p < .005

increase in G^2 value ($\Delta G^2[6]$ = 3.2, p > .10). Partial invariance tests revealed that items 1 and 2 of the Dependence scale were nonequivalent.

For the Personal Punishment scale (see Table 4), the fit of full invariance model for a and b_j was not significantly different from the baseline model ($\Delta G^2[25]$ = 27.6, p > .10). Thus, no items in the Personal Punishment scale displayed DIF.

As shown in Table 5, the results for the Power-distance scale indicated that the change in G^2 value between the baseline model and the full invariance model for a and b_j was statistically significant ($\Delta G^2[91]$ = 503.0, p < .005). However, the full invariance model for a could not be calibrated in this case due to a singular matrix error emerging in the MULTILOG estimation process. Partial invariance tests demonstrated that items 1, 3, 4, 6, 12, and 13 of the Personal Punishment scale are variant across samples.[1]

Purified scales were next constructed by deleting the DIF items from each initial scale. The means, standard deviations, and coefficient alpha internal consistency reliabilities for the purified scales are presented in Table 6. Again, all the reliability coefficients are $\geq .70$ and are acceptable. Additionally, it might be noted that the refined Dependence and Power-distance scales correlate highly with the original scales ($r = .95$ and $.98$, respectively; $p < .001$) in the reduced sample ($N = 377$) but they cannot be considered equivalent measures. With Pearson correlations, the high magnitudes simply mean that the rank-orders of the respondents on the refined and original scales are extremely similar, not necessarily that highly similar patterns of relationships will be obtained with other variables (McNemar, 1969).

CFA of the Purified Scales

A confirmatory factory analysis was undertaken of the purified scales to provide further support for their subsequent use. The three-factor model ($\chi^2[101] = 203.2$, $p < 0.001$) with the combined sample obtained quite a good fit, indicated by a low root mean square error of approximation (RMSEA) (.048) and acceptable values for the non-normed fit index (NNFI) and the comparative fit index (CFI) (.92 and .93, respectively) (Medsker, Williams, & Holahan, 1994). Additionally, all of the factor loadings were statistically significant ($p < .01$) and all of the completely standardized loadings were .38 or greater—except one of .28. Additionally, the correlations among the three latent factors were low and nonsignificant. These results therefore provide some additional support for the construct validity of the new purified scales.

Two-way Analysis of Variance (ANOVA)

Table 7 presents the ANOVA results for both the initial and purified Dependence measures and for the Personal Punishment scale. In these

Table 6.   Purified Scales: Number of Retained Items, Mean, Standard Deviation (SD), and Coefficient Alpha for Each Scale after DIF Item Deletions

Scale	Number of Retained Items	U.S.			German		
		Mean	SD	α	Mean	SD	α
Dependence	4	11.94	3.36	.83	11.94	3.11	.80
Personal Punishment[a]	5	6.23	1.93	.74	5.98	1.73	.71
Power-Distance	7	23.76	6.60	.71	22.73	6.42	.70

Note: [a]Scale not altered from the original version (see Table 1).

Table 7. Summary of ANOVA Results with the Initial and Refined Scales

Parameter	Initial Dependence		Purified Dependence		Personal Punishment	
	F	p Value	F	p Value	F	p Value
Initial (Unpurified) Power-distance measure						
Target	.20	.819	.20	.823	14.83**	.000
Power-distance	5.81*	.016	7.02**	.008	.61	.436
Target X Power-distance	4.21*	.016	5.64**	.004	.11	.899
Refined (Purified) Power-distance measure						
Target	.14	.872	.14	.870	19.41**	.000
Power-distance	7.54**	.006	10.63**	.001	1.98	.160
Target X Power-distance	3.41*	.034	5.34**	.005	3.63*	.027

Note: N = 377; Power-distance = dichotomized Power-distance scale.

$**p < .01$; $*p < .05$

analyses, two independent variables were used: Either (a) influence target and the initial Power-distance scale, or (b) influence target and the purified Power-distance measure.

As show in Table 7, all four sets of results support an interaction effect between influence target and Power-distance for the dependent variable of Dependence. However, stronger results are obtained with the purified Dependence measure than with the initial Dependence scale. Using the initial or unpurified Power-distance measure and the initial Dependence scale, the F associated with the interaction is 4.21 ($p = .016$) but it is 5.64 ($p = .004$) with the purified Dependence measure. Similarly, using the purified Power-distance measure and the initial Dependence scale yields an interaction F value of 3.41 ($p = .034$) but this goes up to 5.34 ($p = .005$) for the purified Dependence measure.

A similar pattern of obtaining stronger results with purified than original measures can also be seen for the Personal Punishment dependent variable (which had no DIF items removed from the initial measure). Here, the interaction F is nonsignificant (0.11; $p = .899$) with the initial unpurified Power-distance scale but a significant 3.63 ($p = .027$) with the purified Power-distance measure.

Plotting the obtained interactions from Table 7, using only the purified measures, yields Figures 2 and 3. As shown in Figure 2, the results for Dependence support Hypothesis 2 for high-power distance persons. There is a clear upwardly-increasing relationship between the strength of the influence target (from subordinate to co-worker to superior) and the

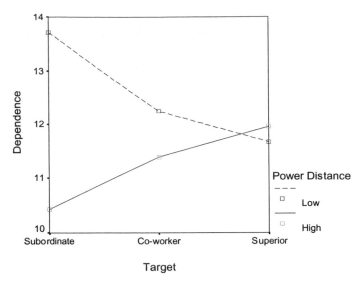

Figure 2. Plot of the interaction of target and power-distance on dependence.

amount of Dependence reported as being used. Figure 2 also shows, however, that the second part of Hypothesis 2 is not supported in that there is a downward-sloping trend for persons of lower Power-distance (the prediction was for no slope or a straight horizontal line).

Figure 3 shows support for Hypothesis 1 with respect to high Power-distance persons. Here, less Personal Punishment is used for the stronger

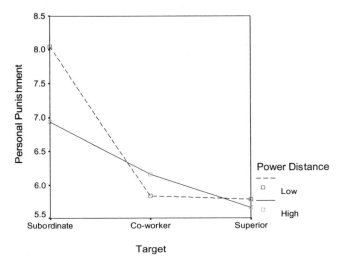

Figure 3. Plot of the interaction of target and power-distance on personal punishment.

influence targets, as predicted. However, the results for the second part of Hypothesis 1 appear to be mixed. Although Figure 3 shows little difference in the use of Personal Punishment by low Power-distance persons for co-worker and superior as influence targets, a substantially higher level of use is reported for subordinate targets. Thus, this part of the hypothesis can be considered only partially supported.

DISCUSSION

In general, our results at least partially supported the two substantive hypotheses. However, and more important, they also showed that use of equivalent measures increased the support for our predictions over what would have been obtained through the use of measures with mixed-equivalence items. Thus, the implications from our study are both substantive (culture moderates the effects of target power on influence tactics employed) and methodological (transnational psychological studies need to ensure scale item equivalence if they are to adequately investigate cultural effects).

We think that the implications of these findings should be obvious and we will therefore discuss them only briefly. For those interested in studying influence processes, our findings provide further support for the framework proposed by Yukl and Tracy (1992) and suggest that, with proper attention being devoted to methodological concerns, their approach may generalize beyond the boundaries of the United States and beyond the context of U.S. culture. Our findings also indicate that the suggestion advanced by Kipnis (1984), that stronger influence tactics are generally used against weaker targets, may be too simplistic to capture the dynamics of power and influence in organizations. Instead, more complex portrayals that include such things as norms and values (e.g., Yukl & Tracy, 1992) appear needed in this domain.

Our methodological findings support the usefulness of IRT as a way of ensuring measurement equivalence and, again, reinforce the conclusion that measurement equivalence should not be assumed. Instead, it should be ensured by appropriate methodologies prior to undertaking any substantive investigation where groups may be different on potentially troublesome covariates, moderators, and/or intervening variables.

Before ending our discussion, there are several limitations that we should mention that are associated with the IRT procedures that we employed. First, the PCA of the Power-distance scale indicated that this scale did not meet the criterion for unidimensionality. Although Drasgow and Parsons (1983) reported that IRT models could be applied to moderately heterogeneous item sets, violation of this assumption could have had an effect on the estimation of item parameters and on the subsequent DIF tests (Budgell et al., 1995).

Second, the concurrent calibration of the IRT model with MULTILOG does not require any metric transformation but relies on anchor items to calibrate parameters on a common scale across groups. However, the existence of possible DIF items in the anchor set may bias the parameter estimates. The IRT partial invariance model tries to test DIF by constraining the parameters of one item to be equal across groups and, at the same time, this item is used as an anchor item to identify a common metric. Thus, the unknown nature of the anchor item may cause inadequate test results. One solution to this problem is to examine scales that include items that previous research has shown to be invariant; unfortunately, this could not be done in the present study, since the measures were all newly-developed.

Third, no holdout samples were used to cross-validate our obtained findings. From this perspective, the IRT procedure that we employed was more exploratory than confirmatory since every item in our scales was checked by a DIF test. However, the results from this study can be used to construct a partial invariance model in which all the invariant items' parameters are constrained to be equal across groups. If this model is supported by another set of samples, we would therefore have more confidence in our results.

Fourth, although the sample sizes used here were acceptable for analyzing the Dependence (6 items) and Personal Punishment (5 items) scales within an IRT framework, the samples should have been larger to adequately analyze the Power-distance scale (13 items). Thus, a replication of this study using larger samples is clearly desirable.

Finally, the Power-distance items have 7 response categories, not the 5 employed on the other measures. According to our knowledge, no published research has investigated the use of the MULTILOG program with items that have 7 response categories. Thus, Monte Carlo and other studies are needed to test the efficiency of MULTILOG in analyzing such items.

In conclusion, although there are recent works that summarize the use of CFA procedures for examining measurement equivalence (e.g., Vandenberg & Lance, 2000), item response theory (IRT) has not received the same attention. IRT is, however, a highly informative and useful methodology that is well suited for the examination and investigation of measurement equivalence. Consequently, additional research that both employs it and that facilitates its further development is clearly needed. We hope that this paper helps stimulate such additional work in the future.

ACKNOWLEDGMENT

The authors would like to acknowledge the constructive comments of Professors Stephanie L. Castro and Christine M. Hagan on earlier drafts of this manuscript. Correspondence should be addressed to Xiaohua Zhou, Department of Management, School of Business Administration, University of Miami, 414 Jenkins Building, Coral Gables, FL 33124-9145. Electronic correspondence should be sent to xzhou@sba.miami.edu.

NOTE

1. A CFA approach was also used to assess the factorial invariance of the three scales. Here, we did not test the equivalence of the intercept parameters. The CFA analysis for the Personal Punishment scale detected no DIF items and supported the IRT finding. It also failed to reject the full factorial invariance model for the Dependence scale and suggested that all the items are invariant across samples. However, this finding differed from the one attained by IRT approach when both the a parameters and b_j parameters are examined. For the Power-distance scale, CFA analysis rejected the full invariance hypothesis and yielded a slightly different set of DIF items than the IRT analysis. The primary reason for the difference between the CFA and IRT results is that the CFA model ignores the difficulty parameters represented by the b_j parameters in the IRT model. Detailed procedures and full test results are available from the first author upon request.

REFERENCES

Agresti, A., & Yang, M. (1986). An empirical investigation of some effects of sparseness in contingency tables. *Computational Statistics & Data Analysis, 5*, 9-21.

Beck, W. (1997). *Hofstede's cultural dimensions as predictors of tactics used in influencing others in organizations.* Unpublished M.S. thesis, Psychological Institute, University of Heidelberg (Germany).

Bock, D.R., & Aitkin, M. (1981). Marginal maximum likelihood estimation of item parameters: Application of an EM algorithm. *Psychometrika, 46*, 443-459.

Brislin, R.W. (1980). Translation and content analysis of oral and written material. In H.C. Triandis & J.W. Berry (Eds.), *Handbook of cross-cultural psychology* (Vol. 2, pp. 380-444). Boston: Allyn & Bacon.

Budgell, G.R., Raju, N., & Quartetti, D.A. (1995). Analysis of differential item functioning in translated assessment instruments. *Applied Psychological Measurement, 19*, 309-321.

Candell, G.L., & Hulin, C.L. (1987). Cross-language and cross-cultural comparisons in scale translations: Independent sources of information about item nonequivalence. *Journal of Cross-Cultural Psychology, 17*, 417-440.

Cheung, G.W., & Rensvold, R.B. (1999). Testing factorial invariance across groups: A reconceptualization and proposed new method. *Journal of Management, 25*, 1-27.

Cohen, A.S., Kim, S., & Baker, F.B. (1993). Detection of differential item functioning in the graded response model. *Applied Psychological Measurement, 17,* 335-350.

Dragow, F. (1987). Study of measurement bias of two standardized psychological tests. *Journal of Applied Psychology, 72,* 19-29.

Dragow, F., & Hulin, C.L. (1990). Item response theory. In M.D. Dunnette & L.M. Hough (Eds.), *Handbook of Industrial and Organizational Psychology* (2nd ed., pp. 577-636). Palo Alto, CA: Consulting Psychologists Press, Inc.

Dragow, F., & Parsons, C.K. (1983). Application of unidimensional item response theory models to multidimensional data. *Applied Psychological Measurement, 7,* 189-199.

Eagle, B.W., Miles, E.W., & Icenogle, M.L. (2001, this volume). Male and female interpretations of bidirectional work-family conflict scales: Testing for measurement equivalence. In C.A. Schriesheim & L.L. Neider (Eds.), *Research in management* (Vol. 1). Greenwich, CT: Information Age Publishing.

Ellis, B.B. (1989). Differential item functioning: Implications for test translations. *Journal of Applied Psychology, 74,* 912-921.

Ellis, B.B., & Kimmel. H.D. (1992). Identification of unique cultural response patterns by means of item response theory. *Journal of Applied Psychology, 77,* 177-184.

Gerstner, C.R., & Day, D.V. (1997). Meta-analytic review of leader-member exchange theory: Correlates and construct issues. *Journal of Applied Psychology, 82,* 827-844.

Hambleton, R.K., Swaminathan, H., & Rogers, H.J. (1991). *Fundamentals of item response theory.* Newbury Park, CA: Sage.

Hellriegel, D., Slocum, J., & Woodman, R. (1993). *Organizational behavior* (4th ed.). Minneapolis, MN: West Publishers.

Hofstede, G.H. (1980). *Culture's consequences: International differences in work-related attitudes.* Beverly Hills, CA: Sage.

Hofstede, G.H. (1991). *Cultures and organizations: Software of the mind.* London: McGraw-Hill.

Howell, J., & Dorfmann, P. (1993). *Cultural Inventory.* Unpublished paper. New Mexico State University.

Hui, C.H., & Triandis, H.C. (1985). Measurement in cross-cultural psychology. *Journal of Cross-Cultural Psychology, 16,* 131-152.

Hulin, C.L., & Mayer, L.J. (1986). Psychometric equivalence of a translation of the job descriptive index into Hebrew. *Journal of Applied Psychology, 71,* 83-94.

Johns, G., & Xie, J.L. (1998). Perceptions of absence from work: People's Republic of China versus Canada. *Journal of Applied Psychology, 83,* 515-530.

Jöreskog, K.G., & Sörbom, D. (1993). *New features in LISREL 8.* Chicago: Scientific Software International, Inc.

Kim, S., & Cohen, A.S. (1998). Detection of differential item functioning under the graded response model with the likelihood ratio test. *Applied Psychological Measurement, 22,* 345-355.

Kipnis, D. (1984). The use of power in organizations and in interpersonal settings. *Applied Social Psychology Annual, 5,* 179-210.

Kipnis, D., Schmidt, S.M., & Wilkinson, I. (1980). Intraorganizational influence tactics: Explorations in getting one's way. *Journal of Applied Psychology, 65,* 440-452.

Lee, C., Pillutla, M., & Law, K.S. (2000). Power-distance, gender and organizational justice. *Journal of Management, 26*, 685-704.

Lord, F. (1980). *Applications of item response theory to practical testing problems.* Hillsdale, NJ: Erlbaum.

Maurer, T.J., Raju, N.S., & Collins, W.C. (1998). Peer and subordinate performance appraisal measurement equivalence. *Journal of Applied Psychology, 83*, 693-702.

McNemar, Q. (1969). *Psychological statistics* (4th ed.). New York: Wiley.

Medsker, G.J., Williams, L.J., & Holahan, P.J. (1994). A review of current practices for evaluating causal models in organizational behavior and human resources management research. *Journal of Management, 20*, 439-464.

Nunnally, J.C., & Bernstein, I.H. (1994). *Psychometric theory* (3rd ed.). New York: McGraw-Hill.

Pfeffer, J. (1977). Power and resource allocation in organizations. In B. Staw & G. Salancik (Eds.), *New directions in organizational behavior.* Chicago: St. Clair Press.

Pfeffer, J. (1981). *Power in organizations.* Marshfield, MA: Pittman.

Reise, S.P., Widaman, K.F., & Pugh, R.H. (1993). Confirmatory factor analysis and item response theory: Two approaches for exploring measurement invariance. *Psychological Bulletin, 114*, 552-566.

Reise, S.P., & Yu, J. (1990). Parameter recovery in the graded response model using MULTILOG. *Journal of Educational Measurement, 27*, 133-144.

Riordan, C.M., & Schaffer, B. (1999). *Cross-cultural methodologies for organizational research using self-report measures: A best practice approach.* Paper presented at the annual Southern Management Association Meeting, Atlanta, GA.

Riordan, C.M., & Vandenberg, R.J. (1994). A central question in cross-cultural research: Do employees of different cultures interpret work-related measures in an equivalent manner? *Journal of Management, 20*, 643-671.

Samejima, F. (1969). Estimation of latent ability using a response pattern of graded scores. *Psychometrika Monographs, 34.*

Schriesheim, C.A., & Hinkin, T.R. (1990). Influence tactics used by subordinates: A theoretical and empirical analysis and refinement of the Kipnis, Schmidt, and Wilkinson subscales. *Journal of Applied Psychology, 75*, 246-257.

Stocking, M.L., & Lord, F.M. (1983). Developing a common metric in item response theory. *Applied Psychological Measurement, 7*, 201-210.

Tepper B.J. (1989). *A replication and extension of the inductive strategy used by Kipnis, Schmidt, & Wilkinson (1980) to derive tactics of organizational influence.* Unpublished M.S. thesis, Department of Psychology, University of Miami.

Thissen, D. (1984). *MULTILOG: Multiple categorical item analysis and test scoring using item response theory (Version 6).* Chicago: Scientific Software, Inc.

Thissen, D., & Steinberg, L. (1988). Data analysis using item response theory. *Psychological Bulletin, 104*, 385-395.

Thissen, D., Steinberg, L., & Gerrard, M. (1986). Beyond group mean differences: The concept of item bias. *Psychological Bulletin, 99*, 118-128.

Thissen, D., Steinberg, L., & Wainer, H. (1988). Use of item response theory in the study of group differences in trace lines. In H. Waimer & H.I. Braun (Eds.), *Test validity* (pp. 147-169). Hillsdale, NJ: Erlbaum.

Triandis, H.C. (1996). The psychological measurement of cultural syndromes. *American Psychologist, 51*, 407-415.

Vandenberg, R.J., & Lance, C.E. (2000). A review and synthesis of the measurement invariance literature: Suggestions, practices, and recommendations for organizational research. *Organizational Research Methods, 3,* 4-69.

Yukl, G.A. (1998). *Leadership in organizations* (4th ed.). Upper Saddle River, NJ: Prentice-Hall.

Yukl, G.A., & Falbe, C.M. (1990). Influence tactics in upward, downward, and lateral influence attempts. *Journal of Applied Psychology, 75,* 132-140.

Yukl, G., Lepsinger, R., & Lucia, A. (1992). Preliminary report on development and validation of the influence behavior questionnaire. In K. Clark, M.B. Clark, & D.P. Campbell (Eds.), *Impact of leadership* (pp. 417-427). Greensboro, NC: Center for Creative Leadership.

Yukl, G., & Tracy, B. (1992). Consequences of influence tactics used with subordinates, peers, and the boss. *Journal of Applied Psychology, 77,* 525-535.